Contents

INTRODUCTION   1

TEACHING DEVICES
An explanation of the main teaching devices used
throughout the book.   3

EXPEDITION
This project prepares students for a GCSE course. The
adventure task builds group identity with an easy role-
play. The teacher can establish a high level of belief in
the drama. The momentum of the journey is interspersed
with opportunities to heighten students' awareness of
prejudice.   7

SOAP
Many students want to make their own soap opera. This
project generates a fuller consideration of real people
and stereotypes than an imitation of TV would produce.
Principal skills are developing more fully rounded roles
and using research.   30

MAKING IT HOME
The title of this project was a Shelter campaign. Here the
concept of home is considered through drama, from the
public issue of homelessness to the personal need for a
home. Communication through space is sharpened in
improvisation.   54

THEATRE-IN-EDUCATION
Devising a Theatre-in-Education programme gives
students a chance to explore creatively the use of form.
In consolidating all the skills taught in the previous
projects, teachers can use their own content or the
sample. This perspective on the popular topic of war
raises questions about loss of life and how we look at
our history.   82

DOCUMENTING DRAMA
Every project has integrated written tasks. This chapter
gives examples of mixed-ability work with advice on how
to improve skills of evaluation. To develop effective
recording of drama, the process, the purpose and the
product are analysed.   101

THE JARROW MARCH
A framework for creating a play using factual material
from history, local or current affairs, or contemporary
themes. The example indicates how the teacher can offer
stimulus and guidance at the same time as enabling
students to create their own presentation.   117

THE TAMING OF THE SHREW

Well, what better text for looking at the role of women in society? This project can be adapted to suit any text being studied. The high profile given to the skill of interpreting the playwright's words opens a way in to the text and identifies its relevance for students.   143

COMMUNITY DRAMA

A collective approach to making drama with, for, or about the community. Using the more open form of community theatre to develop meaningful drama, the form and the content become one. The sample material looks at the relationship between the process of growing up and how different racial groups take their place in Britain, although the structure is designed for any content.   177

PROGRESS?

Literary resources lead this project which uses prepared improvisation to look at lives in the future. The use of language is the skill focus.   211

THEATRE: A COLLECTIVE FORM OF STORY-TELLING

How drama communicates through form is tackled in stages, using a variety of texts. More difficult concepts are introduced, in particular the discovery of the essential truth, as opposed to the reconstruction of reality, in effective communication.   239

A PROJECT PLANNER

An example of how teachers can prepare their own schemes by adapting a content to teach skills, concepts and attitudes.   264

DRAMA 14-16

A book of projects and resources

Pauline Marson
Kate Brockbank
Brian McGuire
Shiona Morton

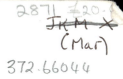

First published in 1990 by:
Stanley Thornes (publishers) Ltd
Old Station Drive
Leckhampton
CHELTENHAM GL53 0DN
England

Col.B 2871 /20. 3.91

British Library Cataloguing in Publication Data
Drama 14–16
   1. Secondary schools. Curriculum subjects: Drama.
Teaching
I. Marson, Pauline
792'.07'12

ISBN 07487 0223-7

Cover illustration by Alan Hood
Cover design by Ned Hoste
Artwork by Philip Page, Merida Woodford, Paul Sexton

Set in Futura and Bembo by ℱ Tek Art Ltd, Croydon, Surrey

Printed and bound in Great Britain by the Bath Press, Avon.

INTRODUCTION

This book is for you. We are all able to generate more effective work when we talk to other teachers. When you teach from this book you are talking to us, listening to our ideas and adapting them for your purposes. You are in charge. The network at the beginning of the chapters allows you to take any route. The skills are identified to support your teaching for examinations. The rationale for each teaching strategy is there to strengthen the educational purpose of the action.

The HMSO publication *Drama 5–16* stresses the need for teachers to formulate a scheme of work which outlines the drama practice in the school, drama's contribution to the school's policy for the arts, its relationship to the attainment targets and programmes of study for English in the National Curriculum and its links with other curricular areas and with more general aspects of the school's provision.

As each National Curriculum document is produced, the place of drama as a learning tool is affirmed. But we know drama is something more, an art form in its own right about culture and about feelings.

This book concentrates on Key Stage 4, where the Cox Report believes 'at level 7 and beyond the claims of drama as a separate subject become specific' (*English for ages 5 to 16*. DES). Each scheme of work can be adapted to fit a modular course. There is ample help with assessment and evaluation. Teachers using this book alongside published curriculum documents will be well equipped to enhance the position of drama in their school's curriculum.

Drama is about people. Social issues can be seen in the actions of individuals. The schemes in this book encourage students to understand drama as a thinking activity, one that is both entertaining and meaningful. In the past, the divide between theatre and drama was important in allowing the development of a supportive theoretical framework for drama in education. This book stands for a consolidation of the two. Getting the best from role-play and presentation means never seeing either as an end in itself but as a means for helping students to distinguish between reality and truth, and to communicate that understanding in a conscious and creative manner.

Our ideas are the result of a dialogue between books that we have read, students we have taught and our work with teachers. Books of practical exercises are useful for the odd tip, though we have learned more from adapting the ideas of Gavin Bolton and Dorothy Heathcote. Watching live theatre has informed our teaching, and our teaching has informed our understanding of drama. This book is the result of our belief that theory and practice must combine before tasks or ideas can be of value to teachers or their students.

The ideas have arisen from our own mixed-ability teaching and have been tried out on teachers' training courses as well as in one another's schools. Whichever examination group you choose, you will find key words and phrases from its assessment objectives to enable you to build the students' skills. You may want to teach the material off the page, or to adapt the resources for a less directed approach. When you are planning, remember to think in terms not only of content, but of skills, attitudes and concepts. Our qualifying criteria for these schemes depended on a set of values by which we operate daily. Each scheme is explicitly anti-racist and anti-sexist; it can be taught as well in inner city as in rural schools. The content encourages students towards emotional maturity within a social framework. Positive images and socially-aware context enable students to experiment with decision-making and to take responsibility for their work. Resources are practical and evocative.

We recognise that written work is the most difficult component for students and teachers alike. We have removed the mystique and pressure from this area by bringing the writing closer to the drama, and so it is easier, more relevant and more highly rewarded by the exams. The tasks are small, aided and closely related to the drama, allowing teachers time to help individuals.

We start with the assumption that most of your students have had some drama experience before the fourth year. The projects develop those skills and leave you scope to assess them. Your role is to plan, to enable, and to prompt critical and constructive thought by asking the right questions. The essential ingredient is improvisation; the method is learning from the relationship between content and form. Every time you teach a unit you could add another box of your own to the network, in response to the way the work unfolds.

We hope this book gives you confidence to expand drama. You are in charge, whether it is a matter of grouping students for a task, or convincing colleagues of the value of your work, of insisting on a good working environment and working clothes for students, or arguing the case for drama for all students. We may not be with you in person but we are together.

Pauline Marson 1990

Teaching Devices

Many of the teaching devices explained below have emerged from contemporary trends in drama and theatre. We have drawn from the work of practitioners in education like Dorothy Heathcote, in theatre like Augusto Boal. You may be already familiar with their work and, like us, have developed teaching techniques to shape your lessons and improve students' skills. As you use these devices you are sure to adapt them to your own style. What is important is that they are all supported by a convergence of theory with practice.

Back-tracking
Replaying a key moment to focus on form and content.

The group is asked to replay a specific part of the drama. This can be done in silence and slow motion, so that actions can be more carefully noted. A high speed version can reveal movement patterns in the space. Normal speed allows students to note the details of words and actions. The actors and the audience have an increased awareness of the situation, the form and the content, and their viewing has been purposeful and analytical.

Brechtian techniques
Brecht's techniques are useful tools for devised drama. The audience become spectators, aware they are watching a play. A more active response is encouraged, ideal for developing students' evaluation skills. Many of the teaching devices here have developed from the theories of Brecht. Your students will find the techniques help give form to their work. They may already use them.

Speaking in the third person.
Using songs to comment on actions or describe emotions.
Using a narrator to inform us of what is about to happen.
Using resources like films, slides, headlines.
Speaking the stage directions.

These techniques and others can be more fully researched in the many books by and about Brecht.

Distilling to the essence
Students need help to discover truthfulness in drama.

As they are working on a scene ask them to distil the whole scene into a small moment, speaking only one line each. They have to retain the atmosphere and meaning. By encouraging them to decide on the indispensable quality in a scene, you help them to discover the intrinsic nature of the interaction. They need to use all the resources available to them – space, speech, movement and timing – to communicate this effectively.

Forum

Involving the whole class in shaping and re-examining the dramatic situation.

The action is stopped to allow the 'audience' to advise the participants about how to handle situations they are in. The technique was pioneered by Augusto Boal. The advisers help to shape attitudes and explore underlying meanings. The whole direction of a drama can be changed by group negotiation.

Framing the situation

The teacher outlines the context of the drama. The boundaries of the situation are given leaving the students to fill in the details.

Freeze-frame, or frozen picture

Students need to focus on an aspect of the drama. Ask the students to create a still picture from their drama. The freeze-frame should have a specific purpose. It could be content-based, looking at a moment in the drama, or form-based, examining physical relationships in the space. This could be a separate task or an intervention in a role-play.

Good questions

A training in simple evaluation in which the performers and the questioners learn more about what and how they are communicating.

After showing some work, stop to ask Good Questions:
- a question must address someone by name.
- everyone in the group must be asked a question.
- questions must not imply an answer, i.e. they must be open questions.

Hot seating

Deepening individual roles and uncovering further information for the drama.

Outside the drama, students are placed in the 'hot seat'. They are questioned by the class and they respond in role. This is unprepared and questioners have to accept the responses given by the student in role. Skilful questioning by the group will enrich the role within a more developed personal profile.

Improvisation

Whether spontaneous or prepared, students work together to create their own drama.

Life rate

Time is a critical dimension in drama. Action can move forward three years in a few minutes giving the drama a non-naturalistic style. At the other end of the continuum is life-rate drama, where time moves as in everyday life. The focus of a life-rate role play is an ordinary, routine interaction and avoids 'big moments'. The emphasis of life-rate drama is not on events but on life style – slowing down the pace deepens belief.

Reconstructing events

Going to another time or situation from the one current in the piece of drama.

Role-play

Students adopt the attitude of another person, rather than trying to become that person. The thought process is fundamental to this technique where the drama unfolds at life-rate. The students have to respond quickly so there is a chance that their own perspective speaks rather than the role. The teacher stands back and lets the drama happen, assessing the direct communication and the degree of understanding. Good in role work has students managing the drama from within by not blocking other students' ideas, but accepting them, at the same time using their role to move the drama on.

An individual scene can be informed by looking at what happened in the past – the recent past, last night, or a greater time span (when the people in the scene first met, for example). This can be an improvisation which develops the present roles, or it can be used to work on characters from a text.

Sound collage

Assembling different sounds to create an atmosphere.

To evoke a specific place, time and mood in a truthful but non-realistic way, students contribute appropriate sounds. Each individual sound is sequenced with the others to make rhythms, patterns and contrasts. The collage can be random or planned. No props are allowed, sounds must be created by voice or body. This makes the work more immediate and brings collective concentration on effective group work.

Spotlighting, or fly on the wall

This is an immediate way to share work in a role-play, particularly when a critical moment has occurred.

Everyone has to stop; the teacher indicates who should continue. A small sample of work is shared by shining the imaginary spotlight on one area of the room. This way everyone can see what is happening in the role-play, or learn from a particularly skilled piece of work. The drama then resumes without losing concentration and momentum.

Teacher-in-role

The teacher adopts a role to act as a stimulus.

This can be used to set up a dramatic context and to open up possibilities at the beginning of a drama by generally addressing the whole class. To deepen and focus work without disturbing the belief, the teacher can adopt roles to work with specific groups in the class, with immediate and direct purpose and results.

Teachers should choose a role of moderate status and not attempt to 'act' or perform. Avoid becoming so involved that the students depend on you.

Thinking aloud

This reinforces role and assesses belief in the drama.

During a role play, teacher stops the action and indicates a student. S/he will respond in role to a question about how they feel or what s/he is thinking. This can be developed into a group freeze with students freely expressing their thoughts aloud as a kind of sound track to the action.

Expedition

NETWORK

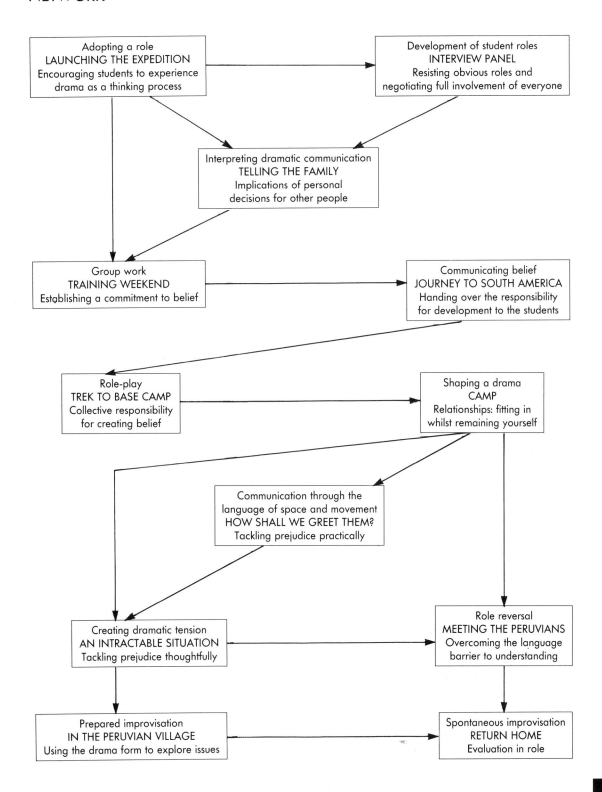

Adopting a role
LAUNCHING THE EXPEDITION
Encouraging students to experience
drama as a thinking process

Development of student roles
INTERVIEW PANEL
Resisting obvious roles and
negotiating full involvement of everyone

Interpreting dramatic communication
TELLING THE FAMILY
Implications of personal
decisions for other people

Group work
TRAINING WEEKEND
Establishing a commitment to belief

Communicating belief
JOURNEY TO SOUTH AMERICA
Handing over the responsibility
for development to the students

Role-play
TREK TO BASE CAMP
Collective responsibility
for creating belief

Shaping a drama
CAMP
Relationships: fitting in
whilst remaining yourself

Communication through the
language of space and movement
HOW SHALL WE GREET THEM?
Tackling prejudice practically

Creating dramatic tension
AN INTRACTABLE SITUATION
Tackling prejudice thoughtfully

Role reversal
MEETING THE PERUVIANS
Overcoming the language
barrier to understanding

Prepared improvisation
IN THE PERUVIAN VILLAGE
Using the drama form to explore issues

Spontaneous improvisation
RETURN HOME
Evaluation in role

This is an effective project for covering all the basic skills listed in the Teaching Devices section.

It enables students:
- to support one another in and out of role;
- to identify issues and principles, make decisions and explore them throughout the drama;
- to face up to their own prejudices.

The theme is an extension of students' own needs as teenagers, taking an independent and appropriate place in an adult world while maintaining loyalties to friends and building a family relationship.

Many of the skills referred to in the text are social and analytical; these are a pre-requisite for good drama. In this project we have drawn your attention to these skills.

The focus for assessment of spontaneous and prepared improvisation will be the drama skills identified here. These skills are the ability to:
- adopt and sustain an appropriate role;
- communicate through the language of space, movement and words;
- work effectively in groups of various sizes;
- evaluate students' own work and the work of others, within and without a role.

Launching the Expedition

OBJECTIVES
During this lesson the students will receive basic information about the drama and help in adopting roles.
- An agreement to believe in one another's roles should be reached through negotiation.
- The beginning of the drama should be clearly identified (perhaps by you, the teacher, leaving the group and returning in role).
- Advise the students to listen for clues from you, and ask questions wherever possible.

1 Teacher in role as UN representative for South America, speaking at a weekend selection conference for a research expedition to Peru. 'I would like to welcome you on behalf of the UN. You haven't met one another, but you will do so during the interview stage of the selection conference. We are grateful that such busy people have been able to take time off work to join us.

'We are impressed by the high calibre of the applicants and congratulate you on getting this far. As you know from our advert, we plan a research expedition. We deliberately didn't give you too much information, because we knew you would have a lot of questions at this stage.'

The purpose of using the teacher in role is to give students information and to give the situation authenticity. You do not need to 'act'; better if you develop a safe situation in which students can feel confident in using their own skills.

Giving students the roles of experts, while gaining information needed for the drama, increases their confidence and the status of their ideas. If someone has the role of a photographer, you could equip him or her with a camera, which will document the expedition and be useful for evaluation later.

2 Questioning in role

2 Students question you in role.
Information to be given:
- Where? Peru, South America. (Refer to map.)
- When? Very soon.
- How much? No cost.
- Who? Only people who can offer expertise or who can learn from this experience can come; they should have either special interests or special needs.

Stress the importance of commitment over expertise. The purpose is to learn from the people there. It is important to see the Peruvians as having a sophisticated but different culture. Invent answers to other questions and use students themselves to answer specialised questions; for example:
Student: What about First Aid?
Teacher: Oh, are you a doctor by any chance?

The purpose of questioning in role is to draw students into the drama. It builds their belief and commitment. It gives students the responsibility for getting the information they need. Working in a large class group, they actively shape the drama by responding to one another.

3 Adopting a role
Supporting one another

3 During questioning, slowly help students to build their roles; for example:
Teacher: Do we have anybody who is a geographer?
Teacher: You look a bit doubtful. Have you been on an expedition before? Are you worried about leaving people behind?
Aim to ensure that everyone has adopted a role.

The teacher should encourage the adoption and gradual development of positive, non-stereotyped roles, which are deepened at students' own pace.
To pitch in with a role is a high-level skill. Sometimes it is

Training Weekend

- Group work
- Establishing a commitment to belief

1 Fulfilling the task while maintaining the role

1 As the students enter the room they begin a training programme. Launch it with strenuous activities. These can include running, stretching, sit-ups, arm exercises.

'Over the years I have learned some useful tips for safe exploration. One is that on any long or arduous journey, the pace must be set by the slowest person. I expect you can all figure out why.' (Allow time for student response.)

'Just follow me and I'll show you what I would do if the third stepping stone was slippery.' Using the outdoor pursuit technique of knowing who is behind and in front of you, a message about a hazard is passed back to the next person.

As the pace changes, the emphasis shifts to the reality of the endurance ahead. The twin ethics of the trip are established: being physically fit and working as a team.

2 Team work
Negotiation
Use of space, levels, resources available in the room

2 Students in role now prepare a guide for other groups (rather like a training video on how to deal with hazardous terrains). In this the team members help one another over a natural obstacle, e.g. a swollen river, dense undergrowth, high altitudes.

Ensure that each group works on a different problem, so that the class as a whole can 'train' for a range of problems by learning from one another.

In introducing and establishing survival techniques, the students are building on their belief in the drama and thinking through some possibilities of action which they may be asked to use in subsequent lessons.

3 Sustaining in role passively and actively
Evaluation in context

3 Watch each group's 'video' in turn. The class evaluates the survival techniques in role.

Watching has a motive as everyone needs to learn from one another. Sharing strategies brings the group together, in and out of role.

| 4 Exploring issues in context | 4 Teacher in role: 'Now you have your basic training, but there are certain issues which we need to tackle before we go.
— How do you feel about leadership?
— What other problems will you face besides the terrain?
— What if anyone is ill while we are on the move?
— Interference in another culture – is it okay to go?'
(Encourage a thoughtful group to take this on.)
— Food? Survival? Living naturally?'
Students should identify and decide upon these issues themselves through discussion together in role.

This work outlines the degree of challenge for students in physical and social terms. By giving consideration to the issues they are likely to face before the expedition begins 'for real', students are encouraged to take thoughtful responsibility for one another. |
| 5 Negotiation in role | 5 Either in groups or as a class, an Expedition Charter based on the discussion is produced for display.
For homework you could ask students to find out something about Peru; this could be from geographical, historical, or cultural sources.

This enables everyone to make a contribution to a written statement about collective responsibility as well as setting the parameters for future action. |

Telling the Family

- Interpreting dramatic communication
- Implications of personal decisions for other people

| 1 Examining and communicating feelings in role | 1 Standing in a space, students recall their role quietly. Perhaps they've just got off the bus and are walking home. As they approach the door they figure out how and when to tell their parents/spouse or others that they are going. Encourage them to think of the impact on the family and |

the relationship. Suggest to the students that their first words on opening the door should give a clue to how they feel. When everyone seems ready, tell the students to open the door and say these first words aloud.

Share some of the statements.

Students see their own decision in the wider perspective of their close relationships.

Asking everyone to speak at once avoids embarrassment and sharing enriches the experience for the individual and the class.

2 Using improvisation to examine a wider range of feelings

2 Pair work. Rehearse a scene which explores the relationship between one of the roles and a friend or family member when the decision to go is revealed. The scene should explore the relationship and feelings.

Time is allowed for students to become involved in the story and to play through the relationship. Freedom from form produces a mass of raw material.

3 Making quick decisions
Giving the content form
Co-operation

3 Ask students to distil the atmosphere into one sentence or phrase each. Their use of space and movement will be important. Allow them about one minute to choose their moment.

Having generated plenty of ideas, students have the confidence to apply form to the content. The essence is captured, all can achieve a good standard and there will be time to see everyone's work.

4 Presentation
Communication through the language of space, movement and words
Discussion
Evaluation

4 See each pair. Ask the class to read the subtext immediately after each scene.
- What do these people feel?
- What is their relationship?
- What clues are there in the way they are sitting?
- Did they say what they really meant?

Evaluation focuses on the subtext, with detailed analysis of the hidden meanings. Thus the process of sharing has meaning for the participants and the audience. It is important to use the term subtext within the discussion so that students begin to use the vocabulary of evaluation.

5 Consolidating improvisation in writing
In role evaluation

5 In role, students write a note to be left on the kitchen table, on the day of departure, e.g. Scot can leave a note for his fiancée to find as he leaves. Yasmin can write a note for a parent to find after she has gone.

All students now adopt their original role to lead into the remainder of the project. Writing within the drama experience gives students greater confidence and improves the quality of their work.

|6| Reflecting in action

6 Working alone in the space, the students mime the packing of one small rucksack with personal belongings.

Here the teacher is enabling informal anticipation of what is to come.
The selection of articles creates possibilities for future work.

7 Ask the students to bring along an article they couldn't do without on the expedition. (This will be used later in 'camp' lesson.)

You are giving the students responsibility for shaping the drama and enhancing the status of the work.

Interview Panel

- Development of student roles
- Resisting obvious roles and negotiating full involvement of everyone

RESOURCES
Application forms from last lesson

|1| Adopting a role

1 Teacher in role sums up from the last lesson.
Ask each person to introduce him or herself to the group and say why he/she would like to go along.

Sharing of information recreates belief in the situation. As the first piece of writing is purposeful and the students can see the relationship between it and the drama, coursework is less likely to become a mere description of events.

2 Discussion
Decision-making

2 After you have heard from everyone, say: 'As you are some of the people who will go, we feel you should help to decide what qualities you want in your fellow travellers. Experience has shown us at UN that groups get along together if they are mixed. Indeed, in terms of sex, age, experience and background, it is a principle of the UN that groups should reflect a mixture.'

Ask the students to identify what makes a good candidate. This should be based on clues you have given last time about respecting and learning from other cultures and being prepared to work with others.

This can be done as a class or in groups. Students should stay in role. Teacher in role can focus on any group or point made.

This formally reinforces the status of the expedition and informally suggests co-operation and support.

The purpose of defining the desirable group as reflecting a social mix avoids an excess of stereotyped 'intrepid explorers'. There is scope to use a variety of working patterns; the discussion could be as a whole class, or in pairs or groups who report back to the class for the negotiated conclusion.

3 Helping one another to reach and maintain good, positive roles
Class co-operation
Sustaining a role or adjusting to a more appropriate role

3 Interview panel Select some candidates for a more formal interview, using application forms and knowledge of roles. Ask students to be an interview panel on your behalf, briefly questioning each applicant chosen, in turn or in pairs.

The aim is to get the person through the interview. For example:
'This application form is very good – just the type of person we need to balance the group.'

The questioning technique allows even the most poorly-sustained roles to be deepened. Select roles that require further development, as well as the clearer roles, for interview. This encourages students to help one another to develop their positive characteristics.

The purpose of the interview is to encourage competition, not with one another but with themselves. They are able to:
- resist easy or obvious roles;
- explore a wider, more challenging range of possibilities;
- re-work a negative choice which might have blocked the drama;
- dispense with a role which was difficult to maintain.

4 'You have all been most successful. I was right about the high calibre of applicants and am pleased to be able to tell you that you are all accepted on the trip. Having got this far I must reinforce the need for *total* commitment. There will be training sessions next weekend and the expedition leaves for Peru on Monday.'

If you have used application forms, you can re-issue them with a stamp/signature in the box provided to show applicants have been accepted.

The stressing of commitment will help in the next lesson.

Journey to South America

- Communicating belief
- Handing over the responsibility for development to the students

RESOURCES
Camera, local map

1 Responding in role to clues

1 As the students arrive, call them over with a flight announcement 'Gate 23 for Lima, South America. Gate 23 boarding now.'

An immediate start generates excitement about the journey.

2 Expressing thoughts and feelings, orally and physically

2 Students arrange themselves for a group photo. (If you can actually take it, do so, and have it developed for later.) Set up a frozen depiction and, by tapping individuals in turn, ask such questions as:
— 'What are you thinking now?'
— 'How do you feel about leaving/arriving in Peru?'

Through your questioning first those who are deeply in role, students help one another build belief in the real implications of leaving home on a risky expedition. Depiction is a useful technique here, reinforcing the idea that they are all one group and allowing focus on a key moment. If you can take a real photo, the belief and status is heightened.

3 Improvising independently of the teacher in a large group

3 Students as a group spontaneously improvise the transition to their destination.

'I'm sure you will all get to know one another during the flight. Enjoy sharing with one another your hopes for the expedition.'

The teacher's role of expedition organiser is being gently phased out, and responsibility for the drama is more and more being handed over to the students.

Allocation of seats by the teacher can allow students to develop relationships which they would not normally initiate themselves.

4 Writing within the drama

4 Students write their first diary entry on the journey.

'Have a good night's sleep. You set off at dawn tomorrow. I will see you briefly then.'

Consolidate the drama experience into a short diary entry. Immediately after reflecting in role and developing a relationship, students are given the opportunity to learn by recording their feelings.

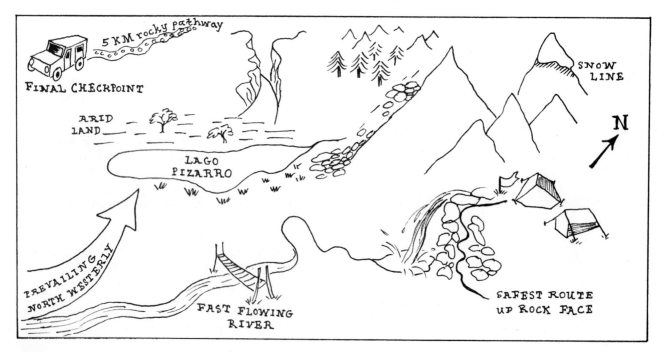

5 Group improvisation in role Using research	**5** In the hotel in Lima, explorers are asked to share their knowledge of Peru with one another. Sharing knowledge of research in groups enhances belief and the status of the students' own work.
6 Imagining the possibilities of the space	**6** Explain that you will have to leave the explorers on their own in the morning. Offer the local map to someone who can use it. Pick out features on the map and point to areas of the room that correspond; for example, as you point to the middle of the room say, 'Be particularly careful of the slippery rocks.' The map represents an imagined interpretation of the drama space. Reward positively those students who have been less dominant by asking them to read the map.

Trek to Base Camp

- Role-play
- Collective responsibility for creating belief

RESOURCES
Tape recorder, local map

---

1 Using space to create a dramatic setting Group work	**1** Students set up the room, out of role, by interpreting the map. They should agree on what to use and how to use it as a whole group. Explain the time allocation – three-quarters of a lesson to improvise, one quarter to evaluate – so that the students can pace their journey. Involving everyone in the imaginative interpretation of the room makes the space their own. Quality of negotiation is important. People must believe in one another's inventions.
2 Listening for clues	**2** In role, you offer last-minute advice for the journey. 'Use the map to lead you on the expedition. You've got a

limited time, you know how long it is till nightfall, you must get to the base camp area using the map, establish camp and be safely settled for the night. Remember the charter and what you learned in the training session. Take my advice, don't wait for anyone, no matter what happens.'

Reminding students to use of space and of time limitations frames the dramatic form. The deliberate emphasis on the primacy of the expedition over the individual is designed to provoke the students to reject this concept of 'survival of the fittest'.

[3] Sustaining belief in the role and the situation
Building on one another's contributions
Use of real time to create dramatic time

3 Now allow students to explore the environment and spontaneously improvise the journey. As far as possible let the drama unfold. Don't be afraid to allow students to solve their own problems in their role-play. If focusing is necessary, these standby devices might be used: freeze; spotlight; thinking aloud. (For definitions of these terms, see *Teaching Devices*, pages 3–6.)
As soon as the party arrives at camp, cut the action.

The project has been quite tightly structured so far; in this lesson it is important to let the drama run. You will see what students make of the opportunities given. In role you have gone into the background; as a teacher you can, too. Step in if students need you, but also let them make their own mistakes.

[4] Evaluation of techniques:
roles (own and others)
use of space
dramatic form
use of time
group work
Critical and constructive thought

4 Everybody then takes part in a major evaluation of drama skills out of role. These areas will probably be covered:
How did we
• use time?
• sustain roles?
• use movement, space, words?
• react as a group?
Did anyone include anyone else who was a little left out?
Did you notice anyone doing anything interesting?
It is recommended that this evaluation is tape-recorded for use when writing up the unit.

The students have been really involved in the expedition up until now. The evaluation looks objectively at drama skills.
Tape-recording this now will help to restimulate students later when they need support for written coursework.

Camp

- Shaping a drama
- Relationships: fitting in whilst remaining yourself

RESOURCES
Model diary entry, personal articles from home

1 Awareness of teacher's evaluation of good drama

1 Read out a diary entry written by yourself which includes incidents from the drama to date.

Focus on the small incidents away from the 'hot spots', and on the work of individuals who do not always approach the centre of action. You can tuck this into an old log book. You are creating an atmosphere and providing a model of written style, namely one that is relevant and analytical with personal judgements supported by sound argument.
Coursework again is an integral part of the drama.

2 Revealing an understanding of the significance of the interaction Using the drama form to explore issues

2 Divide the class into groups for prepared improvisation. The task is to show students their relationships and to use their personal articles in the scene.

As a teacher you need time to assess the process and the product; the students have been given ample stimuli. The articles regarded as precious by each student can give all students a tip about drama form.

3 Using the stimuli in an appropriate and effective manner Using form and characterisation

3 Watch the work in an appropriate way and evaluate in role. For example:
- How have we met our objectives?
- Have we stuck to our charter?
- Is there a contrast between expectations and reality?
- What are we going to do next?

Snippets can give a quick insight into everyone's work. Full playing of prepared scenes takes longer and relies more on respect for others in the class. Either way the sharing opens up possibilities for students to evaluate their own work and that of others.

4 Students should now create a diary entry which records the improvisation.

This is a slightly more complex task than a straightforward diary entry because it is influenced by the class evaluation and the model diary entry heard at the start of the lesson.

How Shall We Greet Them?

- Communication through the language of space and movement
- Tackling prejudice practically

1 Communication without words

1 Without discussion, ask the students to imagine that the drama room is a busy, noisy space, and to move around it, entirely individually creating that atmosphere. They are out of role.

After a few seconds, get them to notice and communicate – without using voices – with a friend across the room.

The launch is sharp, practical and in contrast to the other openers used in this project. This is refreshing and gives a sense of mystery; students do not know what is coming next and will have to think from a different perspective.

2 Interpreting and evaluating a simple task

2 Immediately this is under way, freeze the activity, spotlight individuals and ask the class to analyse their actions. You might like to focus questions on the following areas:
- What methods did people use?
- Which were most effective?
- What do the actions mean?
- How easy is it to communicate without language?

This simple task reveals the meanings in action. The actions can be repeated until the meanings become clear.

|3| Listening actively to pick up clues for development of drama

3 Focus the students on to the Expedition. Explain that it is time to think about meeting the South Americans for the first time. Positively stress that they are intelligent, non-English speaking, civilised people. Pose the question: 'How do we successfully communicate to these people that we come in peace and friendship?'

Aim to reach the conclusion that we need to devise an unthreatening strategy which does not patronise.

Here you positively reinforce the situation of equal but different cultures to reduce prejudice. Students are clear about the setting and attitude required and the evaluation of the outcome will be directly related to 'What does my action mean?' You have made it clear that native-stereotyping is not appropriate. The students will realise that there is a language barrier, so action will need to take on symbolic value.

|4| Group work skills which, in planning out of role, negotiating and working efficiently, are highly valued. Conscious planning and practising the use of movement, space, gesture without words to communicate ideas. Polishing and evaluating ideas in process. Adopting and sustaining a role

4 In small, pre-planned groups ask the students to prepare a very short piece of drama in which they effectively use:
• movement;
• space;
• gesture;
• language;
• roles of expedition members *only*.

You can arrange the groups as appropriate, to mix ability, give a range of attitudes and a good social mix. The organisation and discussion can be free, fluent and speedy. This will focus thought and force decision-making, enabling time to be spent evaluating. The students have been able to experience empathy for people with a different language. They don't take on roles of the South Americans at this stage to avoid stereotyping.

|5| Critical awareness of students' own work in the context of that of others
Watching supportively

5 During a sharing of work, get the class members watching to concentrate on how actions conveyed meaning and indicated attitude. Use the evaluation to decide with the group which techniques were the most friendly.

This lesson may begin to examine hidden prejudice. If you see evidence of this, you might like to put it to the test by replaying scenes, asking the rest of the class to spot potentially unsuitable actions.

Students have to concentrate on the effectiveness of meaning. The emphasis is on simple, well-formed actions showing evidence of thought.

| 6 | Interpreting dramatic action and techniques | 6 | The students write down in one column a list of the actions used, and in another their meanings. |

6 Interpreting dramatic action and techniques

6 The students write down in one column a list of the actions used, and in another their meanings.

This is a small and achievable task for students coming fresh from the experience.

An Intractable Situation

- Creating dramatic tension
- Tackling prejudice thoughtfully

7 Improvisation
Building tension
Rehearsing, polishing
Use of movement, space and words
Meaning implicit in actions

7 Students go straight into groups chosen by the teacher. They begin to prepare an improvised scene which explores a possible tricky situation on the journey, e.g. having eaten poisoned berries for which they possess no antidote, having lost the map.

Brief   The scene should not have an ending. The problem can't be solved by the people involved. The only solution will be to seek help from the locals, but how to approach them is not clear. Use research and experience gained from previous lessons.

The stereotyped situation of the intrepid explorer who brings knowledge to otherwise unsophisticated folk is reversed. By undermining the stereotype we challenge prejudice based on the notion of cultural superiority.

Choose from these two:
(a) Place the emphasis on a polished piece which highlights the building of tension.

Using the drama form to increase tension in stages, we are developing theatre skills by carefully working towards a climax without an easy resolution.
Allow an opportunity for assessment.

(b) Prepare a scene in groups with emphasis on the thinking behind the decision to seek help.

The structure of the scene is shaped by the issue rather than the tension.

Your choice will depend on the syllabus and the needs of the class.

2 Presentation or reporting skills

2 The sharing of work can be either a report of the crisis, or a presentation of the scene. Each group could decide which method suits its work best.

Allowing students to 'report or show' can take the emphasis away from the product, allowing the process to be valued and evaluated. Students who describe their own work to the class are orally evaluating its content and form.

3 Evaluating the drama form and process

3 In note form students record either:
How did the tension build from stage to stage? or: How did the drama help communicate the issue?

Here is an opportunity for students to analyse how ideas shaped by the group worked in action. Writing in note form means that students can concentrate on the analysis rather than their prose.

Meeting the Peruvians

- Role reversal
- Overcoming the language barrier to understanding

RESOURCES
Recording of music from the Andes

1 Extrapolating from experience in terms of form and content

1 Ask students to refer to the notes they have made over the previous weeks in establishing the criteria for effective drama work.
Discuss as a class:
- role-play techniques;

- unhelpful assumptions about the Peruvians which might damage relations;
- where you are up to in the drama.

Written notes are useful in the drama. If students see a purpose in writing, the quality of their work improves. The notes are more than a record of what happened. Evaluation before the lesson begins sets the climate and gives maximum scope for success.

2 Considering the use of language

2 Before starting the role-play in which the visitors meet the locals, the question and use of language needs to be addressed. No-one should speak 'gobbledegook', but use his or her own language. The problems of communication between cultures who speak different languages can be created, and explored, by students pretending to understand only those from their own country. Students should appreciate the many reasons for this.

One of our objectives in this project has been to address cultural stereotyping. The use of language here focuses the twin strands of the issue of stereotyping implicit in the content and the use of a form that makes the drama effective. The power of communication is given to the Peruvians who might otherwise be portrayed as simple folk who grunt. Students are made aware of how language can be used to patronise, or to poke fun at other cultures. This dramatic device allows them to see that the problem of communication is shared by both cultures. Students have a form that both enables the drama to flow and teaches a device that can be used in presentation. It does require concentration but students quickly find they are able to use this form in more complex and sophisticated ways.

3/4 Assessment Point
Step back from the work here and assess your students in terms of the skills you discussed at the start of the lesson. Their commitment to the drama and the intellectual challenge of the criteria established at the start should enable them to work without you.

3 The drama begins by all the students taking on their roles of the expedition members during the last stages of the journey. They role-play for a few minutes.

4 Responding to the music whilst sustaining the role and belief in the situation

4 At a suitable moment, start playing the Peruvian music, then stand back and allow the students to respond in role. Their reaction will be to grow in anticipation with the music and perhaps focus on, or move towards, the source of the sound in the room.

Choose to play the tape at a time when belief is established, but before the role-play either loses momentum or takes off on an over-dramatic course. The music we have suggested is evocative and easily obtainable. The piece gives dramatic shape as its phrasing becomes gradually louder and fuller. We use the structure of the music to allow anticipation rather than realisation so that students have time to consider the implications of their actions. The use of music represses speech, so when students do speak later the words take on more value.

5 Individual reflection. Role-play structured to complement previous activity

5 Freeze the action and the music. Give the students a couple of minutes to think through what they were 'seeing' during the music. Ask them now to move into role as the Peruvians, occupying the area of the room from which the sound had come. Re-play the music and the action; the students improvise the same experience from the opposite point of view.

The next stage is important, so we stop before the climax. Giving students an opportunity for private reflection, without the extra level of interaction that occurs in discussions, allows everyone to practise the skill of personal evaluation in a peaceful atmosphere that arises from the sense of awe created by the music. The decision to have all the students as members of the expedition avoids the need for confrontation which might occur if the class were divided into travellers and Peruvians. The single focus and the space available to the students allows them to develop positive approaches, rather than defensive and territorial stands.

6 Communication of attitudes through words and actions. Evaluation through process

6 Divide the class into half; one in role as the Peruvians, the other as expedition members. Indicate that the students should role-play, without music, the meeting between the cultures, communicating in a positive non-threatening and non-stereotyped way. The process can be stopped and started by both students and teacher until everyone is satisfied that the drama form conveys their message of friendship.

Having set the climate and given the students tools for communication without words, we rehearse the meeting. We practise the skills through a rehearsal process to encourage students to see the developmental nature of rehearsals. The negotiative style is an introduction to forum theatre (see *Teaching Devices* page 4) and enables the students to learn that rehearsals are not merely a process of repetition in which they have to learn the director's plan. The forum allows discussion of the issues. The rehearsal allows students to grasp the language form.

Adapting the Network

- Prepared improvisation
- In the Peruvian village
- Using the drama form to explore issues

- Spontaneous improvisation
- Return home
- Evaluation in role

ADDITIONAL RESOURCE
Photographs of Peruvian boy and girl.

The network lesson plan allows you to respond to the needs of the students, shaping their experiences towards purposeful learning. You might want to work with this material, or feel a resolution had been reached after 'Meeting the Peruvians'. Either way, you need to give yourself time to evaluate the teaching and learning. From this you can decide which action most closely meets the needs of the students and what to look for when choosing the next project.

What skills have been learned?
e.g. Role-play
     Use of language
     Evaluation

Has the story ended for the students?
Was the crisis resolved?
Did the two cultures interact?
Was the experience processed to the point of returning home?

What changes in attitudes have been brought about?
Towards stereotypes?
Towards cross-cultural relations?

What concepts do the students have of a community?
The two final boxes in the network on page 7 were drawn up after evaluating the teaching.

Peruvian girl

Peruvian boy

Soap

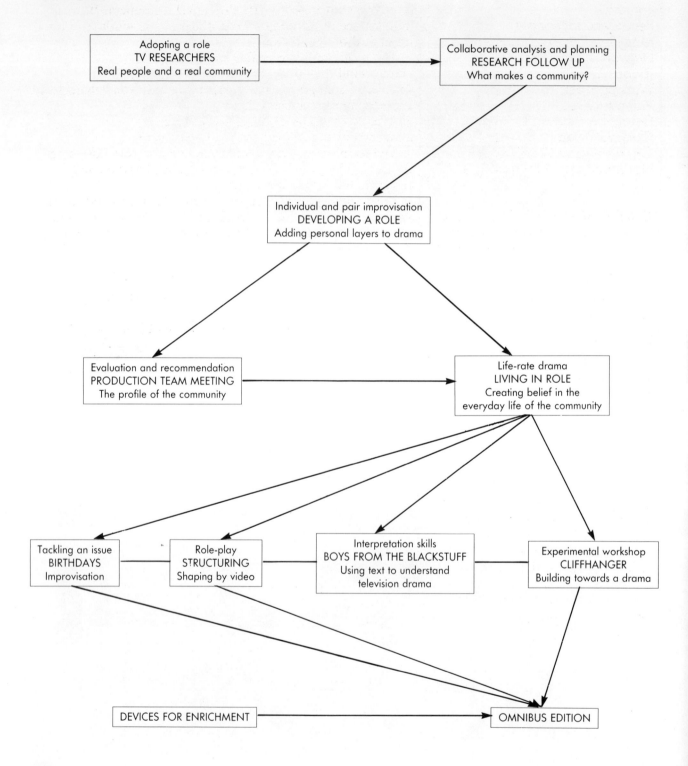

Adopting a role
TV RESEARCHERS
Real people and a real community

Collaborative analysis and planning
RESEARCH FOLLOW UP
What makes a community?

Individual and pair improvisation
DEVELOPING A ROLE
Adding personal layers to drama

Evaluation and recommendation
PRODUCTION TEAM MEETING
The profile of the community

Life-rate drama
LIVING IN ROLE
Creating belief in the
everyday life of the community

Tackling an issue
BIRTHDAYS
Improvisation

Role-play
STRUCTURING
Shaping by video

Interpretation skills
BOYS FROM THE BLACKSTUFF
Using text to understand
television drama

Experimental workshop
CLIFFHANGER
Building towards a drama

DEVICES FOR ENRICHMENT

OMNIBUS EDITION

RESOURCES
Questionnaire (page 32),
cameras
Recorders, notebooks
Miscellaneous small articles
Network 7 profile sheet
(page 38)
Working clock
Video facilities
Extract from *Boys from the Blackstuff* (pages 45–49)
Clip from recent soap opera
Noticeboard used throughout

OTHER RESOURCES
Several organisations can provide videos and educational packs that would support and enrich the students' work in this project. *Stories from the First Estate* records the experiences of the people living on the first public housing estate and is available from Media Arts, Town Hall Studios, Regent Circus, Swindon, SN1 1QF. *Shields Stories* records on video the lives of people in the north east and is available from Amber Films, 5 Side (Rear), Newcastle-upon-Tyne, NE1 3JE.

An educational pack is also available from Granada TV, where you can take a tour of the *Coronation Street* set: Granada Studio Tours Ltd, Quay Street, Manchester, M60 9EA.

Many local libraries will have recordings of 'talking newspaper' interviews with local characters.

Although media studies and drama are examined differently, we cannot underestimate the influence TV has on students' concept of the theatre. This project is designed to enable students to devise their own soap opera. With a high degree of planning by the students, the work requires a good deal of negotiation.

The project aims to enable students to:
- understand the notion of truth in drama;
- challenge stereotypes and devise more individual characters;
- develop and structure a narrative;
- use drama to explore issues and concepts;
- understand and analyse the soap opera genre.

The learning experiences include living in role, assessment through video, the role of directors, improvisation and research into local community.

Throughout the project, the teacher documents the work with very little written work from the students. The students see the value of effective working notes and see their teacher taking this task seriously.

TV Researchers

- Adopting a role
- Real people and a real community

The lesson begins with the class in role as TV researchers, gathering relevant information about their own local community. The beginning of the session prepares them for a visit into the locality. The students can then devise their own soap opera community stimulated by people and places from their research.

RESOURCES

Prepared noticeboard headed 'TV Production Team'
Photocopiable questionnaire
Suggested additional resources:
Polaroid camera, tape recorders, reporters' notebooks, pens/pencils

GCSE DRAMA QUESTIONNAIRE

NETWORK 7

YEAR

Forename _____

Surname _____

Are you aged   10–15 ___   25–35 ___   60–70 ___
                    15–18 ___   35–45 ___   over 70 ___
                    18–25 ___   45–60 ___

Place of birth _____

_____

_____

Age left school _____

Occupation _____

Place of work _____
(if applicable) _____

Area of town _____
you live in _____

_____

Places visited regularly

Favourite place _____

Best part of living here

Worst part of living here

Any other information

1 Role-play

1 As the students arrive, greet them in role. You are a TV producer, they are TV researchers. Allocate them places around a large table on which are displayed all the available resources.

Students are immediately part of a piece of drama, role-playing attitudes not necessarily their own. This is a much more challenging experience than merely being themselves discussing what they are going to do, planning a drama. The resources ready and room set out enhance the status of the drama.

2 Response in role

2 Introduce the meeting with something like this: 'Channel 7 has decided to launch a major new TV project. As yet, specific details are not known, but I have been given the job of co-ordinating you TV researchers to find out as much as possible about the local community and the areas in which its members live. Perhaps we could start by gathering some immediate information from one another now. For example, where do the teenagers spend their time? Where do the parents of those teenagers spend their time?'

Teacher, in role, introduces the first task without revealing too much about the topic as a whole. This is to minimise the risk of students only researching/finding 'characters' and locations within their community which have probably been rather stereotyped in the popular soap operas they watch. They have enough information to be able to explain their drama to their interviewees.

3 Research in role

3 Extend the discussion to include small children, pensioners and so on. Chart the information and display centrally, perhaps in list form with link-ups. For example:

People	Places
teenagers	arcade
toddlers	bus station
pensioners	chip shop

Throughout this unit it is suggested that all the documentation is done by the teacher to provide a model for the students to observe and make use of at a later date. The discussion can be extended until a picture of the community emerges.

4 Negotiating a plan of action

4 Explain that, to do the research properly, students must go out into the community to talk to people, watch them, look at places and record their findings.

Allocate teams of students to tackle the areas we suggest and any others that your particular community offers.
- Photographers to take pictures of people and places.
- Interviewers to question a range of people in the street/school, using the questionnaire.
- Interviewers to tape-record conversations with local people, in their own homes or at work, based on the questionnaire.
- Researchers to visit the Town Hall/Council Offices to find out about housing, population, to get a map of the area.
- Researchers to visit a Job Centre or DHSS to find out employment/unemployment figures.
- Artists to sketch different types of housing, open spaces and other areas.
- Researchers to visit the Police Station to find out about crime patterns.
- Researchers to make contact with community groups.

The success of the research depends on students being prepared to approach the task with a genuine sense of enquiry and interest in the outcome.

Here are some tips for students to ensure they complete the task effectively:
- Telephone organisations to prepare them for a visit.
- Notice if people in the street are prepared to give you time – some people will be in a hurry, or carrying too much shopping.
- Greet people politely. 'Good morning, I'm from school. We are researching for a drama project. Would you mind answering some questions?' and 'Thank you for your help.'
- Use personal contacts in your own area to help to get more indepth information.

Research Follow-up

- Collaborative analysis and planning
- What makes a community?

RESOURCE
Research findings

During this lesson you will challenge the concept of research as simplistic. Students will be pushed to view evidence with a critical eye. Their understanding of the soap genre will be drawn. The concept of a community will be exposed and explored.

1 Critical exploration of evidence

1 In role as TV producer, call a meeting of the production team to consider initial research evidence. Whether the results are sketchy or inspiring, treat the evidence as problematic. Aim to encourage students to see that fact must be processed by their thoughts and feelings before it can work as drama.
    Some questions to address:
- Is this a community?
- Where are its boundaries?
- What groups are found within the community (families, classes, etc.)?
- What messages are there in the day-to-day environment?

    This stretches all the students and introduces the concept of community. The drama is not going to merely reproduce life as though it were fixed, but treat it as changeable. The purpose of interactive research is to discover what questions the soap opera will ask rather than what answers it provides.

2 Analysing in role

2 Divide the researchers into four groups to tackle, in role, the next planning issues.
- What traditions are there in this community?
- What different cultures are found there?
- What characters have we got/do we need?
- What habits/behaviours will our audience recognise/care about?
    Remind students that their task is to advise you on whether this locality will make a good drama.

    After the initial challenging session, working in groups allows more in-depth work by individuals. Students are not merely taking on the mantle of the expert, but applying analysis in role.

3 Sustaining a role/arguing a case

3 Groups report back to the production team, making recommendations that will help shape the drama. Your role can be to bring in comments about existing soaps, suggesting successful elements and new directions. Take notes of what is said.

In role as experts with a specific task, students bring their thoughts and feelings to bear on the evidence.

4 Brainstorm   'A good soap is one which . . .'

Teacher records the students' 'objective' understanding of the genre. Display this and other notes, as the students can use them as a framework for their drama.

5 Explain that next lesson we shall put some of this research into action.

Developing a Role

- Individual and pair improvisation
- Adding personal layers to drama

RESOURCES
Small articles (suggestions in text)
Ten copies of the Network 7
Community Profile Sheet
(page 38)

As students will be working with and developing roles over several sessions, this lesson, in which they adopt their role, is critical. We want the students to see the roles as people who are not stereotypes, or received images, but people with the possibility of change. Television presents people and situations in an influential manner. To get nearer a sense of truth we start with the students' own drama skills.

You will need to provide enough small articles for each student. The articles should be drawn from different social and ethnic cultures. Here is a sample list:

car key	padlock for bike
shopping list	video membership card
business card	cinema ticket
packet of sweets	invitation to a celebration
big can of hairspray	phone message
old photo	clocking-on card
airmail letter from Pakistan	baby's garment
bus pass	toy
Woman's Realm	scarf
UB40	rent book
item of jewellery	pay slip

1 Improvise as an individual, using movement, language and a prop to create meaning

1 Begin the lesson with a 'lucky dip' in which each student picks an object. Keep this random. Students have to make up a piece of drama lasting 15 seconds, using the object and working alone.

Simple shaping and creative use of the article is reassuring in that everyone knows what to do with the object. Those with a more developed dramatic sense will devise a simple but revealing improvisation.

2 Communicating through prepared improvisation

2 Bring the preparation period to an end by asking for the pieces to be performed. Have either the whole class performing simultaneously, or divide it in half.

Asking for individual work to be viewed takes a lot of time and puts a premium on the 'clever' idea, with students performing to the class at the level of their social relations. By asking for a formal presentation, but with you as the audience, the level of work is higher and you can define and comment on effective work.

3 Play the numbers game. You want students to select an age for their character. A free choice usually ends up with an excess of 16–25 year olds. The numbers game puts this right. Each student thinks of a number between 1 and 20. They call it out to you.
  You reply by saying
— 'keep it';
— 'double it';
— 'double double it';
— 'double it, add 6', etc.
The resulting number becomes their age.

Your interaction with the students is slick and fun. You are actually using this game to give an appropriate challenge to each individual.

4 Give the students a few moments to consider silently how they can build the sense of age, experience and outlook into their scene. While they are thinking, pair off the students by escorting one to join another without disturbing the quiet atmosphere.

Students are concentrating on themselves and their work. You are finding worthwhile partnerships without allowing them to opt for friends.

NETWORK 7: Building our community profile

What and who do we want to know more about?

Will audiences care about these people? Give examples

Any promising ideas?

Useful emotional moments

Good characters

5 Shaping a big moment

5 The partners have to prepare a scene lasting no more than two minutes, keeping the two individual components already developed. Locate the scene in the community.

Roles are being developed by interaction with objects, people and situations, though retaining the autonomy of the individual. A snippet rather than a whole event allows for detailing.

6 The scenes must be well-prepared, specifically limited in time, as they are to be brought to the production team. View each scene with the rest of the class in role as the production team. The production team is issued with clipboards to note responses in small groups.

Giving status and purpose to the viewing are vital in terms of making the experience mutually worthwhile and developing evaluation skills.

Production Team Meeting

- Evaluation and recommendation
- The profile of the community

RESOURCES
The completed copies of the community profile sheet
Large sheets of paper

1 Evaluation

1 Using the notes taken last week and the work on the noticeboard, begin to shape the parameters of your soap opera. Tackle these questions:
- People: Believable and representative without being stereotyped.
- Moments: What incidents are worthy of 'close-up'?
- Time: The series is going to run over a number of years. How do we allow characters and events to develop?

- Realism: How will we make the drama convincing and informative about 'real life'?
- Issues: What matters concern today's audience?

The meeting opens, explores and strengthens the students' understanding of the soap genre and their own work. They are developing the skills and vocabulary of evaluation in a positive setting.

2 Devising a promising role from evidence

2 In groups, the team 'designs' households and their histories. These are to be displayed graphically on large poster sheets. Students are to use good characters from last week, but not to plan characters for themselves to play. Each relationship must contain a 'story line', or tip for the actor. Instruct each group how many male/female roles to plan to reflect the class profile.

Objective decisions about roles help the students to adopt a collaborative approach and to give all the roles equal status in their minds.

3 Explain that you will have cast the roles for the start of the next lesson.

Living in Role

- Life-rate drama
- Creating belief in the everyday life of the community

RESOURCE
Large clock set at 5.30 p.m.

1 Use of space

1 Ask the students to read the noticeboard to discover which role they are to play and to help set out the room into public and private spaces. Allow them to get busy at this and choose your moment to call 'freeze'. In the silence, ask each person to adopt the role they are to experiment with in the soap opera, and initially to work with the two or three people nearest them.

This is a random device for grouping students. The roles arise directly from the thinking about space.

2 Life-rate role play

2 Explain that, as the producer, you want to let the drama run for around half an hour, that the half-hour will be drama at life-rate, and that you will be taking notes and watching, though students should try to ignore you. The time is 5.30 p.m. Everyone can see the clock. Agree guidelines for the improvisation. Each student might want to say something about him or herself, or about the space, for information. It is most important to stress that you are looking for details of everyday life. Nothing dramatic is to happen.

It is not often that older students are given the opportunity to become absorbed in a life-rate drama. Giving them this large chunk of time allows interaction of the roles on an ordinary level and is a good foundation for more structured work. Your presence, perhaps with a clipboard, noting down *only* ordinary details and ideas, gives status to the everyday life as a piece of research. Very much in the style of *cinéma vérité*, this drama without form allows the creation of belief in the locality and the people. Your presence, wandering with the clipboard, is a control device and you become the low-key audience for their work. It is vital that you let it run without intervention. Write down problems, or ideas.

3 Evaluation in role

3 When the clock reaches 6 p.m., call the group together as a group of actors. Give them your report back, in role as TV producer. Concentrate on what you got to know about people and their relationships, what promising personal details cropped up, what problems you will be taking to the next meeting of the production team for discussion. Encourage the actors to comment on details they observed.

The students might well be surprised by some of the details you note, particularly if they were fully absorbed in their roles. You are providing a model for evaluation of work and rewarding successful students.

4 Evaluation of skills

4 Around the circle, debrief/evaluate on improvisation skills by each student completing the sentence, 'It helped my drama most when . . . did . . .'

5 Display your notes from this lesson.

Birthdays

- Tackling an issue
- Improvisation

This lesson can be slotted in at one of several points during the project. It uses a simple framework to introduce an issue into the drama. The issue can be chosen by you or the students.

1 Gather the students round and tell them an anecdotal story of a disappointing birthday present you once received from someone you cared about.

Students seem to find little personal stories quite entertaining. "My mother gave me a present of a home-made brown fake fur coat with duffle peg buttons, when I desperately wanted a pale blue zip-up fur fabric bomber jacket . . ." Begin the drama with a real, non-dramatic experience.

2 Ask the students to adopt their role from the soap opera. Call the characters by name and pair them up in pre-planned combinations.

Your criteria might be social or dramatic. Calling the character by name removes the emphasis from the personal, decreasing the possibility of disagreement arising from embarrassment.

3 Spontaneous improvisation shaping drama

3 Allow about five minutes for improvising a short piece in which something unexpected goes wrong on the birthday of one of the characters. It need not be gift-related and a variety of reasons for disappointment is desirable.

After the time limit, allow another two minutes for the pairs to distil the improvisation to its essence. (See *Teaching Devices* on pages 3–6.)

Share the work rapidly around the class.

4 Developing the idea through group work.
Using drama to link the personal with the universal

4 Develop larger groups of between four and six characters – families, or groups of likely friends, or colleagues. Set the groups the task of devising a short scene in which some kind of celebration is ruined by a problem which is completely beyond the control of the characters there.

We want students to move on to thinking about issues, and therefore need to give guidance so that events such as sudden death/fatal accidents are not chosen. Concentrate more on such issues as:
- being unable to leave the home safely – (in strife riven areas);

- converting a building for use as a women's refuge;
- problems in the family, divorce, lack of money due to unemployment;
- confronting an issue in the news.

5 Work will need focusing during the preparation time to avoid melodrama – cliffhangers will be dealt with in the next lesson.

6 Selection and presentation

6 Groups should present a snippet of their improvisations in which the watchers, in role as the TV producers, get a flavour of the situation, but not a full picture. The action should then be frozen and the class 'good question' (see *Teaching Devices*, page 4) the group to find out
- what's going on;
- how they all feel;
- what they think will happen.

This is a way of evaluating and getting the most out of each situation. If the choice can be made, one of the events will lend itself as an issue, and will be taken on by the whole class. This exercise gives credit to *all* the work.

7 Evaluation in role

7 In role as TV producers, discuss the possibilities for the series/soap. Decide on your criteria:
- what is needed to make it more exciting?
- what action will include those characters who are losing momentum?
- what will complement story-lines already in progress?
  Make a decision to tackle one of the issues.

8 Apply it to any of the next suggested lessons.

Structuring

- Role-play
- Shaping by video

RESOURCES
Video camera, cassette and
playback screen

This lesson uses video filming to learn about structuring.
The video camera and playback are used within the
dramatic structure, not merely as a way of recording an end
result.

1 Decide on a public place or a community event where all
the characters devised and worked at by the students in role
might meet. Set up the space to represent this area.

The class can set up the space out of role as a
negotiated task. It is sometimes good for the teacher to
stand right back from this and allow the students complete
freedom and responsibility. Whatever is decided upon must
be acceptable to and believable for everyone.

2 Inform the students that you will be filming their work.
Explain that you will be a 'fly on the wall', just as you were
in the 'Living in Role' lesson. You do not want them to 'act'
any differently; this is a part of a learning process and there
will be an opportunity to refine work later on.

3 Life-rate role-play in greater
depth

3 Allow a few moments for roles to be recreated. Students
enter the space and begin to role-play. The drama should be
at life-rate and not contain any 'dramatic' incidents. It may
link to the issue.

Each student could enter the space in their own time. This
allows people to feel comfortable in their roles before they
have to start playing, is perhaps more 'realistic', and
sometimes gives support to those with few ideas.

4 Once the drama is under way, begin to film as
unobtrusively as possible. Allow the drama to continue for
up to 15 minutes and then immediately watch the video.

Watch the tape at least twice, as the first time students
will only notice how they look.

5 Evaluate and try to discover if:

- it was too long-winded and 'boring' for an audience to watch;
- it was hard to focus on what was happening because there was too much/not enough going on;
- all the characters being in one place was too contrived and too limiting;
- there is a need for short moments of drama, or *episodes*.

All these features are likely to be found in the video. Obviously, the discussion should deal with any issues arising from the viewing which are in need of analysis. Episodes should be understood in the Brechtian sense, rather than the TV half hour slot!

6 Plan a series of episodes with the material available from the role-play. Decide on a location for each one.

Allow a short time for each episode to be planned, but not over-rehearsed. Encourage characters to link over into several episodes. Video the new structure. Watch and evaluate again. Perhaps juggle the sequencing around and discuss:

- the interrelation of the episodes.
- some comparisons with existing TV soap operas.
- what happens if a character leaves one location in one episode and arrives in a completely new one in the next shot? Is this challenging the viewers' belief?

Boys from the Blackstuff

- Interpretation skills
- Using text to understand television drama

RESOURCE
Photocopiable extracts from *Boys from the Blackstuff* by Alan Bleasdale (pages 46–49)

Although not a soap opera, *Boys from the Blackstuff* contains, in a more sophisticated style, many of the genre's attractive qualities: a strong sense of community and place; an on-going saga about a set of recognisable characters who evoke empathy in their audience; an episodic structure set around a powerful issue. The session uses text extracts to examine the form, which can then be applied to students' own soap drama.

Fraud section office

We see the manageress of the fraud section office, **Miss Sutcliffe,** *plus her* **assistant.** *He is in his mid-thirties. He wears a leather jacket and lots of contempt. The office has two desks, four chairs, two telephones on each desk, filing cabinets, a few charts and a large map of Greater Merseyside. Plus a semi-tropical forest of potted plants on every possible ledge and window sill.*

Yosser *is in the middle of a speech and clearly on his way towards breakdown. He is speeding more than ever. As he talks, the* **manageress** *is looking at her* **assistant,** *who looks at his desk. Then they both look at their watches.* **Yosser's children** *are also present:* **Dustin** *at the window,* **Jason** *by the anglepoise lamp and finally his* **daughter** *by a filing cabinet, where she is opening a drawer.*

Yosser: Look, here I am, man. [*He laughs*] A man. A man. With no job. Looking for one. [*He laughs again*] It's like tryin' t' find the Scarlet Pimpernel. [*He moves in*] Have you got a job, gizza job, eh, I'd be all right, if I had a job. Honest. [*He sits*] I'd be all right. [*He shouts*] Oh yes!

[*During the following speech the* **manageress** *goes to the door, opens it and looks out.* **Loggo** *and* **Chrissie** *are leaning against a wall outside the door. She closes the door on them and on her way back she gently closes the filing cabinet and moves the girl away.* **Yosser** *seems finally to have run out of steam. She stands by the cabinet*]

Miss Sutcliffe: Well, that has been very . . . long, Mr Hughes. I don't think we need to trouble you any further.

[**Yosser** *sits there*]

Miss Sutcliffe: You were, after all, only asked here to help our enquiries.

[*And* **Yosser** *sits there*]

Miss Sutcliffe: If you would like to go. Away. *Now.* Thank you.

[**Yosser** *stands. He walks towards the door and opens it. The* **children** *file out.* **Loggo** *and* **Chrissie** *are waiting still.* **Yosser** *addresses them sanely as he goes out*]

Yosser: You're all right boys, you're sound, y' can kid them soft . . . [*He laughs*]

[**Loggo** *and* **Chrissie** *move towards the door, but* **Miss Sutcliffe** *closes the door on them again.*]

Front of Chrissie's house

Two men are standing outside **Chrissie's** *house at the front door. They knock. The door half opens. We see* **Angie.** *She looks at the men, then at the cards they are flourishing. She slams the door fast.*

Gas man: Go an' get a chisel, Jimmy . . .

[*One man turns away and gets a tool-box from the van.* **Angie** *has run around to the lounge window. When she looks out and sees the mate return with his tool-box, she bangs the window*]

Angie: No. Wait.

[*She returns to the hall and opens the door to let them in*]

Fraud section office

Miss Sutcliffe *is at her desk. Her* **assistant,** *in his leather jacket is closing his note pad, in the centre of his desk.* **Miss Sutcliffe** *is slightly distanced from him. He shuffles his papers with an air of finality and puts his pen away.* **Loggo** *and* **Chrissie** *are sitting at the other side of the desk, looking suitably muted. As well as blank. They all stare at each other for a couple of seconds. Both 'couples' exchange looks.*

Assistant: [*Formally*] I think that just about concludes everything.

Loggo: Er yeah. Er all that y've just said, y' know, the mumbo jumbo – what it means is er . . . what does it mean?

[*The* **assistant** *sighs with great contempt.* **Miss Sutcliffe** *intervenes, speaking pleasantly*]

Miss Sutcliffe: I'm sorry, we didn't intend to confuse you. What my colleague is saying is that it is his intention to forward your papers for prosecution.

Loggo: Y'goin' to do us then?

Miss Sutcliffe: Well it certainly looks that way, gentlemen.

Loggo: Ah, she called me a gentleman, now isn't that nice. Chrissie.

Chrissie: Leave it alone, will y'.

Miss Sutcliffe: Wise advice.

Assistant: In your situation.

Miss Sutcliffe: It would be even wiser to listen to it, Mr Logmond.

Assistant: And no doubt impossible for you.

Loggo: Friggin' hell, this is a double act. Or else one's a ventriloquist.

Assistant: That's enough.

Loggo: 'Enough' – from what you've been sayin' it hasn't even started yet. I thought y' would have had y' pound of flesh when y' killed Snowy Malone.

[**Chrissie** *sighs*]

Assistant: He killed himself.

Loggo: Oh aye, yeah. He was always jumpin' from third floor windows – it was his hobby.

Assistant: None of this behaviour is helping you, you know.

Loggo: I wish I was hard. I mean I wish I had a leather jacket like that to make me hard.

Assistant: Just don't.

Loggo: Why – what you you going to do about it?

Chrissie: Forget it.

Loggo: State of it though Chrissie – had to stand on a stool t' reach manhood.

Chrissie: Y' askin' f' trouble.

Loggo: Well. We've already got it, haven't we – so screw them.

[*He turns to the* **assistant**]

Loggo: All right, go on, go'head do what y' please – see if I care, only I'm telling you just

don't walk home alone in the dark, that's all.

Assistant: I hope, for your sake, that's not a threat.

[**Loggo** *shakes his head. When he replies, he does so quietly*]

Loggo: It's a promise.

[**Miss Sutcliffe** *stands*]

Miss Sutcliffe: If I could bring the matter to a close, Mr Logmond, Mr Todd, before tempers get too heated. [*She crosses to the door*] We will keep you informed of the . . . eventualities of this particular case, but . . .

Loggo: Yeah yeah, all right. Don't bother trying to be nice, eh. It doesn't go with y' job. But at least there's one savin' grace – we won't have you minge bags followin' us around anymore, like bad smells.

Assistant: [*Eager to score any kind of point*] I wouldn't count on that, if I were you.

Loggo/Chrissie: You wha'?

[**Chrissie** *stands*]

Chrissie: What? What for?

Assistant: Because of your known and undenied activities, to possibly further the strength of our case . . . and as a deterrent. To you, and the likes of you.

Chrissie: What's your name? Hey? Come on, what's your name?

Assistant: Why?

[**Chrissie** *crosses to the* **assistant**]

Chrissie: Why? Because I'm going to report you, that's why.

Assistant: It won't do you any good.

Loggo: [*Quietly*] I know what will though . . .

Chrissie: [*Leaning over*] No one's followin' me anymore, I'm tellin' y'. No one. Havin' a job's one thing – I'm sure it must make you very proud – but usin' it to persecute people's another. 'Cos that's what y' doin'. Now what's your name?

Miss Sutcliffe: Gentlemen, gentlemen.

Loggo: There she goes again.

Chrissie: *Tell me your name.*

Loggo: Come on, we've told you ours, it's only fair. Play the white man, will y'.

Chrissie: I want your name.

Loggo: So do I. An' that's just for starters.

Loggo: Give us your friggin' name!

Assistant: . . . I don't want to, and I'm not going to. It's not . . . advisable.

[**Miss Sutcliffe** *takes over*]

Miss Sutcliffe: Absolutely correct and proper, although you can have my name if you like, you can even have my address – however, do not hesitate to register a formal complaint – gentlemen – if you feel you have not been treated in a fitting manner. But I do really suggest that our interview is now over.

[*She moves to the door, smiling warily at them*]

Assistant: For the time being.

[**Loggo** *and* **Chrissie** *hesitate.* **Chrissie** *turns to the* **assistant**]

Chrissie: I wouldn't be you. *I wouldn't be you.* Not for anythin'.

[*They move towards the door and go out. As they go* **Chrissie** *says* 'Fascist Bastards']

[*Inside the fraud section office, there is a pause before* **Miss Sutcliffe** *closes the door*]

Chrissie's back kitchen

We see a close up of **Angie**, *who is full of loathing. She and* **Chrissie** *are sitting on stools, facing out.*

Angie: Where were y'? *Where were y'?* Why didn't you tell me?

Chrissie: I forgot.

Angie: *You forgot?* You forgot they were coming to turn off the gas?

Chrissie: I had other things on my mind.

[**Angie** *goes to the sink, leans out, then turns*]

Angie: Yeah well . . . it doesn't matter does it? We didn't have anything to cook anyway.

[*She throws the fridge door open*]

Angie: Half a tub of marg. Monday's milk and a pound of dead lettuce.

Chrissie: That's all right, we'll save on the electricity.

[**Chrissie** *switches the fridge off at the wall plug*]

[*They move into the hall*]

Angie: Until they come to cut that off.

[*She storms past him to go up the stairs*]

Chrissie's stairs and landing

Chrissie *is following* **Angie** *up the stairs.*

Chrissie: Yeah. Yeah! Until they come and cut that off. And then there won't be anything left to cut off, will there, except me. But they can't cut me off though, can they – that's your department.

Angie: I can't cut off what you haven't got.

[*She goes into the toilet. Fast.* **Chrissie** *reaches the toilet door, tries to open it, but then turns away*]

Chrissie: I didn't think you could hurt me any more.

[*He leans against the door*]

Chrissie: But there again, practice makes perfect.

[*We hear* **Angie**'*s voice through the door*]

Angie: Not in your case.

[**Chrissie** *leans against the doorframe*]

Chrissie: Do you sit around all day thinking these things up? Oh that's a good one – that'll hurt him . . .

Angie: No, I sit there and wait for you to do something. You've got to do something.

[**Chrissie** *bangs on the toilet door*]

Chrissie: I *am* doing something. I'm going to court. Then I'm going to get a heavy fine. [*He is walking back and forth*] Then I'll go to jail. [*He kicks the bedroom door*] Do not stop. And you can go and live with your mother – an event you've been looking forward to for some time.

Angie: You know nothing about me, Chrissie.

Chrissie: No, y' right, y' right I don't. Of course I don't. If I'd have known you better, I would have known that. But I have this ability to live with someone for eleven years and not know anything about them. And of course, not knowing anything about you or anything come to that, I don't know what love is neither, do I.

[**Angie** *laughs from the safety of the toilet*]

Chrissie: Well it obviously isn't an empty fridge and the gas cut off.

[*The toilet flushes.* **Angie** *comes out again.* **Chrissie** *is in her way*]

Angie: Let me go past.

Chrissie: And when we get evicted, we'll be standing there in the street well and truly finished with each other. If that's what love's about.

[*He lets her go past into the bedroom where she straightens the bed*]

Chrissie: It's not my fault, you know. *Not my fault.*

Angie: Self pity, that's all I've heard from you for months. And it's pitiful.

[*He follows her and grabs her arm. He speaks with strength and anger*]

Chrissie: Look, Angie – go away, go to your mother's, go to y' sister's, go to the dogs for all I care – but go away. I'd rather have nothing than what I'm getting now. And go on your own if y' want. You don't have to take the kids and look the martyr.

[*He throws her on the bed*]

Chrissie: If you wanna go, go. And hurry up about it.

[**Chrissie** *goes into their bedroom. Closes the door behind him.* **Angie** *looks at the door*]

Extracts from *'Shop Thy Neighbour'*, an episode of *Boys from the Blackstuff* by Alan Bleasdale

1 The students are still in role as TV producers. Announce the session as being a training day in which new techniques will be learned, suitable for applying to the class drama. Explain that, in fact, *Boys from the Blackstuff* is a TV drama, not a soap, but shares some of the same features. Distribute the extracts around the class and allow students time to read through privately or with others. Share the reading in a rolling programme of volunteer groups.

Preparation minimises stumblings and groups become involved with the play, but a class sharing means members can begin to analyse as a whole.

2 Textual analysis

2 Discussion at this point should concentrate mainly on content.
- What attitudes do the characters display?
- What are the relationships between characters?
- What is a fraud office?
- What is the issue on which the scene focuses?
- What similarities can you see between this material and soap opera at this stage?

3 Revealing meanings by practical analysis

3 Continue to work as a class, with volunteer demonstrators enacting moments from the text.
Here we suggest several ways of using the extracts to make teaching points relevant to the students' own drama.

Space   Read the opening scene description and set up the space with whatever props are available. Place characters Yosser, Miss Sutcliffe and kids in space and freeze at a meaningful moment, sharing feelings about the space. The class can offer suggestions for improvements, as in forum.

Meanings are created in the space.

Activate the space, focusing on the issue of unemployment, to allow movement to take on meaning for the people and the situation.

Symbol   Play the lines referring to the assistant's leather jacket; read the description. Discuss the symbolic meanings: power, superiority, tough, rich, trendy, protection, a shield.

This is a simple introduction to the concept of symbolism.

Juxtaposition   In groups, prepare the whole extract and present it. Discuss the power of juxtapositioning in the gas man scene, messages created within it, how we look more closely at what happens next. Introduce the vocabulary.

Humour   'That's all right, we'll save on the electricity.'

'I can't cut off what you haven't got.'
How does the humour relate to the issue?
Does it reinforce or undermine points which are being made?
Is it funny? Do we laugh? Why do we laugh?

Truth   While some groups rehearse the script, others begin a life-rate drama around everyday domestic routines. Remind them of the learning that arose from the lesson 'Living in Role'. Set up a forum to consider which of the two styles more clearly represents the truth.

This is an introduction to a difficult concept of truth in the theatre. The theatre form can present a more truthful and realistic picture of life than life-rate work. The use of form allows issues and attitudes to be pointed and events to become entertaining and powerful, communicating an understanding of life more effectively.

Character   Ask students to find a line which is significant for a character and rehearse it. Play these lines at random round the class, giving students the choice of using their chosen line or mimicking someone else's.
Discuss why we like some people/lines and not others.
How do we identify with characters?
Is it what they say, how they say it, or what it means?
Is it important to identify?
Are the characters stereotypes?

Language   Miss Sutcliffe wields power, or tries to do so, over Chrissie and Loggo. There is sarcasm in the use of the the word 'Gentlemen'. Miss Sutcliffe keeps calm and handles the situation. Her assistant gets agitated and would lose control. Use this as a discussion of register.

Omnibus Edition

RESOURCE
Noticeboard of good moments

To conclude the work, prepare an omnibus edition. Good moments from any lesson are drawn together, using the noticeboards, videos and production notes as reminders.
Time will need to be given to
• negotiate the content and sequence of events;
• rehearse chosen scenes;
• plan links between the scenes.

This process helps develop skills in preparation for shaping drama for an audience. Students regard their improvisations as work in progress that can be revised, played in a different sequence and so on. Thinking of links will be helpful in the future. An omnibus edition is a practical version of what is worth writing about for coursework.

Cliffhanger

- Experimental workshop
- Building towards a climax

The students use the cliffhanger technique – an important feature of all soap opera drama. They learn its subtleties and the ease with which it can so easily be over-exaggerated.

[1] Receptive in-role response

1 In role, explain that ratings are falling due to competition from a rival network. We need to do something exciting and leave TV audiences crying out for more. Suggest a cliffhanger at the end of the next episode.

What is a cliffhanger? Show the example, or talk about one seen recently.

[2] Building to a climax

2 In twos/threes/fours set up an experimental workshop in which students, out of role and unbound by the class soap opera, prepare a range of cliffhangers. Encourage some to be 'over the top'. Allow five minutes to work on this and decide a maximum running time for each example.

Freedom from the soap opera's theme(s), content, characters, will mean that students are likely to come up with creative ideas. By allowing them to 'go over the top', you are able to de-mystify the technique, teach how to use it profitably and how to measure its credibility.

3 Share the work quickly around the class. Enjoy the humorous situations. Discuss, as TV bosses, what might work and what won't.

4 Continuing the experimental workshop structure, divide the class into soap opera-related groupings of up to six people. This will probably be done in negotiation with the class as TV producers. Again, encourage some of the groups to opt for exaggerated cliffhangers.

This might be an appropriate point to end the soap unit, with a fire or other devastating final incident. Otherwise, the characters can be tested on how they cope with serious problems.

Devices for Enrichment

Slot these ideas into the project to tackle specific problems, move the drama on, review and evaluate.

In production team roles:

- One feature of the soap genre is that the community is a safe place; when people move outside it something invariably goes wrong. The device is used to add new tension. The team can discuss this, taking examples from soaps they have seen, before planning a new location.
- The drama can become restricted by too much territorial life-rate work. Use the production team to create greater opportunities for people to meet through a new situation.
- Use the notion of ratings to axe characters and encourage others, e.g. a letter from a fan of someone who is doing good work which is unacknowledged by the others.
- Awareness of audience – Soap audiences are consumers of a product that is shaped and marketed. It is designed to be compelling and addictive. An episode can be targeted to specific audience groups. By stepping into the role of shapers, students become more aware of how their drama is received and interpreted and can begin to plan for a specific interpretation.
- Use of language – This can be a signal of class or cultural origins, as well as an indicator of how formal or informal a character feels in a situation. Use the production team to develop awareness of language by advising of language appropriate to a specific setting or situation.
- Plan different perspectives on a major incident like a crisis, or a cliffhanger. Use the drama to gain a sense of perspective and bias. How would . . . see this?

In soap opera roles:

- Take on a role yourself to challenge responses.
- Make a tape recording of 'local radio news' to introduce an issue or event.
- Use students who were absent to take the role of the returned long-lost relative.

Narrative line   Consistency of characterisation is a feature of soaps, each character having an extended history which is referred to as a means of reinforcing belief. You could insert a device for summing up the 'truth' – for example, a vicar at a funeral talking about the life and times of the deceased. On a smaller scale, a character can inform someone else of a recent or past event. Either of these tasks stretch an individual to shape and present a longer piece. Remember to display your working notebook as a sample of valuable source material for coursework and development of drama.

Making It Home

NETWORK

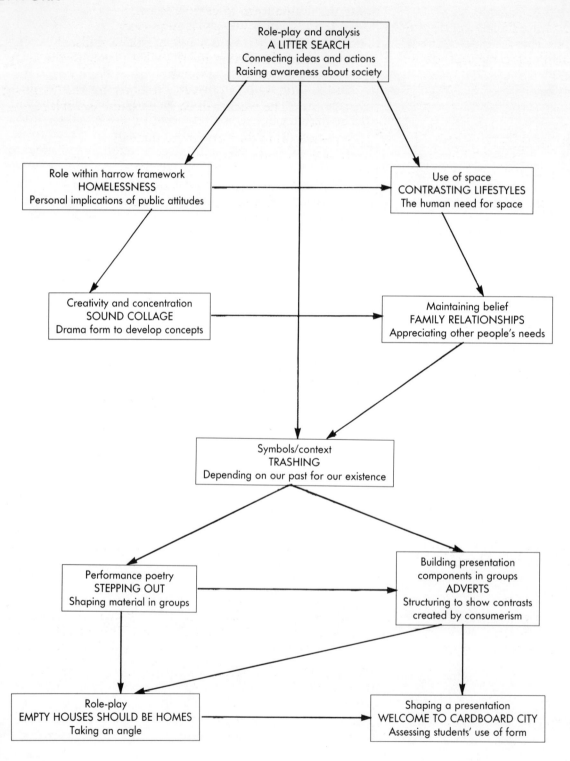

Role-play and analysis
A LITTER SEARCH
Connecting ideas and actions
Raising awareness about society

Role within harrow framework
HOMELESSNESS
Personal implications of public attitudes

Use of space
CONTRASTING LIFESTYLES
The human need for space

Creativity and concentration
SOUND COLLAGE
Drama form to develop concepts

Maintaining belief
FAMILY RELATIONSHIPS
Appreciating other people's needs

Symbols/context
TRASHING
Depending on our past for our existence

Performance poetry
STEPPING OUT
Shaping material in groups

Building presentation
components in groups
ADVERTS
Structuring to show contrasts
created by consumerism

Role-play
EMPTY HOUSES SHOULD BE HOMES
Taking an angle

Shaping a presentation
WELCOME TO CARDBOARD CITY
Assessing students' use of form

This project focuses on role-making and role-taking as basic human experiences, a tenet of the Welsh Joint Education Committee's GCSE. It enables students to
- use the drama form to explore issues;
- develop auditory and spatial awareness;
- experiment with a wider range of drama skills.

From a simple starting point – what people throw away – we explore the concept of home.

All homework tasks provide a resource for the 'Stepping Out' lesson. The work will be given status if displayed by the teacher.

Skills taught in this project are these:
- creating a sound collage;
- use of space;
- evaluation of the uses of the drama form;
- the use and effect of symbols in drama.

A Litter Search

- Role-play and analysis
- Connecting ideas and actions. Raising awareness about society.

From Stage 3 in this lesson, students' strengths and weaknesses can be diagnosed. You can help them to make connections between ideas and action. The skill of adopting a role which builds on research is rewarded. Students learn to use their roles to move the drama on.

| 1 Research | **1** When the class has arrived, set the students the task of finding an item of litter which has been thrown away. Allow about five minutes.

An unusual stimulus generates curiosity and expectation. It is important to wait until the whole class is present in order to gain full impact from this strange request. |
|---|---|

2 Early stages of generating an idea for the drama

2 Assemble the collection. Initiate a class discussion:
What do all the items have in common?
What do they tell us about our way of life?
Are they of any use to anyone?
  Responses to listen out for:
— that they are luxury items;
— that they provide evidence of consumerism;
— that what some people discard, other people use.

  Maintaining the stimulating atmosphere, use students' intellect to 'discover' meanings. As there are no right answers, every student can make a valuable contribution.

3 Adopting a simple role that develops the research theme

3 Students adopt a simple role related to the litter and the analysis of it. Some possible examples are refuse collector, antique dealer, councillor, caretaker, homeless person, environmentalist, shopkeeper, parent.

  This is an opportunity to consolidate thinking and action through the dramatic form.

4 Improvising a simple scene combining role and research

4 Ask the students to record conclusions immediately. Students should write an individual response or analysis. A display of the litter could be individual or collective.

  Encourage the habit of making personal notes during a lesson. There is scope to respond on different levels, but everyone will have begun to record findings.

Homelessness

- Role within narrow framework
- Personal implications of public attitudes

The rubbish was used in the last lesson to raise awareness about society. In this lesson, the personal implications of public attitudes are considered. By taking tramps as a focus, but not contrasting them with an extremely wealthy city gent, stereotypes are avoided. The issue is given more relevance because the students can adopt a role whose views are not very different from their own. The lesson is structured in a series of small tasks, to enable the students to develop roles in greater detail by achieving short term goals.

1 Concentration, confidence and independence

1 On entering the room, students should stand in a space alone adopting a relaxed, balanced position. The teacher speaks in a slow, evenly-paced voice, keeping a low pitch, leaving up to a minute between each request: 'Close your eyes . . . listen to the sounds outside the room . . . listen to those inside . . . and now those inside your body.' Work towards a feeling of weariness: 'You are feeling very rested and quite heavy. Look at the ground and find a place to sink into . . . feel as if the floor is pushing up into your back . . . give up the whole effort of holding yourself up. Give yourself as long as you need to do this.'

Pupils should by now be in a relaxed state on the floor.

Voice helps to create the atmosphere and role. A listening activity focuses attention on the lesson. This is an effective task for improving concentration. The listening will be a feature of the lesson.

The aim is to enable the students to experience the link between physical and mental processes.

2 Adopting a role
Building communication through movement
Group development of common role

2 Explain to the students that they are all asleep after a very hard time. Half the class can continue sleeping and the rest should get up. Brief these students to adopt the role of tired, busy, well-paid and *kind* workers, on their way to the office. Ask them to discuss in role altogether what they would do if they met a 'down-and-out'. Whilst they are talking, herd the other group of students into a corner by approaching them in role: 'Come along now, we can't have you dossing about here. Pick up your papers, come on, get going.'

By adopting a role that reacts to the group of homeless people, you reinforce their feeling of being outsiders.

Keep your eye on both groups and feed in extra motivation if necessary.

Framed as 'down-and-outs', the second group of students are briefed to shape the drama by asking for money for 'a cuppa tea'.
— If the answer is yes, ask for money for a meal.
— If the answer is yes, ask to have a meal in a worker's home . . .
— and so on, pushing for more and more: to share a meal with the family, have a bath, have a bed for the night, stay a few days.
These students should then identify a city office worker to pursue.

When dividing the students into two even groups, you will need to have their skills in mind. If the groups are positioned in such a way that they are balanced, you could simply stand in the middle of the space and address each in turn. Alternatively, you might want to tap specific individuals and indicate which way to go. Look for students using the sense of weariness.

The briefs push back the boundaries of personal space and charity. The next activity unfolds from two perspectives on the common situation. By informing the homeless folk whom among the workers they will pursue, but not giving information to the city workers themselves, you set up motivation in the former and provoke an unguarded response in the latter.

The workers have the confidence which comes from financial security and self-esteem.

---

3 Sustaining a role
Communication through movement

3 Allow the pair work to run for as long as it is profitable (up to five minutes).

It is important that you just let this happen. Resist trying to improve on students' work at this stage. They are assembling the raw material for a prepared piece of drama, both in content and form, by believing in the situation.

---

4 Unstructured evaluation

4 Let all the students talk freely about their experience for a few seconds.

This allows a release from role.

---

5 Distilling to the essence
Using the dramatic form

5 Shape a short piece, keeping roles and partners, focusing on a poignant moment. The drama should contain messages about the ideas considered in the last lesson.

Consolidating the issues and content into an effective, structured form helps the students to see how in drama meanings and means of communication are interlinked.

6 Evaluation of use of space and movement

6 Share the students' work and evaluate it in terms of space and movement: distance; eye contact; physical contact; direction faced; speed.

Refer to 'Teaching Devices' (pages 3–6) for methods of looking at work that fits into the time available.

The significance of movement and attitudes can be reinforced as a function of role and communicator of feelings.

Contrasting Lifestyles

- Use of space
- The human need for space

The objective of this lesson is to enable students to understand the human need for space and to be able to understand and use spatial awareness to communicate. The primary skill here is use of space and setting, which we analyse in detail. Students are using other skills such as communication and use of role.

RESOURCES
Five or six 15m lengths of string
Photograph of family outside tent

1 Establishing an empty space in which the drama can take place

1 In groups of three to five, students enclose on the floor a space with a ball of string (not more than 15m long). The space should represent a home and be the *minimum* size they could live in.

This is a task for active group work and negotiation.

2 Giving the space a believable function
Co-operating in the use of space with others
Structuring use of space to convey an image and an atmosphere

2 The majority of groups should then adopt a role and begin to role-play, living in the space. Another couple of groups meanwhile prepare a live advert, lasting 30 seconds, with a slogan which supports the picture they are presenting of 'happiness in the tiniest home'.

Getting students actively involved in living in the space enables you to brief a small number of groups with a specific task. Developing the theme of contrast from earlier lessons, some students are given a task that uses movement and words to point an issue.

3 The effecting of patterns and space between people to create a stage picture where the context and form are in harmony

3 On completion, signal switching on a TV set, so that students watch the adverts in role.

Watching one another's work needs a purpose in drama. This technique of watching and responding in role maintains belief and heightens the commitment to the work viewed.

4 Consciously structuring space, lines and levels

4 Use the photograph as a basis for evaluation. Those who have been enacting the adverts become 'puppets' for the others to re-shape a moment from their presentation. They should change its basis from one of idealism to one of reality in a series of still pictures.

The students who had worked spontaneously before have a chance to shape a stage picture.

A happy home?

| 5 Evaluation of the use of space | 5 Recorded evaluation, to be completed before the next lesson. Students contrast the use of space in the fantasy world of the television advert and the 'real' one of overcrowded homes. Sketches, cartoons, plans, diagrams, and notes can be used. |

The contrast helps the students understand that use of space has meaning and needs planning to reveal that meaning effectively.

Sound Collage

- Creativity and concentration
- Drama form to develop concepts

Listening was an important aspect of the last lesson. During this lesson we ask the students to consider sounds around them that they don't often consciously hear. The sounds in a home can reveal the way people interact. Time is given to consider familiar sounds and to use the drama form to interpret them.

1 Understanding the relationship between ideas; their relevance to the whole
Processing ideas and understanding from experience

1 Students gather round and discuss with the teacher the project so far: how the collecting of litter gave rise to
- considerations of values in society;
- creating contrasts;
- an understanding of the meanings in space/setting.

Students are encouraged to retain and develop the concepts arising from the situation.

2 Sensitivity and group awareness
Sound and rhythm sequencing

2 Sitting in a circle, the students are asked to recall 'breakfast time' in their home. Focusing on the *sounds* of the morning, e.g. radio on, footsteps downstairs, banging on bathroom door, alarm clock, kettle and so on. Each student should decide on one sound and recreate it using just him/herself, and no props. Working in pairs to create a sequence of sounds would also work well. Play the sounds around the circle, one at a time. Encourage the students to experiment freely with sequencing and patterns. Play the sound collage spontaneously.

This reinforces auditory awareness. As students express their sounds, they will have to listen to one another and time their contributions to fit in with the rhythm of the whole. The piece may well become humorous. It is equally likely that there will be some silent moments. This is fine.

|3| To contribute to group development and shaping roles using sounds

3 Recalling the discussion at the start of the session, in three groups the students now prepare a sound collage of their own which re-creates the sounds of a home, with its particular atmosphere. They should be left to work on this for about ten minutes.

Keep the number of groups down to allow for a workable noise level and for concentration. You will also need time to feed in the next task to each group in turn.

|4| Juxtaposing sounds and movements
Abstracting

4 When a group has a sound collage with a clear shape, ask the students to look at how movement can arise from the sounds. When they have a movement, they can experiment with running the movement out of sequence with the sound; making the movement and sound come from different people; making the size of the movement out of proportion to the sound. Creating an impression, rather than enacting a scene, teaches simple abstracting techniques.

Building on spatial skills from previous lessons, aim for stylised movement that reinforces the patterns and rhythms of the sound structure. This stylisation entails making the everyday action abstract, patterned, but content bound. This technique can be used within rehearsed presentations in the future.

|5| Realisation of ideas
Concentration

5 Share the work around by using each group to run one after the other. The teacher can freeze the action and cut from one to another to experiment with the overall effect.

Playing all the scenes in an orchestrated form allows sharing of work in a limited time and creates a need for sharp concentration.

|6| Free evaluation

6 After a moment's pause, allow open chatter in response to the experience.

Opening the evaluation enables a wider range of responses to be expressed.

Family Relationships

Role-play is used here to enable students to see family relationships from another point of view. Continuing the consideration of space and what it means to people is helpful in building the skill of communicating through space in drama. These roles are familiar to students, giving you scope for assessing role-play skills.

- Maintaining belief
- Appreciating other people's needs

1 Understanding the nature of role-play

1 The session focuses on role-play. To begin with, recap with the students on the elements which make up a successful role-play, for example:
- believing and accepting;
- choosing an appropriate role for yourself and the drama;
- agreeing on a time and space;
- bringing in your own role and including the roles of others;
- moving the drama on naturally.

Evaluation before an activity takes place ensures awareness of quality by focusing on specific skills and techniques of role-play.

2 Adopting a role

2 Divide the class into smaller working groups. Aim to have a variety of sizes and family relationships which reflect the range of households in society. Ask each student to find a place in the family by declaring his/her relationship to one other role only. As each person declares a relationship, the pattern of the whole group changes and finally becomes fixed with the last declaration.

At the same time as creating families other than the typical nuclear family, family members become aware of how others are related to them. Allow the groups to reflect the multiplicity of households in society.

3 Negotiation

3 The groups briefly discuss their circumstances. Not all of the relatives need live with one another and not all of the relationships need be blood ones. Negotiate and build up the space for each of the groups and set their time of day.

Allow time to establish relationships.

4 Role-play skills
In the early stages:
— adopting a role
— creating belief in the space

4 Students role-play life in the home for around 20 minutes. The issues about privacy and togetherness are the subtext of the work.

— establishing realism
— accepting the roles of others
In the later stages:
— sustaining and developing a role
— developing relationships and
  motivation
— maintaining belief
— moving the drama forward
— not being over-dramatic
— being aware of the situation and
  its implications

Give ample time for students to do their own work, while selecting a focus which builds on the use of space (form) and relations (content).

5 Evaluation in role

5 All the parents now team up together. While the rest of the class observe, they talk together in role about their attitudes towards home, focusing firstly on what is good about it and then on what the difficulties are, picking up their experiences of privacy and togetherness.

We have used parents here so that young people all gain a different perspective from their own. The next lesson has the young person as the initiator of actions, informed by this experience. Using listening in role gives a purpose and focus for observing the work of others.

6 Deepening the role and the drama
Using stimulus effectively

6 Using the feelings revealed, the group role-plays now continue.

Understanding and motivation are used on a social and dramatic level. The drama is fed by positive responses as well as those which are too often stressed.

7 Evaluation of relationships and interaction

7 Documented evaluation of the lesson could be in the form of a flow chart, or illustration. The students' role in the centre of the page is interrelated to others with symbols, pictures and statements representing feelings and attitudes. An example is given opposite.

The diagrammatic form is helpful for all levels of ability to conceptualise relationships. The exercise can highlight indicators of the use of space and movement and be developed into a piece of coursework.

8 For the next lesson, pupils should bring in several articles that were more important to them in their past than they are now.

EVERY STEP YOU TAKE

GRAND-DAUGHTER
BY MY 1ST CHILD.
Looks just like Fran, but instead of a quiet girl like Fran she is very noisy and well. Only happy if she has what she wants.

GRANDSON
BY MY 1ST CHILD.
a sweet boy with a great talent of drawing. Very noisy at times, but knows the right time and place of doing things

3rd CHILD
A little boy called Paul, always crying and keeps me young all day. Birth 15 hours.

MY 2nd CHILD
A girl called Anna very sweet first sucks her thumb and will be content just watching me work.

MY HUSBAND.
I met him at a dinner dance and it was love at first sight, but all he does is watch TV all day and doesn't help.

MY 1ST CHILD
a little girl called Fran very quiet and very good was a hard birth 24 hours.

MY SISTER
I fought a lot with her she always broke my toys and crept about me. I've lost contact with her now.

MY SISTER
Very bossy as she was the eldest. always made sure I was alright, very caring.

MY BROTHER
My brother was very quiet and never did much but read and play with his teddy bear called Edward. I see him only at Christmas now he hasn't changed much.

MY FATHER
I was 10 years old when my father was killed during the war. I don't remember him much.

MY MOTHER
She helped me through my childhood during the war. she means a lot to me and my children now.

ME
↓

THE MOTHER IS THE ROOT OF LOVE AND HOLDS THE FAMILY TOGETHER

Trashing

The concept of symbolism is introduced here and the relationship between the past and the present is explored. The techniques of counterpoint and contrast are introduced in an improvisation that is fun and meaningful.

[1] Appreciating the possibilities of using objects

1 Students divide themselves into pairs with their objects from home. The teacher demonstrates the idea of 'Trashing', using an object he/she has brought from home which has been important to him/her in the past. 'I used to love this rubber. I used to love this rubber. I used to love its smell of raspberries, it was always in my pencil case at school. I think it's silly now, I'll throw it away.'

By being a little confidential and revealing, you are setting the tone for their work and giving them a sample idea.

[2] Understanding the focus and boundaries of the task

2 The task is then for one of the pair to become an 18-year-old (a) and the other the same person at a much younger age (b).
(a) tries to throw away aspects from his/her past.
(b) tries to persuade him/her to stop by reminding him/her of the memories represented.
The pairs should spend 20 minutes preparing a presentation based on this symbiosis.

You are setting up an intensive pair-work task. If you have an odd number in the class, ask one student to be the narrative director, i.e. it is his/her life that the others are playing. By describing the task, the teacher limits the amount of content the students have to negotiate, enabling them to concentrate on the form of communication. The scene called 'Symbiosis' from George C. Wolfe's *The Colored Museum* (Methuen, Royal Court Writers series, 1987) will give you some ideas. Symbiosis is a union between two people, each of whom depends for his/her existence on the other.

[3] Using the dramatic form:
— roles and relationship
— use of language, including
  speaking simultaneously,
  repeating lines, etc.
— space
— shape of scene
— timing
— rhythms
— counterpoint
— eye contact

[4] Presentation and evaluation in terms of form

3 The teacher works around the class helping the pairs to use the drama form to their best advantage.

You will be better able to develop skills of form by applying them to students at specific times to meet their needs and abilities.

4 Students present their work to one another. It is evaluated orally (and on paper if approprate) in terms of effective use of form.

Sharing a concentrated and developed piece of work which has been supported specifically by the teacher gives evidence to fellow students and the teacher about the dramatic form.

ADAPTING THE NETWORK

You will know by now which areas are more productive for your students. You could select from these four alternative lessons, depending on the interests of the group and the skills they need to work on. Our principle is to draw from the list of skills under Form and the ideas and concepts under Content below.

Form	Content
Sound collage	Homes
Spatial relationships	Litter
Setting	Homelessness
Patterns } in movement and sound	Family roles
Rhythms }	Adverts
Establishing belief	Meanings in
Contrast and counterpoint	artefacts
Symbols	Belonging
Distilling to the essence	

Choose from the following four sample lesson plans.

Stepping Out

- Performance poetry
- Shaping material in groups

Everyone leaves home, but only a small percentage of children run away under emotional stress. Drama lessons have traditionally concentrated on the more desperate experience, thereby reinforcing the negative. Here we concentrate on the assured stepping out, with the emphasis on competence and confidence. This material will take a couple of hours of lesson time.

OBJECTIVES

- To explore in groups the experience of stepping out.
- To use the forms of performance poetry to contrast with realism.

(Try to have some percussion instruments available, perhaps by encouraging the students to bring in their own.)

SKILLS

- Shaping material to suit the intention.
- Rhythm and pattern.
- Group work.

TASK

Brainstorm 'Stepping Out'. Using the more positive ideas from the brainstorm, each group focuses on a scene set around a doorway of a home. Take a rhythm, such as a rap, a reggae beat, the rhythm of a well-known song, or a voice-over technique. In groups, write a poem about the situation, dubbing words onto the beat. The poems should be simple and designed to be performed. Encourage the students to work quickly, even allowing 'cheating' to make the scan work.

Once the poem is written, juxtapose a rehearsed improvisation on the same topic. Experiment with contrasting for effect. Evaluation could be in terms of how the form affected your understanding of the content.

Adverts

- Building presentation components in group
- Structuring to show contrast, created by consumerism

An introduction to the juxtaposing of scenes to create meanings in the drama. This lesson explores, in a simple way, the concept of consumerism.

The outline could be developed for use over two hours. This can be another useful component in a future presentation.

SKILLS
- abstract/naturalism
- juxtapositioning
- simple structuring
- sound collage
- communication through language of words
- simple presentation

1 The students should spread out around the room. Give them each an age between five and 70 and ask them to think of a luxury product that might be desired, above all else, by someone of that age.

The students then give voice to their 'desires' around the class using the opening words: 'I want a/some/those . . .' Using the same words, change the tone to a whine and then to a demand.

Experiment with a variety of tones used within the group and run again several times to create an effective sound collage.

2 In twos or threes, the students should take one of these 'desires' and adopt the roles of advertising agents. They create a very simple slogan which begins: 'We can offer you . . .'

The slogans are to tempt and persuade. Encourage the groups to experiment with ways of speaking to gain maximum impact.

3 The sound collage could be developed here by combining the 'offers' and the 'desires' and perhaps adding movement.

4 Spread out the selection of available up-to-date adverts and briefly discuss, in relation to the sound collage, why adverts have so much impact.

Adverts create desires, we desire what we see.

Hidden promise that life will change for the better encourages competitiveness and jealousy.

Students should jot down notes from this discussion.

5 Divide the class into groups of three to five to devise a naturalistic family scene in which advertising causes problems. They should aim for a product which is three to five minutes long, spending between 20 to 30 minutes improvising and polishing it.

6 The presentation of the work should incorporate the initial sound collage, the advertising slogans and the naturalistic scenes. Experiment with the structure to create different meanings.

7 Discuss how the juxtaposition creates meaning. The effect of interspersing naturalism with abstract sound comments on and underlines the point.

8 Students write a paragraph exploring juxtapositioning, using examples from the session.

Empty Houses Should Be Homes

- Role-play
- Taking an angle

RESOURCES
Video camera, still camera, notebooks, portable tape recorders, word processor or typewriter. Photocopies of article 'Estate project delayed 2 years'

A text is used to develop role-play in another direction from the same core theme of 'Making It Home'. A newspaper article gives the scope for seeing different perspectives on the same situation. It leads to drama techniques associated with *cinéma vérité* and reportage, and is a model form for coursework recording the role-play itself.

OBJECTIVES
- To explore the relationship between buildings and the lifestyles they allow.
- To use role-play to explore a range of perspectives.

SKILLS
- role-play
- group work
- establishing belief
- taking an angle

TASKS

1 Establish life in a partly empty block of flats. The building is in decline, but the people feel at home there. They are so familiar with the place that they can turn on a light without looking where the switch is. The conditions are poor, but this is their home.

2 Select some students to stay in those roles, observed by the others. At a meeting of the Council Housing Committee the rest of the class is in role as officers and elected members discussing a proposal to convert the whole area into a luxury development. Meanwhile, the policies that lead to long waiting lists leave some people living in very temporary accommodation. Issue the photographs to two small groups. Ask them to take on a role of either a person in the photograph, or someone who is aware of their problems.

3 Using video, tape recordings, cameras and notebooks, a small group, in role as a TV crew, record events unfolding. The people in their flats try to live as normal under the pressure of publicity and poor conditions; the council prepares for a meeting with the developers.

   At this point a number of techniques used previously can be helpful. You could use a frozen picture, distilling to the essence to focus and share work. (See *Teaching Devices*, pages 3–6.)

4 Work the material towards a conclusion. We might all dream of 'rags to riches', but here the buildings are benefiting, not the people. How does the group want the issue to be resolved?

RECORDING THE EXPERIENCE

You have the experience, the techniques used to focus and the records made by the TV crew as evidence of what happened. Ask the group members to write a newspaper article using quotes, headlines and pictures, to present the case with sympathy towards the people they were playing.

EVALUATION

When students use creative writing in drama they begin to process and evaluate the experience. This is much more readily achievable than the task of formal evaluation. Once students have written the articles as a group, these can be produced on a word processor. Ensure everyone has a copy. The evaluation task is then to identify extracts from the 'newspaper' and analyse how these were communicated through drama. This can take the form of notes to accompany the article.

Estate project delayed 2 years

Paul Hoyland

ONE of Birmingham's most dilapidated council estates – Leach Green at Rubery – stands mostly empty, two years after the city council and the Department of the Environment began talks about an improvement scheme.

The council joined forces with a property developer to refurbish the estate and applied for an urban development grant last June.

"We have still had no formal response from the Department of Environment," said a spokeswoman for the council's housing department.

"We have re-housed tenants in preparation for what we saw as a complete revitalisation of the estate, which was built in 1955 and has 118 flats left."

The Department of Environment blamed the delay on the complexity of the project.

"We want to see something done as much as anybody, but it is a very complex scheme with property being refurbished for sale by the developer and other property refurbished for the council to let," a DoE spokesman said.

"We have to be satisfied that the proposal represents value for money and at the moment the ratio of private capital to exchequer is not acceptable."

From *The Guardian*

Welcome to Cardboard City

Students have done much of their learning through acting out. This task gives them an opportunity for independent study in which they investigate, balance and shape material for presentation. The magazine article was selected because of the rich style used to conjure the atmosphere of life in Cardboard City. Recognising that the imagination works by processing and personalising experience, the students have the opportunity to use their improvisation techniques to match their creative intention.

OBJECTIVES
- To enable the students to collaborate on the shaping of an expressive response to the issue of homelessness.
- To provide the students with an opportunity to research and interpret textual stimulus.
- To use the drama form to communicate creative intentions.

SKILLS
The skills students are likely to use are those which have been developed through this unit. They can form part of your assessment criteria. Making these skills explicit to the students is a helpful teaching device, allowing them to take a more active and conscious role in their own development. The evaluation at the end of the work relates directly to these skills.
- **Space**: shaping the use of space for meaning, focus, picture and boundaries.
- **Gesture**: using movement and facial expression for physical clarity and expressiveness.
- **Language**: using language appropriate to role.
- **Role**: synthesising personal experience into a role that shows awareness of motivation within the group; using role to move the drama towards agreed meaning.
- Sensitivity and awareness in the selection and interpretation of raw material to create counterpoint.
- The use of lighting.

In helping students to appreciate just what is meant by these skills, you need to discuss them before the stimulus is given. You might expect responses such as:
Space: How we make our audience know where to look at a special moment by placing the people and objects in the scene.
Gesture: Making an action of kindness clear and using it at the right time.
Language: Some 'dossers' are ex-university dons.
Role: Helping one another by not speaking all the time. In role, hinting at one's background.

Welcome to Cardboard City

Upstairs, in the warm, two make-believe tramps endlessly wait for Godot; downstairs, in the cold, real ones are waiting for soup.

JOHN SWEENEY *waits with them*

IN THE OPEN-TO-THE-WIND concrete crypt of London's South Bank the cold is bitter, horrible; it burns like acid on the skin. As Estragon and Vladimir perplex at the Lyttelton Theatre, flautists pipe at the Royal Festival Hall and film buffs stream from the back exit of the National Film Theatre, a crowd of 20 to 30 men stamp their feet, blow into their hands and wander to and fro. The film-goers gawk at the wanderers, who take care not to notice, and keep apart from each other, so as not to register that they have something in common — they're all waiting for soup.

Pitifully vivid in the stark glare of an overhead security light is a green blanket which has taken human form and is shuddering uncontrollably; by the blanket's fringe lies a jaunty blue blazer with gold buttons, perfect dress for the Rotary Club but piercingly pathetic here, on the hard concrete ground patchworked with puddles of stinking, green piss. But the shuddering thing in the blanket is not purposeless; it too is waiting for soup.

Away from the glare a terraced street of cardboard-fronted hutches distinguishes itself in the gloom: Welcome to Cardboard City. Not dogs, not pigs, but people live here. Some of the hutch-dwellers are trying to sleep, but it can't be easy, with the cold and the clanking of the trains, the screech of car alarms and the wood-on-concrete clatter of the fanatic skateboarders, weaving and dodging only feet away. The racket is worsened by three bawling kids, in the tow of a woman who says she is looking for her husband: "He's got my child benefit card. He sometimes comes here for the soup."

Inside one empty box, the owner has patriotically stuck up a colour photograph of the Queen on horseback; it would look ordinary in a Home Counties saloon bar amidst the horse brasses, but here it screams blasphemously, a weird echo of straight-laced domesticity. On the front of another hutch, a house-proud owner has scrawled "The Boss Taff Says Keep Out." Behind a third, a candle flickers underneath the sloping roof, the light of which illuminates "Elvis" drawn on the side of a cardboard coffin-bed, and, alive but terrifyingly motionless, a bearded man, whose face remains as still as an icon even when our eyes meet.

Suddenly, the City bursts into energy with the arrival of the first soup wagon. It's like one of those ads on the telly where as soon as someone pours a noxious fizzy drink the party comes to life. The hutch-dwellers emerge, more men appear from nowhere hurrying hungrily to the van, even the shudder casts off the green blanket and shows itself to be Sophie, the only bag lady present, who casts an almost completely round, tragi-comical shadow with the clothes-on-clothes she wears to dull the cold. Filthy-faced, she mutters mad words and darts suspicious glances all around her while drinking her soup from a toy bucket. Sophie is the worst case: wretchedness with a capital W.

The soup is worth waiting for, though it feels odd, and rather disturbing, that the young woman volunteer from the Bondway Hostel pours it out without giving me a second glance. But then, why should she? Many of the men look better dressed than I do. It's good, thick stuff with bits of veg and chunks of unpeeled potato to chew on. It warms the hands through the white styrofoam cups, which hurts, as they had quietly lost their feeling with the cold.

Empty cups

The soup breathes warmth into the men, who start talking and joking and tossing the empty cups at each other. A new knot of men swirl round a volunteer who is doling out sandwiches from a black plastic rubbish bag; soon the volunteer walks away, leaving the men to jostle and shove and good-humouredly cuss for food.

With the soup the wanderers peel off their anonymity and become human and different. Labels like tramps, dossers, even the prissy "gentlemen of the road", don't stick so neatly to individuals. Dave, a tiny but irrepressibly sparky, bespectacled Scot wearing a bright yellow anorak with "Murphy" written over his prominent hunchback, part of a group of five respectably-dressed Scottish blokes who were "skippering" (sleeping rough) by Blackfriars Bridge. A slightly menacing ginger-haired skinhead wearing bobble cap, combat jacket and jeans; who would have thought this neat-looking tough lived in a cardboard hutch?

And what about these two, discussing God and Mrs Gorbachev with dry, donnish wit? Tom Maher, aged 49, an immaculately dressed, intensely religious yet droll London University graduate (Soviet economic studies), whose devotion to the Virgin Mary led him to live with the dossers in Lincoln's Inn and Sarath, a raggle-taggle-haired, bushy-bearded Singhalese, bright-eyed and startlingly articulate, the one black tramp present. "I lost my job about a year ago." He agreed that there are very few Asian or West Indian tramps around, but denied that he came up against much extra unpleasantness because he was black. "It's the same as normal life, I suppose," he said, with laughing eyes, before heading off to Oxford Street, in search of a warm shopfront.

The Bondway van drove off, to be replaced moments later, hilariously too soon, by a wagon carrying a handful of cherubic waist-haired women and sparsely bearded seraphim, all smiling stuck-on "He is with you" smiles: a Christian soup from the University of London. Palates were a bit jaded by now, but their soup was dutifully downed and, a few sulphurous looks apart, no one tweaked the angels' wings.

The students departed not long afterwards, leaving half-eaten loaves of bread and the concrete speckled with crushed styrofoam. One of the Scots charitably said that last week the students had been great: "There was a bloody good sing-song and dancing and all." Sophie disappeared underneath a gaudily-decorated plastic-covered walkway which led to the Artistes Entrance. Only a few years ago home might have been some dark, window-barred psychiatric unit; there Sophie would perhaps have been pumped full of liquid nosh, but at least she would have been warm.

There is some fancy multi-million-pound scheme to develop the South Bank which will mean the end of Cardboard City in a few years' time. Or rather it won't. They will just pick up their cardboard and walk, to find somewhere else.

After midnight, underneath the full moon, the bandstand in the middle of the lawyers' park is a beer-can strewn necropolis, full of near-corpses, the only sign of life the glowing red pinpoint of a fag end, gleaming dully from beneath plastic sheeting thrown over a bench. Lincoln's Inn is labelled as the place for the hard men, the lads who drink "jake" or surgical spirit.

According to Dr John Balaza, a GP who specialises in treating the homeless in the East End, drink and psychiatric problems afflict more than two-thirds of his patients. "It's easier to medicalise the problem than to work it out. Underlying everything is poverty. We can help a few people very much, but for the majority we can do next to nothing."

One of the Bondway volunteer soup-dispensers agrees with this realistic but depressing outlook. Ruth Yearley, the woman who poured the soup at the South Bank, works by day for a marketing firm which handles the Sunsilk hairspray account. "I don't kid myself. I've got all the yuppie trappings, apart from a compact disc player. This is just scratching the surface." What do the people at work think? "They don't know."

Not knowing and not wanting to know is a more common response to these pathetic, mainly unlikeable, often foul-smelling and mind-twisted but *human* beings. No doubt when the various factors come into play and the number of homeless begging on the streets becomes unsightly, compassion will be dusted off. Meanwhile, our homeless suffer cruelly.

Last word to Arthur Wallace, a 66-year-old homeless Glaswegian ex-labourer, who was sheltering from the cold and hiding from the security men in a dark recess of the Lyttelton Theatre cafe at the National. Clean-shaven (for his brush-up he goes to the Leicester Square all-night toilets at four o'clock in the morning), neatly clothed with long white hair swept back, Arthur looked like a twin of the very first Dr Who. He hadn't slept for three days or eaten for one. Because he'd lost his teeth Arthur rolled the tuna sandwiches the *New Statesman* bought him into little balls, before popping them into his mouth. He got more satisfaction from the food than any person for whom I have ever bought a meal.

"You feel that you are not wanted, eh? I always try to keep myself respectable, but it's not very easy. What gets to me is when you see people hurrying home on a night like this, and you've no home to go to. It makes you think."   □

From *New Statesman*

Improvisation: Not using 'real' time. Talking directly to the audience.
Lighting: Using the right amount at the right time to add meaning to our ideas.

LIGHTING

If this is the first time your students have used lighting, these key points are worth drawing to their attention.
- Blackout is the most important lighting feature. Once you have darkness, the smallest light is effective.
- Safety factors.
- Torches have the advantage of being used from any angle and can be shone on a smaller space.
- Matches give a warmer but flickering light.
- Contrast the degree of light to suit the piece.
- Develop lighting ideas alongside the drama, rather than add them later.
- Keep to a few effects for impact.

TASK

Either read or issue copies of the article to the group, editing it to suit their abilities.

Brief the class in groups to devise an improvisation that uses the article and the skills. Explain that they will need to pass several stages to achieve this. This work could be prepared over three or four hours. Allow students to process the work independently so they have ownership of their own work. Your interventions will be as teacher rather than director, and can be made to the whole class or to each group as appropriate. In either case, only introduce a stage after the previous one has been explored.

Stage 1: Investigate the text, searching for ideas that consolidate previous work and have personal appeal.

The students will identify a selection, including some of these examples:

Cultural contrasts: The National Theatre audience or Sunsilk advert. TV crew. Role – labels don't apply to individuals.
Equality: The life of the black tramp, the implications for a family, the male/female ratio.
Consumer society: styrofoam (irony here), beer cans.
Lighting: 'Suddenly lit as day.'
Home: 'They will pick up their homes and walk.'

Stage 2: What do we want to say?
A flow chart or diagram will help to record ideas so that students can refer back to them or add extra details. This is a poster form of working notebook and helpful for collaborative tasks.

Stage 3: Developing roles

Use the evidence in the text and imagination to consider motives and histories. Students will be able to use some of their own experience and it might be helpful to draw to their attention some of the common human experiences they will have shared with homeless people. Remind them of how difficult it is to get up in the morning when they feel cosy in bed, or how reluctant they sometimes feel to take off their coats in class. Good questioning (see *Teaching Devices*, page 4) will enable them to see the link between comfort and security and to consider what it must be like to own only a few articles and to have a movable home. The articles give the security and the home is where the heart is.

This task helps the whole group develop fully rounded roles. The students are in role with a partner who is a fellow 'dosser'. The exercise is played twice. The first time one tramp describes a specific experience which happened earlier that day. The friend helps the story develop by good questions. Let this end before giving the opportunity to reverse roles, so that each student gets complete attention for his/her ideas in turn.

Stage 4: Exploring the context

Find the appropriate situation to communicate the decision made at Stage 2. The students should be encouraged to experiment with different approaches. It is quite useful at this stage to consider the degree of naturalism needed. Is this a narrative? Does it happen in real time? What do we need to believe in?

Here is a piece of writing recording how some students approached this task.

Among the glitter and tinsel of the wealth and selfishness of a money-ridden society "the others" suffer.

The white marble covered floor of the shopping precinct is taken for granted by the feet which clatter over it all day, but for Emma it's home.

The floor, that's cleaned once a day, sparkles in grotesque contrast with her huddled screaming figure. She hasn't washed for three weeks.

All plastic and no heart, the mannequins stare doggedly down at her. Covered in furs and unnecessary frilly lingerie, they don't shiver or scream like Emma.

"I left them bloody bars behind . . . and them prissy doctors . . . bastards in white coats. I won't . . . I'm better off now than I ever was." She broke off to return to her incessant screaming. From the muck and filth, she believes she is somewhere better.

I was politely asked to move over by an oh-so-calm WPC and an irate shopkeeper.

"She's already been in causing havoc; it's the middle of the January sales, it's no good for business."

Ever the diplomat, the WPC, just answers "All right, Madam, everything's under control." And then in a harsh tone to Emma, "I've warned you, one more chance, just cut the screaming."

Amid the chaos of the January sales, passersby, simply preoccupied, hurry off to their next bargain. £2.00 off this, £3.00 off that, makes no odds when you haven't got anything. A stray child wanders over to stare at Emma. She stares back. A protective parent pulls the child back. Out of the homeless society, Emma hollas.

That night Emma was arrested. For what . . .?

Fran, 4th Year

Stage 5: Techniques
All the teaching devices used in these units are applications of the drama form to teaching. It is worth while pointing this out to students, as they will be very familiar with thought-tracking, tableau, distilling to the essence, and these are tools for their work, as well as for teaching.

Stage 6: Getting the moment right.
Once the improvisation has an overall shape, encourage the students to take a closer look at those moments that are most significant. They can help one another to check that all the skills identified have been considered.

Stage 7: Making it run smoothly.
This stage is sometimes dealt with so soon that Stages 3, 5 and 6 get left out, or is sometimes not given enough time. It helps to give status to the work if groups are given time to ensure that all the people are pulling towards a common goal and all the objects in the space are serving their function.

SHARING THE WORK
Ask the students viewing the work to think about questions while they watch.
'What was the improvisation saying?' (*Content*)
'How could we tell what it was saying?' (*Form*)
'How was the meaning carried?'

EVALUATION
Evaluation should be in terms of the skills identified at the start of the work (i.e. how meanings are created in drama), as well as a consideration for the implications of those meanings. A structured evaluation task could be undertaken in groups so that the students have the opportunity to learn from discourse. All these questions refer to positive

examples. Depending on your coursework needs, students could evaluate their own work, or the work of others. The final questions on the sheet refer to the process and so can be left out for evaluation as a member of the audience.

Evaluation sheets such as these are a great help to students needing support in processing their learning. They do sometimes hamper the more able who can respond quickly and effectively but are not free to express their greater insights. You could reserve the handout until after these students have made a personal response, using it as a back-up extension task.

WELCOME TO CARDBOARD CITY: Evaluation

Preparing this work

What was the most effective moment in the drama?

Here are stages you went through to make that moment. Note down how the idea grew at each stage.

1. The article: What inspired you?

2. The message.

3. The role.

4. Working on the idea together.

5. Using drama techniques to shape the idea.

6. Getting it right.

Why did the moment work well?

What was the meaning of this improvisation?
What did it tell us about life?

Space

On a separate sheet of paper, sketch the space used.
Sketch the heads of people, showing where they were looking at an important time in the drama.

Role

What did you know about . . . . ?   How do you know?

Language

Write down some words used in the drama.
Write a few ideas about what these words show.

Lighting

Sketch or write when the lights were used. What difference did this make?

Why did the lights make the drama better?

Gesture

Give an example of movement that you remember. What did the drama make you think?
What techniques were used? What did this mean to you?

Improvisation

How did the drama make you feel? What did the drama make you think? What techniques were used?
What did this mean to you?

Theatre in Education

NETWORK

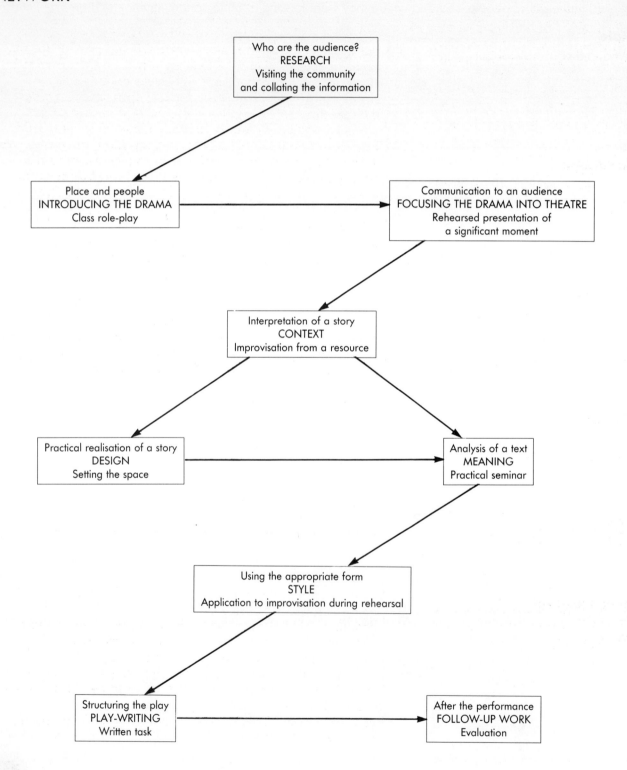

Who are the audience?
RESEARCH
Visiting the community
and collating the information

Place and people
INTRODUCING THE DRAMA
Class role-play

Communication to an audience
FOCUSING THE DRAMA INTO THEATRE
Rehearsed presentation of
a significant moment

Interpretation of a story
CONTEXT
Improvisation from a resource

Practical realisation of a story
DESIGN
Setting the space

Analysis of a text
MEANING
Practical seminar

Using the appropriate form
STYLE
Application to improvisation during rehearsal

Structuring the play
PLAY-WRITING
Written task

After the performance
FOLLOW-UP WORK
Evaluation

RESOURCES

Cameras, questionnaires, tape recorders, TV and video, art materials, junk resources
Pictures of beach (page 85)
A well-remembered role-play
Guardian newspaper article (page 89)
Photographs of sets; art materials
Extract from *Our Day Out* by Willy Russell (pages 94–5)

THEATRE-IN-EDUCATION

This chapter is a flexible framework. A sample theme moves through a series of stages which a GCSE group could successfully use to devise a Theatre-in-Education programme for primary school children.

Working for an audience of five- to ten-year-olds gives the students the opportunity to research and provide for the needs of specific clientele. They can draw on their own rich experience of childhood and apply their drama skills. A large empty school hall is the perfect 'open space' in which the students can experiment with practical theatre design.

Theatre-in-Education, rather than Children's Theatre or Pantomime, forces the students to think more for themselves within the unfamiliar structure. It introduces them to the Brechtian theory that theatre is not 'just' entertainment but is also a powerful learning force, and that good theatre embodies both.

Theatre-in-Education tries to combat stereotypes and negative images in a theatrical framework which is exciting and non-patronising. The sample programme takes the form of a play with participatory features and some element of follow-up work with the children.

It might be argued that investigating war at all often reinforces it as a dramatic and exciting phenomenon, but as students often ask to do so, here is the opportunity to redress the balance by revealing a less popularist view. The newspaper article which is provided as the context for the suggested theme tackles the issue of war by undermining its positive characteristics.

Research

- Who are the audience?
- Visiting the community and collating the information

The students research the prospective audience's interests. The sample structure sets up a series of tasks for small groups. The students share with one another the wealth of experiences they have had and learn that children of the same age have a huge range of likes and dislikes.

The research material is collated and recorded using art techniques familiar to primary school children. This is a fun, practical way to underline the importance of visual communication. This is later developed in terms of theatre in the lesson on design.

SUGGESTED STRUCTURE

Research

Places to go: playgroups; primary school classes/
playgrounds; public playgrounds; children's libraries;
toyshops; children's TV.

Questions to think about

- What do children like doing/eating/reading/watching?
- Are there lots of differences between boys' and girls'
  behaviour?
- Are some influences harmful/good for children? Why? What
  are they?
- What can you remember about your own childhood?
- What games did you and your friends play?
- What do your brothers/sisters and their friends enjoy doing
  most?

Collating information

Using the art rooms would be an advantage here. Aim to
create a huge display in primary school style, with pictures,
paintings, models, paragraphs of writing, which shares
'What we have learned about children'.

OUTCOMES

The students will have a clearer idea of 'where their
audience is at'. Some more specific learning outcomes might
be emphasised. As a way into the theme, a discussion or the
display could focus on children's enthusiasm for:
Discovery e.g. link 'pop-up' books/hide and seek.
Adventure e.g. link TV story lines; exploring unfamiliar
environments.

Introducing the Drama

- Places and people
- Class role-play

RESOURCE
Picture of a beach

Role-play is used to generate ideas. Students are given a
location in which to introduce people and to improvise
relationships and experiences. The form allows for
maximum student freedom and subtle teacher input and
guidance. A beach is an impersonal place. There is a wealth
of possible drama. The physical location frees the drama
from being necessarily domestic and provides plenty of scope
for design at a later stage. It provides the basis for the
suggested theme, but will stimulate plenty of other ideas
too. Recording the drama is necessary for the next lesson.

SUGGESTED STRUCTURE

Individual work
— lying on a beach in the sun;
— trying to keep warm on a cool day;
— dipping toes into the cold water;
— licking an ice cream.

Class role-play
This could be framed as a school trip, on a Spanish resort beach, or a local beach with few tourists. Ages could be suggested, perhaps everyone is a child, or family units are fixed first. Alternatively, there are no constraints and free, life-rate role-play is begun, with inputs at appropriate moments.

Techniques to use
- teacher in role;
- freeze and spotlight } to highlight good practice, significant
- frozen pictures   } moments of drama relationships
                          developing;
- hold some students back and introduce them in role as the drama is under way, or flagging;
- watch for tensions and dramatic moments arising and focus on them;
- introduce tensions or a dramatic moment in or out of role;
- question in role during the drama or at the end.

Recording the drama
- real/imaginary photographs of significant, interesting, funny, or poignant moments of drama;
- writing postcards in role;
- writing or drawing moments in a series of boxes rather like a photo album.

OUTCOMES
After evaluating the role-play in terms of what possibilities have been generated and developed, the students should be aware of the need for:
- characters to care about, with personal pre-occupations and tensions;
- a sense of place and some of its possibilities;
- the combination of these for the beginning of a story which would interest an audience of children.

These may be tentative or well-developed depending totally on the nature of the role-play experience. It may be the point at which students negotiate plot, characters, contexts, concepts, styles for themselves.

Focusing the Drama into Theatre

- Communication to an audience
- Rehearsed presentation of a significant moment

RESOURCE
A well-remembered role-play

The beach role-play is shaped into pieces of theatre. The improvisation has been a meaningful piece of drama for the participants; in this lesson the students turn it into drama which has meaning for an audience.

SUGGESTED STRUCTURE
Pair and/or group work.
Each takes one of the moments from the role-play and experiments:
- distil to the essence;
- change physical and spatial positions, e.g. lie in the sand, climb up a cliff (floor could be cliff face);
- change timing – leave pauses;
- concentrate on eye contact;
- consider suitability for children.

Prepare a short piece for performance. Make decisions about space, contact, timing, emotional level, movement. Make this a rigorous process.

Ideas to feed in

If ideas are wearing thin, or have no mileage for the Theatre-in-Education programme, introduce a metal detector, buried 'treasure', or message in a bottle, or other suggestion, during the experimental work.

Presentation

Presentation should be emphasised and featured. To give the feeling of a horizonless beach/seascape, which will be useful in the design concept later, give the groups as much of the drama space as possible to perform in. The audience could sit right at the edges of the room.

OUTCOMES

Students should be aware of the process a piece of drama has to go through to become a piece of theatre. They should understand that it all comes from them and their ideas, but ceases to be merely personal in performance and becomes part of the audience, too. From these two practical sessions there could be some scenes or beginnings of scenes from which a play can be structured.

Context

- Interpretation of a story
- Improvisation from a resource

RESOURCES

Guardian newspaper article of 15.11.87, 'Forgotten GI heroes honoured'
A selection of 'in-role' diary entries from people named in the article

The place, people and theatrical moments are given a context. The context arises from a piece of content, a newspaper article, with a selection of possible story lines.

FINDING YOUR CONTEXT FROM A RESOURCE

You could:
- prepare a scaled down, simpler version of the article:
- prepare a selection of in-role diary entries written in the 1940s by some of the people mentioned in the article (e.g. Mrs Dorothy Seekings, Mr Manny Rubin).
- feature one of the sections, e.g. 'Three years ago Mrs Dorothy Seekings renounced her wartime promise of silence. She told of piles of bodies in American uniform being brought ashore for burial.'
- interpret the article by drawing out all the implications:
  — the cover-up;
  — inadequacy of training;
  — negligence of officers in charge;
  — blunders mean loss of lives;
  — it was not just the Germans who were 'baddies';

— Ken Small's publicity stunt;
— different viewpoints on the incident depending on the level of involvement;
— does the fact that the victims were American have a significance?

SUGGESTIONS
Introducing the resource
- Students could initially interpret the article or diaries themselves. The role-plays, group improvisations, or play structures are completely negotiated by the class as a result of the analysis and interest.
- Teacher in role could introduce a 'discovery' and feed in the details as one of the local witnesses.
- Teacher in role asks lots of questions and raises lots of issues. Role-play/group improvisations. Set some of the students up with roles and information to introduce during the drama.
- The scene on the beach at the memorial service.
- Kids on holiday making discoveries in the sand.
- Local inhabitants in the 1940s after the tragedy on the beach.
- American base during the war, during or after the incident.

OUTCOMES
Students need to understand that a play has a context, as well as characters, location and plot. The question of interpretation of a story comes up in later sections, when meaning in theatre is examined; here there has been a simple introduction in the analysis of the newspaper article.

Patience rewarded: Ken Small's campaign to honour the forgotten heroes is rewarded yesterday as he reads the newly unveiled plaque at Slapton

Forgotten GI heroes honoured

By John Ezard

A 43-year-old wrong was, in the words of the man who uncovered it, "made right" at an emotional, rain-swept dedication service on a Devon beach yesterday. More than 400 people watched as the Last Post was sounded and a memorial plaque unveiled in Dartmoor granite to 749 American GIs who died in one of the worst and most secret allied disasters of the Second World War.

The ceremony honoured the victims of a story of blunder and bad luck which had remained almost as hidden as the fictional plot of the Jack Higgins novel, *The Eagle has Landed*. The scarcely trained, young, forgotten Americans were killed in a D-Day landings rehearsal which took more lives than the attack for which they were preparing.

They died under fire from three German torpedo boats which burst in on the exercise, in their own crossfire from bullets only their officers knew to be live, and because they were so inexperienced that they fitted their life jackets round their waists rather than under their arms. After their landing craft were sunk, hundreds were found floating upside down.

The calamity nearly caused the Normandy landings to be abandoned. It happened at Slapton Sands, between Dartmouth and Torcross, on a South Devon coastline which had been almost cleared of villagers. The beach, raised and crescent-shaped, was picked as a replica of Normandy.

So deep was the affection the young soldiers and their cause evoked in Devon that the few locals who knew of the disaster were persuaded by officials to keep silent. The secret began to unravel 20 years ago, when Mr Ken Small moved to Devon and took up beachcombing.

"I found live cartridge shells, bullets, shrapnel, military buttons, men's gold signet rings on the beach," he said. "Obviously something major had gone on." In 1971, divers he hired brought up a Sherman tank.

Three years ago, a local woman, Mrs Dorothy Seekings, renounced her wartime promise of silence. She told of piles of bodies in American uniform being brought ashore for burial.

Yesterday, a survivor of the exercise, Mr Manny Rubin, aged 64, said, "There were blunders, but I guess they were just put aside over the years."

Mrs Stella Rouggly, of Missouri, whose brother, Howard, died, said: "I still have some bitterness at the way the whole thing has been covered up for so many years."

From *The Guardian*

Design

- Practical realisation of a concept
- Setting the space

RESOURCES
Photographs of sets

The lesson tackles some basic concepts of design. Practical creative tasks are suggested and, through realisation, could develop into a set which is interpreted in the students' drama.

The work needs to be practical; it is only by using and experimenting with the materials that the students understand and appreciate the possibilities and effects. Through teaching design it is possible to introduce the theatrical concepts of naturalism and symbolism.

This set created a 2 dimensional effect. Our production was based on a photo story similar to what you might find in a magazine so our set was deliberately false with the brightly coloured wind break and the blue sea.

This was al very corny and related to the purposely overdone clichéd play.

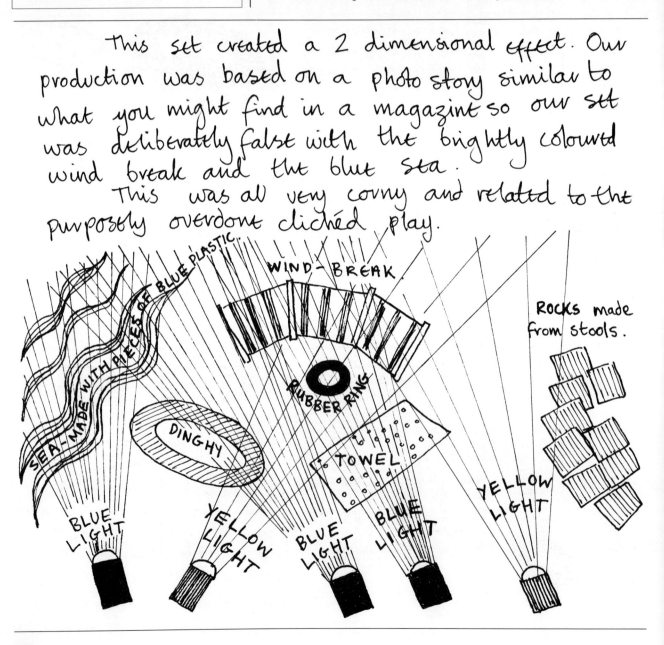

SEA-MADE WITH PIECES OF BLUE PLASTIC.

WIND-BREAK

ROCKS made from stools.

RUBBER RING

DINGHY

TOWEL

BLUE LIGHT

YELLOW LIGHT

BLUE LIGHT

BLUE LIGHT

YELLOW LIGHT

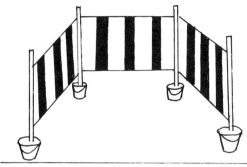

We made a windbreak out of sugar paper and wooden poles. This made a simple background for our play and continued our theme of a beach. We used simple bright colours to make it look summery and tropical. The buckets stood the windbreak up and also carried on the theme.

To add authenticity to the set we used rubber dinghies and rings.

In our set we used mostly things that symbolise the beach. Nothing was used to make up a beach, but just to give an idea of the beach.

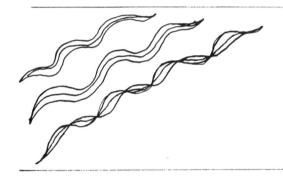

Similarly we used clear blue plastic cut into wave patterns to symbolise the sea.

We used some lighting to set the atmosphere. A blue light to put over the sea and a yellow light for sunlight on the beach.

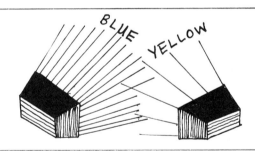

BLUE YELLOW

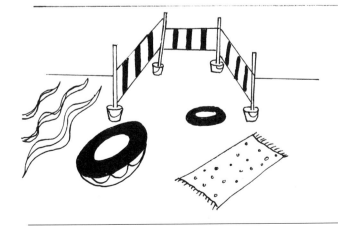

The final set looked like this. The props like the dinghys were not set straight, but crooked. This gave a casual effect overall. As you can see the set symbolises the beach and we hoped would give an idea of a beach scene.

AREAS TO COVER

Beach setting

Suggestion: Reality itself cannot be created. It is not possible to create a real beach in the space and an attempt to do so, completely naturalistically, will look feeble. So, make suggestions of a beach; include pockets of reality.

Practicality: A touring show set must be easily dismantled and fit in a van or car. It must be erected quickly, probably built cheaply, and enable all the audience to see and feel part of the play without the luxury of raised seating.

Audience: The audience is an important element of Theatre-in-Education. It can be featured in the design – as part of the shape of the stage area (thrust, round, proscenium arch style, triangle, semi-circle, clusters, star shape), and as part of the concept (sand dunes, waves, in a boat). The audience of children for whom the programme is devised will appreciate parts of the set which 'appear' or are 'revealed'. An image of buried treasure can be realised here.

Symbol: Some of the programme's concepts can be symbolised in the design – the limpet sticking to the rock/ the old man who wants to leave history where it is; flotsam and jetsam floating in the tide/history which is there for the grabbing/the symbols of the dead men.

Texture: Sets should look touchable (texture gives an atmosphere).

Shape: Shapes in the design might follow a line or contrast with one another.

Floor: The floor is often forgotten and can be made a strong feature. A pile of sand will look very effective. If the audience is seated around the action, thus restricting the use of tall or large pieces of set, the floor offers most potential.

Lighting: Simple lighting effects might be possible with a flood, footlight, blue gel, and a screen or plain wall to create the idea of seascape.

Uniformity: Any addition which is not part of the design concept looks most out of place. Go for simplicity.

SUGGESTED STRUCTURE

Experiment with short-term goals and tasks. Give design briefs, tackling several of the areas to cover, to small groups, and share the final products, or, as a class, build up towards a group set.

Use:
- drawings, sketches, paintings,
- models: cut out a piece of cardboard for stage shape, and realise the set on top of it. Try it to scale.
  Build the real set full size.

Meaning ──────────────────────

- Analysis of a text
- Practical seminar

RESOURCES
Extract from *Our Day Out* by
Willy Russell

In the first lesson on context, the students were touching on meaning in drama/theatre by drawing out the implications of a content. Here, in a practical examination of a text, meaning, underlying action and dialogue is uncovered and emphasised. It is revealed that a piece of theatre must contain deeper, more universal meaning than is just relevant to the characters which function in the specific plot.

SUGGESTED STRUCTURE

Perhaps two students could prepare a rehearsed presentation, or the class could be divided into pairs and all prepare the text extract. The focus of the presentation should be on the meaning behind the text (or subtext), as opposed to the performance skills of the pair at this stage.

In a forum, with the practical example available for delving into, these questions might be tackled:
- Did we care what happened? Why?
- Whom did we care about? Why?
- Only one? Or the other one, too, in a different way? Why?
- What does the extract tell us about their relationship?
- What does it tell us about relationships in general?
- What does it tell us about their individual lives?
- What does it tell us about people's lives in Britain?
- Do you 'recognise' the characters?
- What does the cliff edge symbolise?
- What does the holding of hands symbolise?
- What does Briggs's gesture, holding out his hand for Carol, symbolise for them, for teacher/pupil, for middle-/working-class, for adult/child?
- What is the significance of Carol 'calling the shots' for Theatre-in-Education/a children's audience?

OUTCOMES

As a result of this analysis of *Our Day Out*, the students should, orally, and with practical reference, be able to apply the knowledge they have gained about meaning behind text to a piece of their own theatre. It might be a suitable opportunity to ask them to prepare a scene, or to polish one up for class examination.

Briggs *appears on the cliffs and sees* **Carol**.

Briggs: Carol Chandler, just come here. Who gave you permission to come on these cliffs?

Carol (*moving to the edge*): No one.
She turns and dismisses him.

Briggs: I'm talking to you Miss Chandler.
She continues to ignore his presence.
Now just listen here young lady . . .

Carol (*suddenly turning*): Don't you come near me!

Briggs (*taken aback by her vehemence, he stops*): Pardon?

Carol: I don't want you to come near me.

Briggs: Well in that case just get yourself moving and let's get down to the beach.

Carol: You go. *I'm* not comin'.

Briggs: You what?

Carol: Tell Mrs Kay she can go home without me. I'm stoppin' here, by the sea.
Pause.

Briggs: Now you just listen to me. I've had just about enough today, just about enough and I'm not putting up with a pile of silliness from the likes of you. Now come on!
He starts towards her but she moves to the very edge of the cliff.

Carol: Try an' get me an' I'll jump over.

Briggs *stops in his tracks, astounded and angered.*

Briggs (*shouting*): Listen you stupid girl, get yourself over here this minute.
She ignores him.
I'll not tell you again!
They stare at each other. It's obvious that she will not do as he bids.
I'll give you five seconds! Just five seconds. One, two, three, four, I'm warning you! . . . Five.

Carol: I've told y', I'm not comin' with y'. I will jump y' know. I will.

Briggs: Just what are you tryin' to do to me?

Carol: I've told y', just leave me alone an' I won't jump.
(*Pause.*) I wanna stay here where it's nice.

Briggs: Stay here? How could you stay here? What would you do eh? Where would you live?

Carol: I'd be all right.

Briggs: I've told you, stop being silly.

Carol (*turning on him*): What are you worried for eh? You don't care do y'? Do y'?

Briggs: What? About you? . . . Listen, if I didn't care, why would I be up here now, trying to stop you doing something stupid?

Carol: Because if I jumped over, you'd get into trouble when you get back to school. That's why Briggsy, so stop goin' on. You hate me.

Briggs: Don't be ridiculous. Just because I'm a schoolteacher it doesn't mean to say that . . .

Carol: Don't lie, you! I know you hate me. I've seen you goin' home in your car, passin' us on the street. An' the way you look at us. You hate all the kids.

Briggs: What . . . why do you say that?

Carol: Why can't I just stay out here an' live in one of them nice white houses, an' do the garden an' that?

Briggs: Look . . . Carol . . . You're talking as though you've given up on life. It sounds as though life for you is ending, instead of just beginning. Now why can't . . . I mean, if that's what you want . . . why can't . . . what's to stop you working hard at school from now on, getting a good job and then moving out here when you're old enough? Eh?

Carol (*she turns and looks at him with pure contempt*): Don't be so bloody stupid.
She turns and looks out to the sea.
It's been a great day today. I loved it. I don't wanna leave here an' go home. (*Pause*). If I stayed it wouldn't be any good though, would it? You'd send the coppers to get me, wouldn't y'?

Briggs: We'd have to. How would you survive out here?

Carol: I know. (*Pause*). I'm not goin' back though.
She kneels at the cliff edge, looks over.

Briggs: Carol . . . please . . .

Carol: Sir . . . you know if you'd been my old feller . . . I would've been all right wouldn't I?

Briggs *slowly and cautiously creeping forward, holding out his hand.*

Briggs: Carol, please come away from there.
She looks down over the cliff.
Please.

Carol: Sir . . . sir you don't half look funny y' know.

Briggs (*smiling*): Why?

Carol: Sir you should smile more often. You look great when y' smile.

Briggs (*holding out his hand*): Come on, Carol.

Carol: Sir . . . what'll happen to me for doin' this?

Briggs: Nothing . . . I promise.

Carol: Sir, you're promisin' now, but what about back at school?

Briggs: It won't even be mentioned, I promise . . . *His hand outstretched. She decides to believe him. She reaches out for his hand. As she does she slips but he manages to lunge forward and clasp her to safety. He stands with his arms wrapped around her.*

From Our Day Out by Willy Russell

Style

- Using the appropriate form
- Application to improvisation during rehearsal

The features of Theatre-in-Education programmes which have been described so far are not exclusive to that form. Any piece of good theatre should have a context and a design concept which embody meaning. The techniques suggested in this lesson set the piece of theatre more specifically in the genre of Theatre-in-Education, drawing on several Brechtian techniques. The examples are developments from the suggested theme.

AREAS TO COVER

Story-teller

The story-teller uses direct address to provide a narrative and social link between audience and play. S/he might befriend them, draw them into the play and allay fears. The story-teller can be used to comment on the action. Here is an example.

The story-teller is an old woman, loosely based on Dorothy Seekings from *The Guardian* newspaper article. She talks to the audience in direct address. She introduces herself to them as the story-teller and starts to befriend them and draw them into the programme by chatting naturally (although with preparation) about holidays, adventures and buried treasures. She questions and encourages two-way dialogue. At a pre-determined moment, she introduces the actors as actors, and identifies the characters they will be playing. The play begins and the story-teller watches with the children, stopping the action at points to flashback (see below), or enable actors to change roles, or even take part in the play. The role offers an opportunity for a student to make good relationships with the children and to control the performance.

Actors represent characters

Acting must be truthful; recognisable characters must be devised. The children need to identify with them and be at times immersed in the action. At the same time, children must be aware that these are actors playing a part and not the people themselves. With flashbacks, the actors may need to play more than one character, which is potentially confusing.

A simple way of ensuring success is for the actor to address the audience out of role with something like 'I am Nancy, I'm going to play Dad now.'

Flashback

Flashbacks can add an extra dimension to the action, which can, for the main part, take place in a short time-span. It allows the structure of the play to be tight and the sections of interaction to be detailed.

The main body of the play takes place in the present day. The plot centres on a group of children who find 'buried treasure' from 1944. The flashbacks can comment on the action as contemporary film footage might, thus making history live and full of impact. When juxtaposed with the story-teller's comments and the real life scenes, flashbacks carry meaning. There is scope for using counterpoint, e.g. modern children swimming in the sea on holiday – 'Don't go too far out, kids!' Flashback to the young GIs trying to fit their life jackets on wrongly.

Open ending

As the play is part of an educational programme, it should not contain all the answers. It should be structured to encourage the children to think and question, and to realise that the answers to many of the questions raised lie within themselves.

The issues might be:
— Should history always be uncovered? Look at the view point of:
   the old man who says ''Tis best to leave things be';
   the story-teller who wants to 'renounce her wartime promise of silence' and the kids on the beach who have uncovered evidence of an unknown World War II blunder . . .
— Are events inevitable?
   Could the events of 1944 have been changed? Look at the viewpoints of:
   the stubborn commanding officer who wouldn't listen to advice from Danny, the young soldier;
   the old man who says, 'It was just a blunder, it was just one of those things that happened during the war';
   the kids who think the tragedy could so easily have been averted.

Play-writing

- Structuring the play
- Written task

It is at this point that all the strands from the previous lessons should begin to come together in the form of a finished play. You might choose to work on a class play, involving all the students, in which they will rely on you as their leader – useful if the class is unsettled.

Otherwise the class could be divided into small groups, working separately at first, but using one another to try out ideas when needed. Competition between groups can be avoided and an atmosphere of mutual support fostered if the groups are brought together often.

Meaning	Plot	Form
	A summer's day, present day.	
Responsibility which goes with knowledge.	Story-teller meets audience, introduces actors who are in a tableau.	direct address
	Three children playing on a beach, story-teller's grand-daughter tells them to find out as much as they can about the beach, 'Leave no stone unturned.'	action
Could history have been averted?	Sea, sand, ice cream, teasing, running, arguing.	actors represent character
	Meet old man on walk up beach.	
Children are seen to be responsible and useful.	Make discovery – message in a bottle, metal detector buried in the sand.	counterpoint
	Swimming. Drowning soldiers.	flashback
War is not just about heroes.	Danger, one kid won't listen. Commanding officer won't listen to GI complaints.	tension
	GI is story-teller's sweetheart.	open ending
History relates to you and your times.	Old man is shown kids' discovery. Anger; he knew; says, 'leave history alone.' Story-teller argues with old man. 'Don't bury your head in the sand.'	frozen picture
	Old man accuses story-teller of having known what would happen from sweetheart. Did nothing to stop it.	symbolism
	Children stop old people arguing. Try and decide what to do.	

The issues and teaching points need to be clarified in the structure of the piece. A suggested written task helps the student chart the progressive relationship between form and meaning. In this lesson, too, the suggested theme is developed.

SUGGESTED STRUCTURE

Whether students are working as a class or in small groups, the work needs to be fairly tightly structured. Use improvisation, discussion, forum, video, evaluation, recording on paper during the rehearsal process. The techniques and concepts tackled previously can now be appropriately applied to the product.

WRITTEN TASK

Example structure (see opposite)

This is flexible, with no prescribed sequence. These are just a few ideas related to the newspaper article. Students can develop their presentation from the chart.

OUTCOMES

As a result of this section of the work, which might take between two and four weeks, the students should be ready to present their work. It might be that they take responsibility for the negotiation with the primary school staff, too.

Follow-up Work

- After the performance
- Evaluation

A Theatre-in-Education programme which raises questions and issues is not complete unless there is structured opportunity for the children to follow up the experience of watching the play. This is very important for the GCSE students, too. All the suggestions provide very valuable feedback to the actors.

Generally speaking, a Theatre-in-Education programme should be presented to a small group of children, no bigger than one class. A larger audience decreases involvement, active interest, potential audience/actor relationship, and minimises the choice of possible follow-up activities.

SUGGESTED STRUCTURE

Open ending

If the ending is left completely open, the story-teller can negotiate with the children what they would like to happen/

think should happen. The actors can then perform one of two or three pre-rehearsed endings, sharing the consequence of action and choice.

Discussion
Discussion of issues raised could be controlled by the story-teller, out of role, in a large group, or in small groups with actors, out of role, supervising a group each.

Hot-seating
Again controlled by the story-teller, out of role, in a large group, or in small groups controlled by actors in role.

Children's drama
Working with your students or with one another, the children devise work which presents their view of the plot or issue.

Children's writing
Suggest that the children could write letters to characters or actors, out of role, expressing their opinions.

Documenting Drama

I find drama extremely enjoyable. I've always found drama is a way of communicating with other people. In this year's drama class there is a lot more writing involved, but that doesn't put me off as it's not like work.

We write things down to help us remember what we have done and to help us understand what we are doing. And to show others what you mean. Express our thoughts, so that you have a reason for everything you do.

These extracts from students' work at the start of their fourth year exam course help us to establish why we ask students to write in a subject where learning by doing is the maxim. This book, and our teaching, operates from the principle that all students can learn more about themselves and their drama by purposeful writing. The tasks arise naturally from the practical work and are used to develop practical skills. Students are rarely asked to write merely to record an ephemeral experience for posterity. Their writing is interactive, with themselves, with one another, with the teacher and with the drama.

Students are taught that drama is a thinking process and, as they take on the challenge of exploring through drama, their skills of evaluation are consciously developed. The examples given in this chapter speak for themselves. The work is sometimes taken from students' working notebooks – good quality, hard-backed exercise books which the students use throughout the two-year course. The durability of these books indicates to the students that their notes have status, have value within the drama, and form a process of discovery. Their notes give the students ample support when compiling a piece of coursework for examination, when the audience for their work is someone who has not shared the experience with them.

If you can share your lesson plans with the students, making your intentions clear, they will feel more actively involved in the thinking process, rather than that they are jumping through a series of hoops with some skills but no connection. Making the skills explicit and the criteria open consolidates learning and gives students the vocabulary with which to evaluate the drama. Written tasks should be given in a 'user-friendly' atmosphere where students feel safe. The more they do in class and with the support of one another, the better the basis for their individual reflection. If you think creatively about the tasks you set and the resources at your disposal, you will be able to encourage students of all abilities to record and analyse their achievements.

WRITING TO DEVELOP A ROLE

These examples were all part of a process of deepening roles based on the units in this book. Their principal purpose was to enrich the drama. They of course provide a healthy resource for a piece of documented coursework. At the end of a unit, students have a fuller picture of their development and can link pieces together, reworking some to meet examination requirements. They are not facing that awful empty sheet of paper, with so many hundreds of words required. By engaging in written tasks, they find that their roles become more fully defined and so meaningful to them.

In a whole-class role-play which might go on for several weeks, students may wish to adopt a role using a name other than their own. When students were asked to make badges showing their role in the factory and indicating something about their characters to others, one wrote:

The badges made the factory set and the improvisation began to take shape. My character Nicola Hayes turned up for work as usual, tired out from the exciting mysteries of the weekend. Worn out before she arrived, she had little time to care for the impending doom for the over-fifties. Taken up with her discussion with her work mate Dick Andrew's discussion on his wife's birthday present, our little corner of the factory began to feel like 'home' and as a result the drama became more realistic.

Letters written in class can be received by other students in role. This is an extension of the role development they do when role-playing together.

So far so good. Researching our role was easier working with someone else in role. Because you can say things you wouldn't say out of it.

This example from the *Jarrow March* chapter (pages 117–42) alludes to pair work and could be used as a narrative/spotlight in a presentation to communicate to the audience the passing of the journey.

Dear Lily,

How are you? I am fine but feeling a little exhausted by now. How are the children? God, I hope you're all fine up there. The march is going well so far. We are now in Barnsley. All the way, people have been supporting us with money and encouraging us to continue our march. We are all being fed, would you believe? I'm sorry about our little misunderstanding before I left, but perhaps now you realise why I felt I must come. I have become great mates with the men of my platoon. We confide in each other our feelings and keep each other's morales high, cheer each other up etc. Everything was going fine but we have heard a very disturbing rumour. I was told that the government won't see us and that they don't care how far we have marched. Well, there is no way we are turning back now so we will make them see us. They will have to listen to our case. I still feel that we will bring back good news and Jarrow will become a prosperous town once again. We are just about to eat our meal now so I must close.

Love

George

XXXXXX

PS I never stop thinking about you and the children. I pray that you are all well. Miss you!

This example from the *Theatre: A Collective Form of Story-telling* chapter (pages 239–63) shows how the students took charge of the situation and suggested a new direction for the drama.

Seam Sew,
Department 031,
Formby Street,
Liverpool,
L22 1PZ.

17/11/87

Dear Editor,

We are writing to you to inform you about the disgraceful behaviour of the management, here at 'Seam Sew'.

We participate in the department of Hems, where we have worked for 20 years. Never in my whole career have we witnessed such disgraceful Employers. We being the employees are organising a petition against the fact that they are sacking all workers over 50 years of age.

We were not given any full warning that this decision may ever occur, so as you can understand we were very shocked and angry. The question that has bothered us greatly 'How are they going to cope?' This question concerned us very much so we decided to meet and discuss this situation with the management. We were astonished. We expected our management to be very sympathetic, but instead she was very cold-hearted and her main concern was the amount of money she will save by doing this.

I truly hope that you print this letter and meet, to see for yourself what our management is really like.

Yours faithfully

Angela Baxter
Linda Davies

Mrs Angela Baxter and
Mrs Linda Davies

In both examples, students are adopting an appropriate register to communicate with their audience. Pointing this out to them will help them use language more consciously in practical work. In a lesson you may not always want to give time to extended writing tasks. A note left on the kitchen table in *Soap* (pages 30–53) fulfils the same function.

Mum, got £5 from your family allowance, pay you back soon. Gone to pub. Lance.

Dear Chris
I've gone to Mams for a week or two. Claire is with me. Love you. Angie xxx.

TO LANDLADY PAY DOUBLE NEXT WEEK YOS

James
Sorry. scrap dinner. Got an urgent case. Really sorry. Love Frances x

A diary entry encourages reflection in role. A role can be deepened by being committed to paper. This diary entry, like Joy dreaming in 'Poor Cow', lacks formal structure, allowing the feelings in role to be expressed with the fluidity of thoughts.

Diary

Went to the Office today might go to Jail got to go to court soon, all because of one stupid mistake chrissies wife hates me propaly but i cant change history so not to go to chrissies house no more i bet noone likes me could end it all bet i have other things to do in Life had a benny on one of them women at the office wish i could do other things better but i dont care no more im good at some things not many but i can think of some well i must go now anyway.
PS I wish chrissie never asked me to help him now im really going down just because of one stupid mistake but one thing that gets me i say they never liked me of course i mean terry and jane they never did like me well i think thats enough must go now.

The act of writing this helped the student develop the manic insecurity in Yosser.

Angie's 'Road of Life' (page 106) has a sense of developing motivation. The character is seen changing, not a stereotype whose only existence is this moment.

When a role is based on research, as shown in the *Community Drama* chapter (pages 177–210), students need to process the role for themselves. After an improvisation, reflective writing can help get to the reasons for how someone feels.

Sometimes I blame my mother for not thinking about how people would treat me. I try to fit in. I make friends but as soon as they find out my father is white they no longer wish to know me. I just want somebody to tell me 'Where is this place that I will fit in, where I will find true friends and happiness', 'Where is my Motherland?'

When the students have been aware of your lesson plan, their own work on building roles reflects stages of development.

I felt that my character developed within four main stages . . .

1 Developing a basic character, name, age, sex, status and personality.
2 Developing the character, making friends in role, meeting the manager and being told things in role.
3 Developing a family background.
4 The arguments in a canteen and feeling a character change.

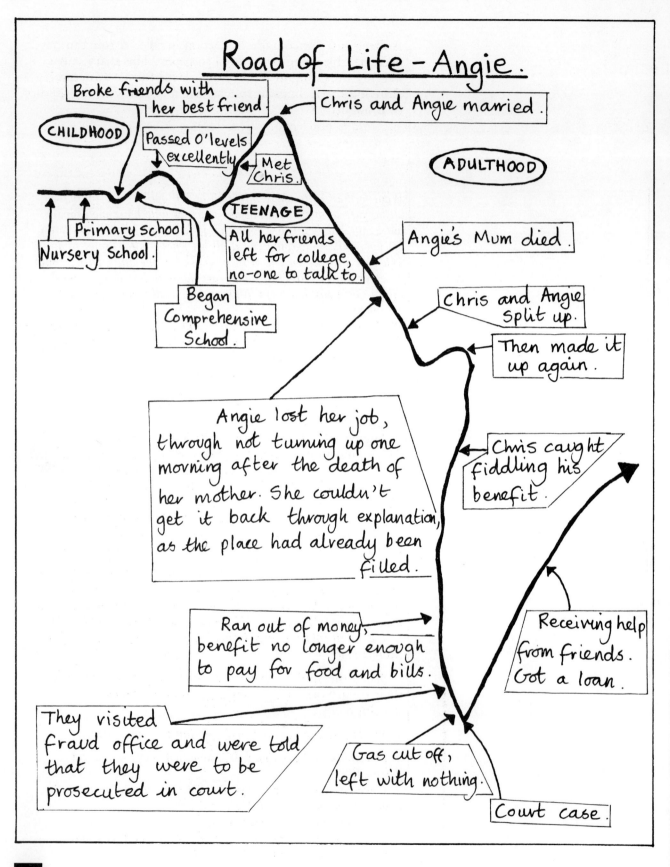

Stage One
  The first stage of developing my character was deciding on an age, name, sex, character and way to act in public. Very quickly I decided on a basic character upon which I could build different things to help me create a realistic and natural person.
  I tried to develop a character very different from my own, but through the very first scenes I was to make decisions and answer questions as I would have myself and not as my character . . .
  I feel that trying to play a character that has a different but not set character to myself is very difficult. It is hard not to play yourself when you have been allowed to choose your own character and been left to develop your own feelings and emotions.
  At this first stage I think I was struggling to create a position and role for my character in the factory . . .

Stage Two
  . . . I felt that when the manager walked around the factory looking over our shoulders I was feeling very confident in role and I was saying things without having to really think about them first. . . . Another thing that helped to make my character realistic was that I wanted to make a good impression on the manager. . . .

Stage Three

Stage Four

The next stage that stands out in my mind is one in which I felt a . . . definite character change.

The canteen arguments between the lower and upper class workers changed my character. Due to the arguments I feel that my character became more aggressive and firm. I was not pleased with the change but I feel that the circumstances made me act in a different way. I know that here there was a definite character change because I felt it within me.

From these extracts you can see what might appear to be a confusion in terms between role and character. In fact, the context is generally right; as the students sharpen the definition of their role and live in it for a while, it becomes a character. In role work, students adopt an attitude rather than becoming the person. At the other extreme lies a character created by a playwright. In between is an enormous range of subtleties, and it is in this interesting and formative ground that our students live most of the time.

WRITING TO DEVELOP TECHNIQUES

The 'bubbles' method can be used to show the thinking in role. This approach is helpful in teaching subtext and heightening students' awareness of the drama skills they use to communicate this.

A photographer's motives are revealed in *Making It Home* (pages 54–81).

Getting behind the text is useful in *The Taming of the Shrew* and *Soap* chapters (pages 143–76 and 30–53).

BEING IN THE PRESS MEANT THAT YOU COULD FIND OUT EXACTLY WHAT EVERYONE FELT.

The *Community Drama* (pages 177–210) experiment with tables showed how use of space affects audience response.

In analysing how space is used, an unsuccessful experiment can be as useful as a successful one in producing a positive analysis.

The group work involved in this improvisation would have been tremendously improved if we had used the space to more advantage. We couldn't communicate properly and this developed into two separate conversations at different ends of the table.
As a result of this misuse of space many dramatic opportunities were lost, because of the lack of eye contact and general atmosphere created by space. For example, the authority and tension of the Chairperson and atmosphere didn't develop because the space didn't allow her total control of the meeting.

Fran's use of space had become more sophisticated by the fifth year. Here she describes how the use of a title for a freeze frame added irony to the drama. Fran is able to use the drama form to explore issues and to reflect on the meanings created.

I thought that to become a young person on the dole would be an interesting and learning insight into life after school. I tried to develop a realistic role, using media and other sources, where you enjoy yourself as well as coping with the financial and emotional problems of being unemployed.

Who wants to be a millionaire, as a title for our illustration, made us more aware of our difficulties not only with money but in society. Millionaires are always accepted; dirty, poor people aren't. Using this opposite title made the audience more aware of our problems and made them more sympathetic to our cause. It highlights the vast difference in lifestyles, attitudes and prospects between the haves and have nots.

Two fourth-year students are already beginning to use techniques and the appropriate vocabulary three weeks into the course.

. . . creating a flashback. Nicky and I tried out freezing for five seconds and then continuing the drama at another point in time.

A symbol is something that represents something, a teddy bear is a symbol of the past, reminding you. It might represent a meaning of feeling that you can't touch. One play to show this was by Matt and Shane . . . in the flashback they showed Matt was very insecure . . . clinging to the teddy for help and support. Whereas in the future he can appreciate being relaxed and what people go through.

WRITING ABOUT THE DRAMA PROCESS
Understand it, try it, rework. Believe!

With this you have to communicate your ideas. Concentrate. Think it through. Discuss. Understand. Try it out – rework.

Encourage your students to make notes together. This is particularly helpful in group work, where a recording of a discussion, or a piece of drama in note form, or a tape can help students to see themselves more objectively.

Good moments – The way I was eating and Liz's and Kelly's reaction to me. How something as simple as a newspaper can be used.

First time – Went exactly as it would in real life, but couldn't really be understood as drama. The space was too small for everyone to fit in, the protesters were too close to the Mayor.

The second time, though, we were able to direct the noise level in the area we wanted it. Being the press meant that you found out what everyone felt. The second time people mingled more and listened to each other, giving more of a view . . . I think the first one was 'real' and the second one was 'drama real'.

With some prompting discussion from the teacher, Clare is not far away from appreciating the difference between truth and reality in drama and the use of the photographer in generating form. Positive marking is a form of teacher interaction with the students' work. If their work comes back full of red ink, the only message students are likely to receive is that they have failed in their task. Equally, when spelling mistakes seem to warrant more teacher-attention than the development of analytical thought, students will equate good work with neatness and accuracy. Spelling errors can be tackled separately from the discussion of the content.

Setting the right kind of dialogue with students about their work will help them meet the demands of the syllabus. The less literate have already achieved a series of small tasks which arise directly from their drama experience. Put together, perhaps using a word processor to help with the spelling, presentation and reworking, these form a series of mini-evaluations that only need linking to show a non-narrative approach that is reasonably coherent. If students are aware of the criteria and the regulations, they will be more satisfied with their work. If students are unable to stick to the word limit, it is possible that they haven't achieved the required balance between writing about themselves and writing about drama. Giving them the criteria, and a highlighter pen, will help them find out what they are saying about drama and re-write it in a more concise form. The quality of their work will increase as they think through the editing.

Knowing the criteria also helps students whose work is either so refined that it reads like a theoretical exercise, devoid of concrete examples, or so involved in the narrative line that analysis is at best deeply buried. Make the job of revising 'finished' work a creative task, having the context of the drama itself. Do some more improvising until a point can be recorded effectively. This next piece of creative work effectively describes the drama experiences.

'Brief Encounter' scene.
The tramp and passer-by was again the subject of our drama. I was the passer-by, Liz was the tramp. She lay asleep covered in newspaper for warmth, I hurried home, newspaper under my arm in 'sophisticated' style. I tripped over her legs, cutting my leg badly.

Through the pain I had a terror for this dirty person trying to console me, trying to apologise. I could only mutter, 'No, don't touch me' and try to get away. Obviously some kind of alcoholic, she had been sleeping with a bottle. While trying to console me, she raised the bottle to her head. Terrified, I screamed,
'No, don't hit me', maybe a natural reaction, maybe typical stereotyping. I felt threatened. I could see from her look just how offended she felt, but because she raised a bottle I assumed she was going to hit me. Because she was dirty and smelly, I assumed she

was violent, though she was caring and well-mannered. I was deceived by her appearance and my unfounded judgement. 'Hit you', 'hit you', was all she could say.

These examples of students' writing around the criteria are from the first term in the fourth year and were a self-evaluation task.

The help of people coming up to me and making me believe in myself and in them helped to sustain my role. . . . When there was the hot seating and we got chosen into groups no-one picked their friends, they picked people who people had never been with before. When we were all in one class group we all listened to each other and talked at everyone and not just Ms Marson! If you were in role and you showed your feelings really well, everyone believed in you.

Research of this kind is very useful, so that we can set the right atmosphere and get our facts right. The atmosphere is extremely important in drama. We have learnt to set this mood simply by believing in our roles.

Now, being able to analyse stories has helped me to dig deeper into my thoughts and discuss them with myself or others. This is a better way of solving problems or finding out what I need to know. Sharing my work with others is very important to me. If I can work with someone else, I feel like I have broken down barriers. And I like this feeling. It's good to know that others can share their thoughts to make the improvisation more realistic.

Role: *Sustaining my role in this project became easier as I began to develop my role in writing and imagining my home surrounds, friends outside work and discussion at work. The role became difficult to sustain when I felt the character I played was doing something I wouldn't naturally do. Then I had to concentrate and believe totally in my character.*

Space, Movement, Language: *The space in this particular improvisation was very important. In a factory space, movement and to some extent language are very uniform and controlled. The spacing of our factory, rows of machines, offices and a canteen helped our movements become more uniformed and realistic in a factory situation. In the canteen the language and movement became more natural and less institutionalised.*

Exploring Further: *The factory improvisation and its theme of age discrimination made us think from different points of view about issues such as the YTS scheme and factory management. We were made to look rationally at the situation and decided what would be good for the factory. Communicating these ideas within your character, sometimes being institutional because of the character you play, gave an overall impression of factory life, the different ways of life, views and needs of all employers and the community in general.*

It is really important to support students whilst they write, rather than leave them to produce a considerable percentage of their examination marks at home. A good atmosphere is helpful, with everyone being given valid challenges. This is an extract from an extension task given in class to someone who was more literate than the others. The thinking developed her analytical skills and the piece formed the stimulus for the next lesson.

ACAS (Advisory, Conciliation and Arbitration Service)
Report of Seam-Sew Dispute
This dispute has now lasted for 4 weeks. Our services were called upon at the end of week 3. The following is our report of the situation and possible solutions.

The Employees' Situation
The workers (members of the National Union of Factory Employees) have decided to strike. The decision to strike was made after the alleged disgraceful behaviour of the management. The issue which caused such a dispute was the proposed sacking of all the factory employees over fifty years old. The workers feel that this action is unjust as the fifty-year-olds would be replaced with unskilled, untrained YTS people, and therefore the presently high standard of work at the factory would diminish. Other workers feel the sacking of the over fifties is just taking young people off the dole and replacing them with old people with families and dependents . . . The workers say they tried to discuss . . .

The Management's Situation
The management feel this move is necessary to keep the factory at its present high standard. Taking on younger people for training means that their wages have to be paid and government incentives in money form would clear the company's overdraft. They feel the clearing of this overdraft is essential if any jobs are to survive . . . The management feel that the workers are acting irrationally and not looking to the long term improvements . . . A questionnaire to the workers in an attempt to understand the emotions was refused.

ACAS's possible solutions to the NUFE v Employer's Dispute
1 *That voluntary redundancies should be asked for.*
2 *The over fifties should be kept on as maybe part-time training officers, at a higher rate of pay for more responsibility.*
3 *A substantial 'golden' handshake should be offered to the redundant and investment facilities or company shares.*
4 *The company should find other means to relieve their overdraft, perhaps increasing the efficiency of other parts of the factory, e.g. cafeteria, cleaning and supply, and not resort to age-ist methods of solving problems of their own inefficient management.*
That concludes the ACAS official report.

WRITING ABOUT LIVE THEATRE

This can be the most difficult task in examination terms, but is often the easiest for teachers to assess objectively. Students can get very distracted by the thrill of the coach journey, or become so absorbed in the theatre experience that being analytical evades them. When they have the support of a series of development tasks, the most important of which is their own drama, then seeing how a theatre piece communicates with its audience becomes much clearer.

Writing an open response is a risky but worthwhile activity. This can form the basis of a coursework unit and allows individual interpretations to develop before the influences of the group are brought into play. Talking over responses can develop the thinking of the talker and the listeners. Perhaps sit the group down with a tape recorder running while they tackle a question or two. Questions devised to meet the potential of the piece of theatre are the most helpful. A group could address each in turn, or focus on one and report back to the class. Try to keep the questions open.

'What did we see on the stage?' (Design.)

'How did the relationship between ——— and ——— change during the piece?'

'How was the message woven through the piece?'

Perhaps use a list of questions the students have raised themselves. (Giving them the vocabulary of evaluation throughout the course makes criticism easier.)

The subtext of this production was how different types of people exploited, and maltreated the angel for their own benefit. It revealed the different stages of greed and selfishness that people went through to own, profit from, or eat! Each character had different reasons for wanting to say 'It's mine, you haven't got one, I have!' . . .

The symbols used in Windfall *underlined the theme and meaning of the whole play, e.g. sunglasses were used several times and became a motif of an unidentifiable character. The glasses added a type of mystery to the visual image of the play. Poverty and Greed were used to represent images of different types of person, e.g. Greed; this was identifiable on stage by a clean, white, tablecloth with knives and forks. Movements of the hands shown by the licking of fingers added slight humour and expressed the love of food exceptionally well. Poverty was also shown by body movements, this time by the scraping of a finger around the edge of a dustbin, in a disgusting manner. To create these two powerful images, the actors exaggerated all their body movements and facial expressions . . .*

The man was very convincing, especially at playing the weak, dying angel. It was a fantastic piece of acting when he had to exert all his energy to bang the drum at the fairground. His facial expressions showed pain and frustration produced by squeezing his eyes tightly and wrinkling his lips in agony. The three actors . . . had to be excellent at 'ensemble playing' and were able to overcome all the problems of performing in open air, such as the wind. . . . The two women having to adopt many smaller roles, having to change costumes quickly, swopping characters all the time. The portrayal of the Mafia involved identical movements, stereotyping their image.

An annotated poster can help the students identify meanings in the play. Sketches, diagrams made of special moments in the play, a graph showing high spots of feeling, the thoughts of a character, are all helpful in encouraging students to see the creative details of the theatre experience.

Perhaps the most impressive thing about the play is the set. The director has opted for a set which shows everything, and although this gives it a rough and ready look the design is perfect for the play. It makes it that bit more interesting to watch. The lighting is clearly visible and there is a large scaffold structure in the left hand corner that houses the orchestra, who are almost as prominent as the actors themselves. Large chunks of the play are set at the Aldwych tube station (in fact the director actually considered the possibility of performing it at the real Aldwych), and to facilitate this dramatic change from the outside world to the underground, a large grey blanket, with the word Aldwych on it, is suspended across the stage.

To help students write in detail about a moment in the play, recreate that moment in class. Use improvisation to consider how movement was used in acting style:

One of the most striking features of The Threepenny Opera *was the use of actors to play pieces of machinery, and we were asked to get into groups of 4 or 5 and reconstruct a piece of machinery depicted in the play. The group I was in decided to be a lift. I found this a rather hard idea to get used to but the rest of my group seemed to take it in their stride and encouraged me to take part. My job in the lift was to be the control panel and megaphone which told passengers to 'Mind the doors'.*

Improvisation can be used to research into someone's character:

After about five minutes of questioning, the investigators were called back to report their findings to Ms Adriani, who was playing the head of the inquiry into Brown's character. Everyone seemed to have got much the same answers to their questions. Yes, Brown was corrupt in some way, but what was more interesting was that all those questioned, with a few exceptions, were very reluctant to answer questions.

Encourage students to identify with the characters and the issue, because a feeling response is vital.

Doctor Foster's Travelling Theatre

Lives Worth Living

When I heard that we were going to watch Lives Worth Living *I started to wonder what the play would be about. I had the idea from the name that it would be about some people's lives being wrecked. I really wasn't too far wrong! When I saw the set I knew that it was going to be the seaside. In fact I was a little surprised at the amount of space they used. It was quite small, but maybe they wanted to create the atmosphere of a crowded beach. . . .*

When Mark walked onto the set, I kept quiet, I wasn't quite sure whether he was going to be some kind of person that takes the mick out of the mentally and physically handicapped, or in fact a physically handicapped person. . . .

A song was chanted in the background that went something like this 'Tescos, Tescos, where spassis get their best clothes!' This really annoyed me and made me feel really sorry for Mark. The feeling that Mark was useless went away when June tried to put her deck chair up, but couldn't, so Mark did it.

The theme question was 'Should Mark go to Northfield?' The play really made me think. At first I thought yes, but then started to change my mind a bit. Why should he? but why should Julie be trapped by having to look after him? Mostly the arguments came down to money. I couldn't believe that the handicapped get £4 a week! It's terrible, he couldn't even afford a tent, let alone his own flat!

Once students have identified what they feel is important about the play and considered how that was communicated to them, they have the raw material for a personal response, together with sound analytical judgements to communicate to an examiner.

The Jarrow March

NETWORK

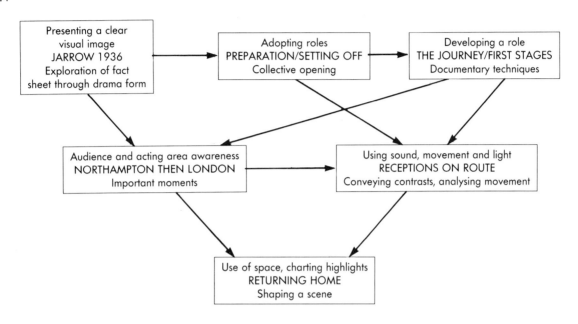

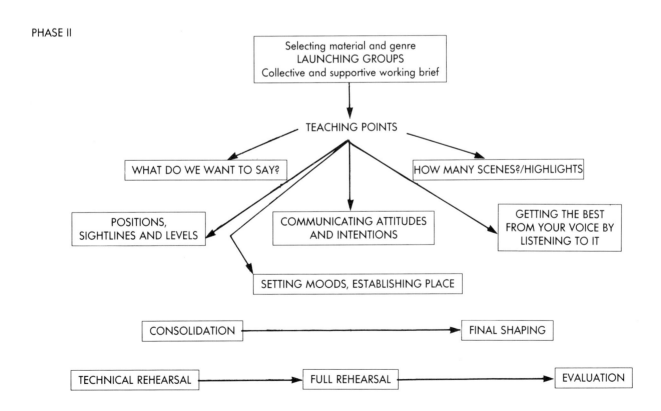

117

This chapter shapes a rehearsed presentation from role-play to performance. The teacher has a central role to play in enabling students to work independently. They are given support in terms of research, improvisation, shaping, technical devices and rehearsals. The students own the work. The teacher provides the framework. Phase I stimulates ideas whilst teaching presentation skills. Phase II (page 133) is a series of teaching points to be introduced to the whole class or to groups at the point of need. The students are given short-term goals to help with planning and motivation. A collective atmosphere is set up where mutual support overrides competition.

The Jarrow March illustrates this technique. You can use it for any other stimulus.

SKILLS

- Imaginative use of space and movement.
- Development and integration of roles within a drama.
- Use of language as related to the role.
- Integral written and oral work developing positive appraisal of own and others' work.
- A supportive and effective contribution to the group presentation.

Complete free choice for students can make it difficult for them to focus on *any* area. The advantages of approaching the rehearsed presentations through theme work are these:

1 Various narratives and issues can be presented to the students for consideration.
2 Theme work enables the students to focus on material they consider interesting.
3 The exploratory work can be made in more depth.
4 The presentations can be easier to stage.
5 Students are not working in isolation. Theme work can generate a 'whole group' atmosphere where there can be natural links and the students can be supportive of one another.

The teacher and students will go through the following stages:

1 Selection of a theme.
2 Exploration of a theme.
3 Focus and selection.
4 Initial development of content.
5 Shaping.
6 Character development.
7 Further shaping and development of form.
8 Technical rehearsals.
9 Polishing rehearsals.
10 Presentation.
11 Final evaluation.

Select a theme that has relevance for your students and their audience.

Themes derived from stimuli	Music/Lyrics Newspapers/Magazines Television/Video/Radio Novels/Poems/Plays Photocopies/Paintings Drawings/Sculpture	

These can provide a suitable framework but the teacher must be careful to promote worthwhile content.

Place as a linking theme	The Beach Market Place Community Centre Railway Station

Basic questions can be a good starting point. For example:
What is responsibility?
How do we act when we are responsible?
When are we responsible?
Why are we responsible?
What are the direct and indirect effects of responsibility?

Concepts and attitudes	Responsibility Friendship

Social issues	Leisure Famine

These offer more opportunity for research.
Factual evidence will help to give the work effective content and will promote credibility in the drama.

Humanity projects	The Jarrow March Spinning and Weaving

SUMMARY OF WRITTEN TASKS
Slogans for and against the
march
Diary of a marcher
Preparation of a column for a
newspaper based on an
interview with a marcher
Written comments on the
effectiveness of the presentation
piece
Graph of improvisation highlights
and notes
'What do we want to say?'
diagram
Scene synopsis
Graph of highlights
Structure notes
Notes on students' own
contribution
Evaluation work

THE JARROW MARCH

What is important about the march was the spirit behind it and the town's need to make a positive statement about unemployment. It was a joyous celebration of determination, conflict and harmony – in fact, the essence of exciting and motivated drama.

The available documentary evidence is stimulating, as would be a local historic event where your students would be able to undertake first-hand research. It is drama across the curriculum.

Resources: The information is taken from The Bede Gallery's *The Jarrow March 1936*; text by David Dougan 1976, with additional help from Vince Rea. Music – Alan Price 'Between today and yesterday' 1974 Warner Brothers.

Jarrow 1936 ——————————

- Presenting a clear visual image
- Exploration of fact sheets through drama form

RESOURCES
Fact Sheet 1 (copies for all
students)
Marker pens
Cartridge paper, to be used for
Ideas Sheet.

Through role-play students consider their own experiences of hunger and the information on Fact Sheet 1.
- In role as someone in Jarrow in 1936, one partner acts as a general dealer, the other asks for credit.
- Students prepare freeze frames to show clearly the content of life in Jarrow in 1936.
- Class role-play: The rumour of the Jarrow March.

Students prepare a very brief improvisation that shows the effect of the rumour on a family.

Ask the students to begin some research on the 1930s, looking at the lifestyles of ordinary people.

Anything the students feel could be explored further should be noted on the Ideas Sheet and displayed. Other ideas can be added as they occur. Research and input are important and the teacher may wish to organise a visit that will help with research. Encourage students to take notes and look for dramatic possibilities. Organise the visit after the drama work has begun. The drama creates a learning desire and students are alert to their needs and interests.

Presentation techniques
- Freeze frame
- Research

Fact Sheet 1

The Jarrow March

Background information

In 1931 Jarrow steel works closed. In 1934 Palmer's shipyard closed. These two closures meant a total loss of 8000 jobs. Other dependent industries, in particular engineering, suffered. In 1936 there was 51% unemployment in Jarrow. It had been as high as 74%. Thousands of skilled men were unemployed and no-one could predict when there would be a change for the better. Malnutrition, although not obvious, was affecting school children. A local headmaster commented that the children tired very easily. The infant mortality rate was an alarming 10%. The 1931 election returned a National Government, with Ramsay MacDonald as Prime Minister until 1935, when Stanley Baldwin took over. For nearly everybody social mobility was out of the question. The North West, Scotland and Wales were equally depressed. From 1930 there had been a 10% reduction in the wages of state employees, such as teachers. Unemployment benefit had been reduced from 17 shillings to 15 shillings. Many women were removed from the unemployment register. It was considered that they had not worked long enough to warrant entitlement. After 26 weeks of unemployment benefit the Public Assistance Committee insisted on the Means Test. This was a humiliating test that scrutinised all the family before any further benefit could be paid. Pensions and children's errand money meant reductions after the test had been applied. For many there seemed little hope. Ellen Wilkinson, MP for Jarrow, said, 'Jarrow as a town has been murdered.'

Concerns about the March

The Bishop of Durham called it 'Mob Pressure which could lead to grave public confusion and danger'. Other marches had often resulted in bloodshed. Agitators infiltrated them. Even the Bishop of Jarrow was doubtful as to what the march would achieve and at first Alderman Thompson, Mayor of Jarrow, thought it would exploit the unemployed. The editorials were less than favourable. Many said it would be a pointless journey. The marchers would not be available for work, therefore there was a possibility that unemployment benefit would not be paid.

More confident views

It was not a hunger march. It was a means of presenting a petition asking for the right to work. It was to be a town march. It would represent Jarrow. The march would not be affiliated to any political party. It would be well organised with sufficient funds. Only the physically fit and those willing to accept discipline would be selected. It would offer purpose for a short while in some men's lives. 'All legal methods in and out of Parliament have been tried. Nothing now remains for us but to place our case before the citizens of our country.'

Ellen Wilkinson, MP for Jarrow
The Times, 26 October 1936

Preparation/Setting Off

- Adopting roles
- Collective opening

RESOURCES
Fact Sheet 2 (copies for all students)
Cartridge paper
Photograph A
Sacks (if possible)
Box to represent the petition box
Camera (if possible)
Strips of card

Make banners to be used on the March.

Pair work: One student takes on the role of someone wanting to go on the March. S/he discusses it with a member of the family.

Class role-play: Marchers have been selected. They select their platoon leaders, sacks are distributed. Marchers return home to inform their families of the selection.

Role-play informing the family: Marchers assemble the next day. They are rallied by Councillor Riley and Ellen Wilkinson, teacher in role with the petition and the 'oak box'.

Freeze frame 1: The marchers setting off.

Freeze frame 2: The crowd waving off the marchers.

Take photographs of the freeze frames. This is a good opportunity to capture some of the work. Get the students to note down their thoughts. The thoughts in the freeze frames and the photographs can be added to the Ideas Sheet.

Presentation techniques
- Using properties right from the start helps students become confident in their use.

Photograph A

Fact Sheet 2

On their way
The date 5 October 1936 will long be remembered by the people of Jarrow. After a service in Christ Church the whole town turns out to wave off Councillor Riley and the selected 200 marchers. An oak box containing the petition and 11,000 signatures is to be carried the 291 miles from Jarrow to London where it will be presented to the government.

The best of plans
Ahead of the marchers is a bus with a crew of four, a driver, a cook and two organisers. They will ensure that areas for lunch are negotiated with local farmers, accommodation is checked, mail is collected and constant contact with Jarrow is maintained.

Marchers well fed
Often the streets are lined with well-wishers as the marchers continue their crusade. In many towns meals have been provided free of charge.

Conference for Ellen
Ellen Wilkinson left the marchers so that she could attend a labour conference at Edinburgh. She will rejoin the marchers at Harrogate.

Well but smiling
The Jarrow councillors arrived at Edgware yesterday. Final preparations for the speech making at Hyde Park will be made. Using their groundsheets to keep off the rain the marchers will enter London today. 'We've had three days of rain on the march,' said one of the marchers. Another marcher said, 'Brave faces are called for, but there is a lot of good humour to keep up our spirits.'

London at last
On 4 November the petition was handed to government officials. Overcome with exhaustion and emotion, Ellen Wilkinson collapsed weeping. She left the Chamber, but returned to cheers. She declared that the government should help Jarrow. The town needed work. After presenting the petition the marchers left. Some commented that it had all seemed an anti-climax, but they had achieved their goal. They had drawn attention to the needs of Jarrow.

Welcome back
After thirty-two days the marchers returned to Jarrow. The welcome was overwhelming and emotional. Ellen Wilkinson said: 'This is the beginning of the fight for our right to work. It is a great night for Jarrow.'

Less money, more poverty
One day after the return of the marchers the Assistance Board reduced their unemployment payments because they had not been available for work.

The Journey – First Stages

- Developing a role
- Documentary techniques

RESOURCES
Fact Sheet 3 (copies for all students)
Writing paper/diaries
Pens
Sacks
The petition box
Tape recorders

Bring last lesson's freeze frame to life.

The marchers leave Jarrow. By evening they are at Chester-le-Street where they sleep in a church institute.

Next day at 5 o'clock they rise, wash and eat breakfast. They begin their diary. The teacher needs to remind the students that they have their individual lifestyles in Jarrow. Their diary will cover recent events, but there should be personal notes as well. These will help develop the role.

Just before Barnsley a rumour starts. The government will not meet the marchers.
— What will they do?
— Is there any point in going on?

A reporter from the local newspaper, *The Shields Gazette*, accompanied the marchers all the way. In pairs, the students set up an interview with a marcher. Particular attention should be given to the marcher's opinion on the recent rumour. It would be helpful if the interview could be recorded.

Written tasks: With a partner the students prepare a column for *The Shields Gazette* based on the interview.

Presentation techniques
- Diary – as a monologue
- Newspaper – Brechtian techniques

Fact Sheet 3

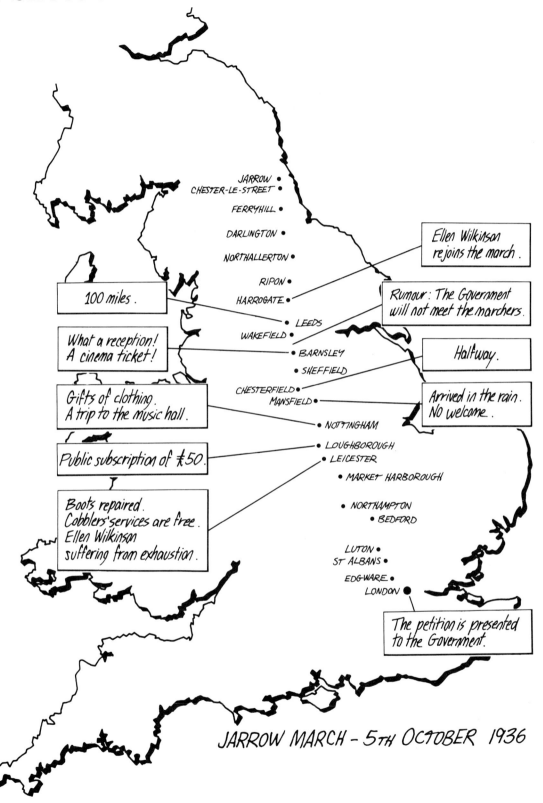

JARROW
CHESTER-LE-STREET
FERRYHILL
DARLINGTON
NORTHALLERTON
RIPON
HARROGATE
LEEDS
WAKEFIELD
BARNSLEY
SHEFFIELD
CHESTERFIELD
MANSFIELD
NOTTINGHAM
LOUGHBOROUGH
LEICESTER
MARKET HARBOROUGH
NORTHAMPTON
BEDFORD
LUTON
ST ALBANS
EDGWARE
LONDON

Ellen Wilkinson rejoins the march.

Rumour: The Government will not meet the marchers.

100 miles.

What a reception! A cinema ticket!

Halfway.

Gifts of clothing. A trip to the music hall.

Arrived in the rain. No welcome.

Public subscription of £50.

Boots repaired. Cobblers' services are free. Ellen Wilkinson suffering from exhaustion.

The petition is presented to the Government.

JARROW MARCH – 5TH OCTOBER 1936

Receptions en Route

- Using sound, movement and light
- Conveying contrasts, analysing movement

RESOURCES
Lanterns with different coloured gels
Video equipment

Class role-play: The marchers arrive at Barnsley. The people of Barnsley are hospitable. When they arrive in Mansfield it is cold and wet. No-one greets them.

Discuss the marchers' contrasting feelings.

In small groups, the students prepare six steps that show the marchers happy and six steps that show the marchers sad. Arm movements and gestures are added. All movements are slowed down and exaggerated.

The students prepare six movements that show the people of Barnsley pleased to welcome the marchers (e.g. hand clapping, arms raised). These are followed by six movements that show the attitude of the people of Mansfield (e.g. turning their backs, hands that push away the marchers). All movements are slowed down and exaggerated.

As the marchers meet with the people of Barnsley, then those of Mansfield, use lights with different coloured gels to emphasise the change.

Problems for the students:
— What colour gels in the lights?
— Can the colours be symbolic?

How should the meetings be staged? Students can experiment with sound collage, even using brief statements. These will have to emphasise the contrast in attitudes of the onlookers.

If possible, video the final result. Play back and discuss what was effective about the piece.

Presentation techniques
- Lighting
- Sound collage
- Video

Northampton Then London

- Audience and acting area awareness
- Important moments

RESOURCES
Letter (for teacher's role-play)
Fact Sheets 1, 2 and 4
Photograph B

Brief class role-play: After walking 21 miles in one day, the marchers are in Northampton. The teacher, in role as a marcher, reads out a letter from someone in Jarrow. There is a rumour going round Jarrow that the marchers are not being fed.

Students prepare improvisations based on the role-play on:

(a) handing over the petition to government officials;
(b) arriving at Marble Arch;
(c) the Jarrow speakers in Hyde Park;
(d) viewing one of the sights of London.

The main purpose of the improvisations is to structure the action. It can be agreed what kind of relationship should be set up with the audience, deciding from that where to seat them.

Presentation techniques
- Setting

Photograph B

Fact Sheet 4 ——————————————————————

THE JARROW MARCHERS

I'm one of the Jarrow Marchers, and I'm proud to say I am,
I've been fed like a fighting cock, on Beef and Eggs and Ham,
We started off from Jarrow Town, a palefaced hungry band,
With all the population out, to shake us by the hand.
But as we left our homes behind, determination grew,
On every face, to show the world, what Jarrow lads could do.
Well led by 'Marshal Riley' a Leader and a Man,
With 'Game Wee Ellen' by his side, to carry out her plan.
From dawn to dusk we marched along, with smiles upon our faces,
We had our smokes and cracked our jokes, in scores of different places.
Each morning saw our tramp begin, each evening saw it end,
With blistered heels to bandage up and ragged clothes to mend.
We passed some pleasant country scenes, and left them with a pang,
But the finest sight throughout the march was O'Hanlon and his gang.
With steaming Dixies on the fires and tons of food for all,
We just sat down and knocked it back, like the lads at Finnegan's Ball.
Then came 'Post Master' Symonds, with his little job to do,
He'd shout your name, up went your hand, and he your letter threw.
Then out upon the road again, Pat Scullion, shouting loud,
'Fall in your sections there, you chaps, don't mingle with the crowd.'
For five long weeks we marched along, and had a glorious time,
As all good things come to an end, so must my little rhyme.
But not before I've sung my praise for Jarrow's Fighting Mayor,
Who left his work to cheer us up and joined us here and there.
I'll now pipe down and thank all hands, from Doctors down to Waiters
Who did their best to cheer the lot, of Jarrow's Bold Crusaders.
We did our bit, we played the game, in spite of all our 'Blarney,'
So farewell lads, the best of Luck, from John J. (Smiler) Harney.

This poem is dedicated to the 200 Jarrow Men who marched to London during October, 1936, and Presented at the Bar of the House of Commons a petition on behalf of their fellow townsmen asking for their right to work to be recognised.

Written by Mr. John J. Harney, one of the marchers.

Petition of the people of Jarrow praying for assistance in the resuscitation of Industry in Jarrow

TO: The Honourable the Commons of the United Kingdom of Great Britain and Northern Ireland in Parliament Assembled.

The humble petition of inhabitants of the Borough of Jarrow sheweth as follows:–
During the last fifteen years Jarrow has passed through a period of industrial depression without parallel in the town's history. The persistence of unemployment has reduced us to a deplorable condition – homes are impoverished and acute distress is prevalent.

Included in your petitioners are highly skilled shipyard and engineering workers who formerly obtained employment at a shipbuilding and iron works which at one time employed some thousands of the town's work people, and from the shipyard of which there have been launched many fine ships for naval and mercantile purposes, and the site of which works now offers an unexcelled opportunity for industrial development.

In the year 1931 the iron and steel works closed, and, except for one brief period, have remained closed ever since and are now in process of demolition.

In or about the month of October 1934 the shipyard known locally as the Palmer Yard was bought by a company named National Ship-builders Security Limited, whose objects include the buying up of shipyards and subsequent disposal of the same subject to prohibition against shipbuilding therein for a period of forty years. The Palmer Yard was disposed of by the company subject to this prohibition.

Your petitioners through the Town Council objected to H.M. Government against the imposition of such a restriction which it was urged was contrary to public policy, and which in fact was and is a crushing blow to Jarrow which is a shipbuilding town. Your petitioners and their forbears have taken a pride in their work with an anxiety that the fine record of the yard and of the town should not be lost, but the traditions of the past carried to the future. By the imposition of the restriction, all chance of employment at their own work in their 'own' yard is denied them.

Your petitioners wish humbly to point out not only the effect of a prolonged stoppage on the technical capabilities of those who are skilled tradesmen and the physical and mental strain upon even the strongest of men in facing, as heads of families, a future prospectless of work and black with unlimited care and want but also the disastrous effect upon the youth of the town who, owing to the restriction of facilities for their being apprenticed, are tending to grow up with no trade to their calling.

Your petitioners have from time to time been buoyed up with hope from statements concerning the re-starting of the Palmer Works. These various statements recede without realisation and your petitioners' anxiety for the future increases.

Jarrow is in the special area of Durham and Tyneside but the reports of the Commissioner appointed by H.M. Government to deal with the special areas of England and Wales make repeated reference towards the inadequacy of the powers imposed in him to deal with the areas.

Wherefore it is with the deepest concern not only in their own plight, but for the nation, that a town should be for so long a period stricken with unemployment and a valuable opportunity for industry left unavailing, that your petitioners humbly and anxiously pray that H.M. Government realise the urgent need that work be provided for the town without further devastating delay, actively assist resuscitation of industry and render such other actions as may be meet.

AND your petitioners as in duty bound will ever pray, etc.

SIGNED by the under-mentioned, being inhabitants of the town of Jarrow of the age of 18 years and over.

Returning Home

- Use of space
- Shaping a scene

RESOURCES
Cartridge paper
Marker pens
Fact Sheet 2 (teacher only)

Ask the students to imagine that, as some of the marchers, they have returned to Jarrow. Everyone is at the railway station to meet the special train. People cried, laughed and cheered. It was an emotional welcome.
- How would the marchers feel?
- What will people say?
- What will be the marchers' feelings when they step inside their own house? Friends, neighbours will want to know about the March.

These thoughts will help prepare the students for the improvisation.

In groups of at least six, the students prepare an improvisation that shows the marchers at home. Family and friends are gathered.

Present the improvisations. After each improvisation the other students identify examples of good use of space.

Students prepare a very brief improvisation which shows the marcher at home seven days after the return from London.

Pair the groups. The aim is to graph the highlights of the piece. For example, group 1 graphs group 3 as follows:

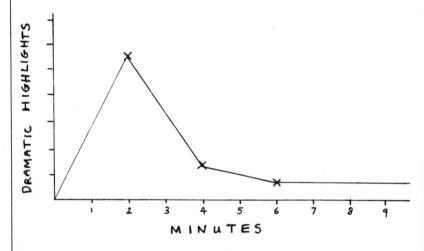

Graph to show the frequence and degree of dramatic highlights

Highlight 1 is when ....

Highlight 2 is when ....

Presentation techniques
- Shaping a scene
- Supporting one another in role so that no prompter is ever needed

Launching Groups

- Selecting material, and genre
- Collective and supportive working brief

RESOURCES
Cartridge paper
Marker pens
Ideas Sheet

1 Have two or three sheets of cartridge paper ready. Gather the students round you. Explain that you are going to display on the paper their ideas for the rehearsed presentations.
What was our work about?
What other possibilities arise?
Consider:
- ideas outside the drama – e.g. while the marchers are *en route*, what events could be happening in Jarrow?
- issues and concepts that have been raised – e.g. rumours, contemporary resonances, the subtle presentation of businesses turning away marchers.
- particular characters – e.g. Ellen Wilkinson
- the National Government – discuss the implications of greeting its members.

Ask questions so that the students are aware of the dramatic possibilities of their work. Discuss ideas in groups of mixed ability.

Throughout this lesson mix groups, encouraging students to support their friends without necessarily working with them. Aim to finalise your groupings based on how the students have operated over this and previous lessons.

2 With new groups, students discuss how each group might complement the others by linking content, theme, plot.

3 Finalise the groups, each group now having the benefit of the discussions with others.
Present the students with the examination requirements.
- Number of students per group.
- Performance time.

- The presentations may be performed for an examiner, but the students may want to invite an audience and devise their work for that target group.
- Consider genre as a way in which the same stimulus can be presented differently. Comedy? Documentary? Dramatic rhyme? A narrator?

Once the groups are organised, then the students should be free to discuss and try out various ideas. Make it clear to them that, by the end of the lesson, each group should be pursuing an idea.

If students make their own choices they will be more committed to their projects. Unless the syllabus requires the teacher to direct them, the teacher's function is to promote good work by guiding, advising, motivating the work, taking on roles, questioning, and discussing with the groups.

Spend time with each group discussing its ideas. Try to steer the groups away from what may be problematic or uninteresting situations, such as certain domestic scenes; static situations; stereotyping; over-stylised presentation; and over-complicated plots.

Present further input to support groups in difficulty, e.g. the poem written by one of the marchers (Fact Sheet 4). How can this best be presented?

Show the students the network for rehearsals. It is important that they are aware of a structured format. The network is a useful reference point which will indicate direction. Depending on the form of the presentation, students may need to spend more or less time on different aspects of the shaping process. Teachers will find it easy to use the lesson notes to feed in necessary information at appropriate times.

Students taking on design have been in on the original conception. They need to devise themselves a programme along the following lines:

1 Consider what atmosphere, meanings, style the drama conveys.
2 Note information about the presentation(s) the actors are working on.
3 Design light/sound plot, set, or costumes/properties in the context of the demands of the piece.
4 Share designs with actors recording developments.
5 Construct set.
6 Try out with actors. Record success/problems.
7 Check original concept. Is it still appropriate?
8 Record final design details.
9 Organise and prepare for final dress rehearsals and presentation(s).

Teaching Points

RESOURCES
Paper
Marker pens

WHAT DO WE WANT TO SAY?

1 Begin the lesson by asking the students to decide on a working title for their dramatic piece.

2 Ask them to write this down in one sentence.

3 Is there a subtext? Can they write that in one sentence? Display the work in diagrammatic form.

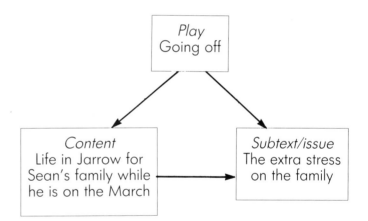

The dramatic piece will be communicated to an audience. Clarity is the basis of communication. The diagram gives focus as the students work on the piece.

Ask the students to bring a scene synopsis of their dramatic piece for the next lesson.

RESOURCES
Paper
Marker pens

HOW MANY SCENES? HIGHLIGHTS

1 Students hand in their scene synopses; then prepare to present up to ten minutes of their dramatic pieces. While the students are preparing their work, go through the scene synopses. See what advice you can give on the structure. Sometimes students will present too many scenes, making the storyline disjointed and working against the building of dramatic tension.

2 Students present their work. As in the 'Returning Home' lesson, groups draw a highlight graph of another group's work. If there are no real highlights, then the piece is lacking in dramatic tension.

If the highlights are at the beginning only, then it is unlikely that the piece will keep the attention of the audience.

The students sit in their groups to discuss structuring problems. Spend time with each group offering advice when possible:
- Would a change of mood benefit the piece?
- Are students clear about the beginning, middle and ending?
- How will sound and lights be used?
- How will the pieces link together?

The students should make notes on the structure of their dramatic presentations.

Presentation techniques
- Highlights
- Structure – preparation for linking group pieces

RESOURCES
Video equipment
Photographs B and C

POSITIONS, SIGHTLINES AND LEVELS

The techniques used here help to teach students who lack awareness of visual meaning how to use space more effectively. Students already capable of appreciating this will need much more subtle teaching and more rigorous analysis.

Show the students the photographs.
- Who do they think is the most important person in the frames?

Photograph C

• How is focus achieved within the natural 'feel' of the shots?

　With the students, decide on the acting area and where the audience will sit, bearing in mind the genre of the piece. Ask the groups to decide upon the most important or exciting moment from their dramatic piece. In the acting area, the students present a freeze frame of the moment. Other students comment briefly on the blocking.

• Check sightlines by appointing students to sit around the room.

• Are there improvements that could be made?

• What is the picture saying?

　Different levels can be used to emphasise status as well as creating interesting visual images. Using their characters from their dramatic presentations, each group makes a freeze frame that will show at a glance the status of the characters in relation to each other. Try to use a variety of levels, and bear in mind status has a lot to do with how you feel. Ellen Wilkinson handing over the Jarrow Petition to a government official may feel pride, or may be made to feel inferior.

　Space in the acting area can be used to confirm the dramatic story visually. If the dramatic piece concerns a conflict between a marcher and his family who disapprove of the march, the family could be grouped together and the marcher isolated to the left or right.

Groups present a three-minute extract from their piece. Video it. On the playback stop several times. Freeze the frame. Students should offer constructive criticism on the use of space.

Alternatively, if the piece is to be presented in the round, or video is not available, as the groups perform call 'Freeze!' Other students check sightlines and make brief constructive comments. Be careful that this process does not restrict expressive movement. Sometimes grouping hides a character for dramatic purpose.

Ask students to make some notes on their own movements throughout the piece.

RESOURCES
Video equipment
Pens
Appraisal sheets

COMMUNICATING ATTITUDES AND INTENTIONS

Begin with a discussion. Points to consider when developing a character are these:

Movements

After marching 21 miles, how would you take off a pair of boots?
Consider what motivates a character's movement.
How would Ellen Wilkinson make her way to the rostra at Hyde Park?

Gestures

Body language can indicate a person's attitude. Closed gestures, arms folded, can visually confirm 'I'm not interested'. In Photograph B Ellen Wilkinson clenches her fist in order to visually confirm her belief in her rhetoric. The marchers would become very close. Sometimes communication would be as simple as eye contact.

Would there be other signals/gestures that would be meaningful to all the marchers?

Language

The Geordie accent may be difficult to imitate and could lead to stereotyping. Discuss what truths are important to you; the right register, for example, is more important than colloquialism. How a person speaks is affected by how he or she is feeling at that moment – nervous, happy, and so on. During the early stages of improvisation, students often 'pick up' on the previous spoken line; it gives them time to think on the spot. This can be developed creatively into positive speech patterns.

Awareness of character's attitudes and intentions

What are the character's fears, hopes, needs? These all affect movement, gesture and language. Know what the character is thinking. How have the marchers been changed by their experiences? Be sensitive to the action and react.

Use of space
If the character is not directly involved with the action, find a place to be that reinforces the focus and the meaning of the scene.

The following exercises may be helpful:
(a) Take the characters from the dramas and put them in new situations – for example, two of the marchers in a pub at Barnsley.
(b) As a television/radio/newspaper reporter, interview the characters about themselves and incidents in the drama.
(c) Video extracts from the dramatic presentations. Freeze the frames. Ask the students what are the character's thoughts at that moment.

The students could make notes on their characters, using the appraisal sheet.

RESOURCES
Appraisal sheets

GETTING THE BEST FROM YOUR VOICE BY LISTENING TO IT

1 Picking up cues.
Ask the students to choose a short extract from their dramatic presentation. In a space with a partner the pairs go over the dialogue from the piece, overlapping cues.
Cobbler: It'll cost you sixpence.
Marcher: That's a good deal.
Cobbler: It's a worthy cause.

This helps attune the students to listening to the spoken word and makes them aware of keeping the pace of the piece.

2 Choose another short extract, about six lines.
Can the students identify where pauses may be effective? For example, the cobbler may pause before the word 'sixpence'. Tape the extract and evaluate what the pause means.

3 Listen to the tape for clarity and pace.
If the pace sounds right to the students, they are probably talking too fast. Remember, the audience only gets to hear the line once.

What about volume? Experiment with the volume control on the tape before playing the extract live again. Try to use the full voice range.

APPRAISAL SHEET

Group/Student _____

BLOCKING IN	Sightlines Levels Movement from place to place In the action Out of the action
GESTURES	E.g. Do we believe in these actions?
LANGUAGE AND VOICE	Natural? Believable? Suitable Any special language use (e.g. repetition)? Affected by mood? Use of pause? Clarity? Inflection? Volume?
TECHNICAL	Links Sound Lighting/Blackout
CONCEN-TRATION	Staying in role Reacting to events Alert to cues Entering/Exiting in role
COSTUME	Accuracy Meaning Colour/shape/details
	Properties

Monitor _____   Date _____

SETTING MOODS, ESTABLISHING PLACE
Music
Music selected for links should be reflective of actions past or future and should underline the mood of the piece. For example, Alan Price's 'Under the Sun' catches without being over-sentimental the mood of a marcher who leaves an ailing relative to go on the march. Rehearsed presentations based on the Jarrow March could begin with Alan Price's 'Jarrow Song' and be linked with traditional Tyneside songs.

Sets
Very simplistic sets can often be as effective as elaborate ones. Simple colour backgrounds can give a unifying feel to a set of presentations. The colour(s) can also be symbolic of place or mood – for example, yellow for a beach, happiness and sunshine. The Jarrow March could be set against a large projected route of the march, with slogans around the space.

Lights
Intensity and angle are the variables. A spotlight for a direct address to the audience; twilight enhancing the uncertainty felt by the marchers; sharp angles for contrasting views. Simplicity should be your principle. Will lights enhance the meaning?

CONSOLIDATION
Consolidate and evaluate, using video, or presentation to the class. The students may have to choose extracts rather than the whole piece so that everyone gets help.

During the playbacks, students make notes on their own and others' presentations. Use the appraisal sheets to prompt discussion. Finalise running order. Devise links between groups, or pauses for the examiner to mark.

FINAL SHAPING
During this lesson all performing takes place in the agreed acting area and is played out to an imaginary audience. Only the beginnings, endings and any complicated scene changes take place.

Topping and tailing each presentation allows the links to be made between them so that some of the work is prepared for the technical rehearsal.

A good, competent start will help settle nerves. The Jarrow marchers make their way to the acting area, passing the audience, and eventually taking up a position in the acting area, facing out, to the playing of the 'Jarrow Song'.

RESOURCES
Video equipment
Appraisal sheets

Students could establish a freeze frame, then lights and music could fade. Lights could come up on Tom's family as they are discussing the march.

Similarly, there should be a strong ending, perhaps involving all the students in a freeze frame with the lights fading to a placard, symbol of hopes dashed.

TECHNICAL REHEARSAL

The aim during a technical rehearsal is simply to go from the beginning of the whole presentation to the end, checking scene links, music and sound cues. The majority of the dialogue, apart from cues, is omitted. It is difficult for students to be getting on with any other work. It is a matter of being ready when you are needed. Students responsible for lights/sound and stage management should have all cue sheets prepared.

This is a collective process and helps to set the atmosphere of serious endeavour that will give confidence to everyone in performance. Routines and responsibilities are the factors leading to calm competence from which artistic flair can grow.

FULL REHEARSAL

Agree on the aims of a dress rehearsal:
- getting it right;
- seeing the piece whole and complete;
- the last time to check details;
- going for pace, tempo;
- audience response;
- last chance to see one another's work as audience;
- checking that intentions are met;
- putting all the ingredients together, except the examiner.

Conduct this rehearsal in as supportive a manner as possible. Only fine tuning can be achieved at this late stage. Refer back to all of your experience from the first role-play. Draw concentration from a thinking through of the process. How did we get here?

Feedback minor tips, positive encouragement. Reward students who have absorbed the importance of routine regard for details.

Aim to get a degree of anxiety for performance which is high enough to achieve peak performance, but not so high as to generate stress. Your voice in feedback can be an important factor in this, and can be 'replayed' immediately prior to performance.

On the day

Students should check all properties, costumes, lights and sound.

Gather the students together for a final briefing. Balance your talk to stress the process and the product. Go over what the rehearsal process was about. Pick out key experiences and describe them positively. How this drama belongs to us. How we've made it together, just like the marchers. Special moments of support, creative ideas you wish to reinforce. Tell the students that our job now is to communicate all that process effectively to the audience. The audience have only one opportunity to understand all the thinking and creating done over several weeks. Special tips for that include:
- speak so the audience can hear and understand;
- support one another in role, especially if mistakes are made;
- it is too late to make any changes;
- enjoy the performance, all have worked for it;
- remember to organise clearing away for the next group.

Recreate positive experiences from the dress rehearsal and the process of devising.

RESOURCES
Paper
Pens
Completed appraisal sheets

EVALUATION

1 Allow some general class discussion on the presentations.

2 Ask each group to consider:
- audience reaction;
- differences between the final rehearsal and the performance.

Allow 15 minutes for each group to produce a written statement. Ask the students to read out their statements. Other groups could offer relevant comments.

Evaluation is a difficult process with subjective responses tending towards the 'all or nothing' model. By beginning with the security of the group statement, students should feel some sense of immediate success, and be able to follow up with greater objectivity.

3 Individually, students write an evaluation based on their own experience in the performance incorporating and considering the group's written statement and other students' comments.

4 Using the statement and working notes taken during the process, write an extended evaluation of the process and presentation.

This gives the students the opportunity to be more reflective and less inhibited with their statements.

The Taming of the Shrew

NETWORK

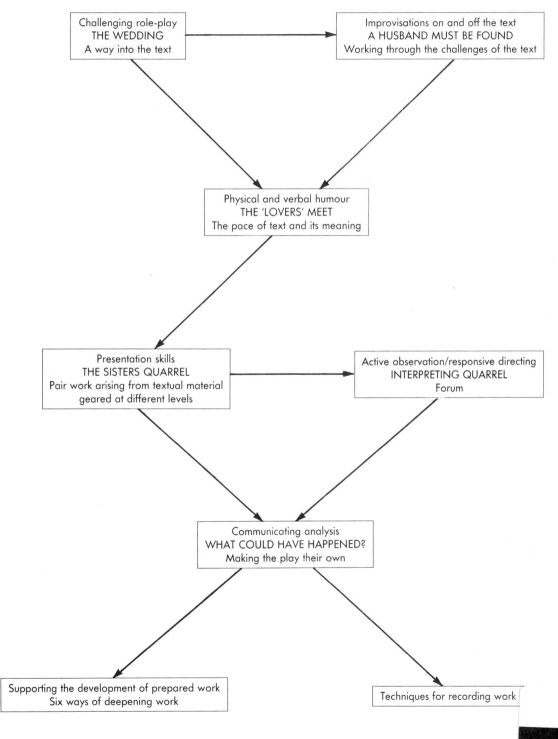

RESOURCES
Wedding invitations (page 146 –
these could be photocopied on
to coloured paper and sealed
with wax)
Guest list
Magazine article – the story of
the text (pages 150–51)
Act I, i, lines 48–58, 80–83: A
husband must be found
(page 151)
Act II, i, lines 181–258: The
'lovers' meet (page 155)
Act II, i, lines 1–38: The sisters
quarrel (page 162)
Picture story of the sisters'
quarrel (pages 164–5)
Contemporary script of the
sisters' quarrel (page 166)
Poster paper, felt tip pens

SUMMARY OF WRITTEN TASKS
Letter in role to problem page
Replying to letters as advisers

READING
The Taming of the Shrew,
Act III, ii: The appointed day;
preparation for the wedding
'Clamorous Voices'
Shakespeare's Women Today by
Carol Rutter and Faith Evans,
Women's Press Ltd, 1988.

This project sets out to demystify Shakespeare, indicating ways into a text which can be adapted for other plays. The intention is not to perform the text, but to interpret it, and in doing so to understand the nature of the theatre. The text becomes a tool in developing techniques and understanding social relations. A play has no life until it is processed; that process is a meeting of the culture of the play with the culture of the interpreter. Katharina is a stroppy teenager resisting demands made on her. We've used magazine style reading and writing to represent the teenage culture and encourage the students to develop a discerning approach to their reading of magazines and the text.

Looking at any Shakespeare text can be difficult, though students often regard it as a great leveller in mixed ability classes; they are all in the position of facing language complex in its construction. *The Taming of the Shrew* presents an ideology that rests on the 'right' of men to control, patronise and bully women. Our approach is to use the text to open the issues of gender roles and use the forum theatre to enable the students to analyse meanings and actively to reshape situations. In doing this they will face their own prejudices and use the drama form to modify their understanding of the social world.

This project will enable students to:
- work within a challenging role;
- discover layers of meaning in text;
- use text to learn more about themselves;
- understand how humour can be used to reinforce or subvert beliefs;
- extrapolate from the theatre to life, from the personal to the universal;
- use the forum theatre to learn that meanings in the theatre are created by an active and conscious process, and that a play is not merely a consumable product;
- prepare, present and record a piece of drama.

How did you help create tension?
What have we learned about comedy?
What have we learned about rituals?

Deal here with what students who are not in principal roles can do to feel involved and maintain belief in the drama. Unlike role-play, a play is often structured in such a way that everyone cannot be involved to the same extent.

10 Explain that the work has arisen from a scene in Shakespeare's *Shrew*, and that the next few weeks will be spent finding out why things happened as they did. Issue the magazine article as private reading (see pages 150–51). 'We are not going to act out the play, but to understand it was written in a time different from our own. The magazine article will help you understand the story Shakespeare told. Our work will have the benefit of progress and analysis.'

Katharina Minola:

a woman of action reflects on her life in times of change.

When Katharina was being brought up by her wealthy widowed father in Padua, the city was full of wealthy young men looking for excitement. Padua was the in place amongst the leisured classes with its reputation for the arts, its university and its free and lively atmosphere.

Young women, frustrated by the out-of-date attitudes of their parents, and often pursued by undesirable men, submerged themselves in music and reading as a release. Women, that is, except Katharina Minola. Katharina was angry, enraged by her father insisting she married before her younger sister Bianca, enraged by the crude labelling of ageing chauvinist creeps like Gremio. Gremio thought that just owning a smart town house and a 'des. res.' in the country made him Exec of the Year. Fed up with being regarded as stupid or wild, Katharina ended up taking it out on her sister.

So what of Bianca Minola? She was every bit as beautiful as her sister, but much preferred a quiet life. She was passive rather than assertive, more inclined to opt out rather than take direct action. Not like her sister who smashed a lute over Hortensio's head when his disguise as a music teacher wasn't matched by his sense of rhythm. Katharina didn't realise it at the time; it seemed like all the fellas were interested in her sister; though Bianca wasn't interested in them – you wouldn't have been either! The men had the philosophy 'drink together, fight apart' and often talked of love in terms of hunting and sport. Even younger, more educated men, who believed in doing their own thing, often resorted to this when in all male company.

The sisters were under pressure 'cos in those days marriage was as much about a business deal, the dowry, fixed by the fathers in advance, as about love.

But Petruchio was different. He met Katharina on her own terms, and boy, was it stormy! He was determined to be married, he needed the cash, and Katharina was quite a challenge. Katharina was reluctant to say exactly why she had agreed to marry him though she did tell me about the wedding itself . . .

Picture the scene, Katharina in her dress, all the guests waiting . . . . Petruchio turned up late, looking like he was wearing the complete stock of an Oxfam shop. He was rude to the priest and kissed her *very* passionately in the church! He refused to go to the reception. Yes, Petruchio was known for being unconventional, but this was going too far.

Katharina lived through a very difficult period. Petruchio couldn't settle in to an equal relationship with his wife. He refused to let her eat food because it wasn't cooked well enough, and made such a scene about the way the bed was made that she didn't get any sleep either.

Katharina was loyal to Petruchio even when he started behaving badly in public. She even found herself being rude to Bianca's father-in-law in the street rather than continue to fight with Petruchio. Bianca got into problems, too. Lucentio, from Pisa, had to pretend to be a teacher to be allowed anywhere near Bianca. His servant disguised himself as Lucentio to keep up appearances. When Vincentio (his dad) found out about this – after they'd secretly married – he was none too pleased. Still, that's another story. And all the time Petruchio would argue the sun was the moon as though it were a game.

The more cerebral Katharina Minola has bounced back. She has found pleasures in her marriage to Petruchio and has certainly outgrown her angry young woman stage. The question is, has she compromised too far?

The Taming of the Shrew

BAPTISTA
Gentlemen, importune me no farther,
For how I firmly am resolved you know;
That is, not to bestow my youngest daughter
Before I have a husband for the elder.
If either of you both love Katharina,
Because I know you well and love you well,
Leave shall you have to court her at your pleasure.

GREMIO
To cart her rather. She's too rough for me.
There, there, Hortensio, will you any wife?

KATHARINA (to Baptista)
I pray you, sir, is it your will
To make a stale of me amongst these mates?

BIANCA
Sister, content you in my discontent.
Sir, to your pleasure humbly I subscribe.
My books and instruments shall be my company,
On them to look and practise by myself.
                    Act I, Scene i, lines 48–58, 80–83

A Husband Must Be Found

Here are two simple approaches to the content of the play. Students apply these to a text extract which reveals that Shakespeare's sources are rooted in folk lore, under which are universal truths about parent/child relationships.

1 Using sharp, clear, precise physical expressions to create meaning in a moment

1 Divide the students into pairs. With a time limit of about five minutes, ask them to prepare several still pictures. Each one should show the first meetings/proposals between a hero and heroine of a fairy story. Share a few around the class.

The quick, fun task initiates thinking about the old-fashioned, usually sexist, approach to relationships in fairy tales. Sharing ideas reveals possibilities.

2 Spontaneous improvisation

2 Students continue to work in their pairs, and start to improvise freely situations between parents and their teenage children in our society. They should focus on typical clashes which might include arguments on parental rules, attitudes towards boy/girl friends, sisters/brothers, imposed on sons/daughters. Ask at least one group to illustrate a moment when a parent embarrasses a teenager in front of friends.

This introduces a modern context in which the play can be understood specifically in relation to the text extract which follows. Relating to students' own experience means deeper analysis is possible later.

3 Distilling to the essence

3 After about five minutes' improvisation, ask the students to distil the essence of their work. The work can be made of good quality in a short time by choosing a moment of drama which contains no more than two lines. Watch each pair. Ask the students to look for general trends.

The task for the spectators encourages a 'conscious learning' approach to drama.

4 Simple textual analysis and character study	4 Read the text extract aloud with clear vocal differentiation between characters. Invite the students to explain what is happening, first generally and then specifically, line by line, translating into modern English. Discuss how each character feels about the situation, about each other and themselves. Make lists which contain words which describe them.
	Teacher reading means the students receive an accurate oral interpretation of the text, which will maximise their understanding. By doing their own translation of meaning, they feel more confidence in their own ability. By doing this in a class group, it is possible for you to have some input into the interpretation. The word lists provide the basis for a more detailed analysis of character and will be useful for referral.
5 Practical interpretation of text and character	5 Allocate each student the role of either Katharina, Bianca, Baptista, or Gremio. Working individually on their lines, ask them to experiment with ways of communicating clearly the feeling of the character.
	Each student should be challenged but not overwhelmed by the task.
6 Effective communication of text and character	6 Spotlight interesting or effective examples, encourage the development of physical communication and encourage an exaggerated interpretation of these characteristics: Baptista as pompous, patriarchal, hard. Gremio as a fool, *nouveau riche*, sexist, rude. Katharina as wild, angry, embarrassed. Bianca as meek, humble, pathetic, weeping.
	Spotlighting enables you to make teaching points briefly without interrupting the work for too long. Exaggeration is freeing for the students and encourages them to see the range of possible interpretations of the character.
7 Drawing together strands which contribute to interpretation and understanding	7 Pick the most exaggerated of the four characters and ask them to present their work together. • What was revealed about the people and their situation? • How did exaggeration create meanings? • How do the improvisations at the start relate to the text?

Allowing the students to see how acting style affects meaning is a useful, critical skill. It helps students to see that theatre is not merely a presentation of how life is, but that this has been given meaning by interpretation. It will enable them to see and make links between the social or real world and the world of the theatre.

8 Ask students to write a letter from one of these four characters to a problem page, asking for advice in dealing with their problem.

The 'Lovers' Meet

- Physical and verbal humour
- The pace of text and its meaning

RESOURCES
Text extract (Act II, i, 181–258)
Problem page letters from last lesson

1 Active listening

1 Give a demonstration with a student of the language style of repartee without specifying a quarrel or even using a competitive tone. Merely say that each person must use a word or phrase that the other person has just used in the dialogue, for example:
(a) I had eggs for supper last night.
(b) Well, I don't like eggs but I enjoyed my hamburger.
(a) Enjoying hamburgers is okay if you're not vegetarian.
(b) My cousin is a vegetarian.
   Ask the students to experiment with this in pairs until they are quite fluent.

Before introducing the pace and competition of a quarrel, students are given time to concentrate on listening and replying in words received.

The Taming of the Shrew

Petruchio
But here she comes, and now, Petruchio, speak.
Enter Katharina
Good morrow, Kate – for that's your name, I hear.

Katharina
Well have you heard, but something hard of hearing;
They call me Katharine that do talk of me.

Petruchio
You lie, in faith, for you are called plain Kate,
And bonny Kate, and sometimes Kate the curst.
But Kate, the prettiest Kate in Christendom,
Kate of Kate Hall, my super-dainty Kate,
For dainties are all Kates, and therefore, Kate,
Take this of me, Kate of my consolation –
Hearing thy mildness praised in every town,
Thy virtues spoke of, and thy beauty sounded,
Yet not so deeply as to thee belongs,
Myself am moved to woo thee for my wife.

Katharina
Moved, in good time! Let him that moved you hither
Remove you hence. I knew you at the first
You were a movable.

Petruchio   Why, what's a movable?

Katharina
A joint-stool.

Petruchio   Thou hast hit it. Come, sit on me.

Katharina
Asses are made to bear, and so are you.

Petruchio
Women are made to bear, and so are you.

Katharina
No such jade as you, if me you mean.

Petruchio
Alas, good Kate, I will not burden thee!
   For knowing thee to be but young and light –

Katharina
Too light for such a swain as you to catch,
And yet as heavy as my weight should be.

Petruchio
Should be? Should – buzz!

Katharina   Well ta'en, and like a buzzard.

Petruchio
O slow-winged turtle, shall a buzzard take thee?

Katharina
Ay, for a turtle, as he takes a buzzard.

Petruchio
Come, come, you wasp, i'faith, you are too angry.

Katharina
If I be waspish, best beware my sting.

Petruchio
My remedy is then to pluck it out.

Katharina
Ay, if the fool could find it where it lies.

Petruchio
Who knows not where a wasp does wear his sting?
In his tail.

Katharina In his tongue.

Petruchio   Whose tongue?

Katharina
Yours, if you talk of tales, and so farewell.
She turns to go

Petruchio
What, with my tongue in your tail? Nay, come again.
He takes her in his arms
Good Kate, I am a gentleman –

Katharina   That I'll try.
She strikes him

Petruchio
I swear I'll cuff you, if you strike again.

Katharina
So may you loose your arms.
If you strike me, you are no gentleman,
And if no gentleman, why then no arms.

Petruchio
A herald, Kate? O, put me in thy books!

Katharina
What is your crest – a coxcomb?

Petruchio
A combless cock, so Kate will be my hen.

Katharina
No cock of mine, you crow too like a craven.

Petruchio
Nay, come, Kate, come, you must not look so sour.

Katharina
It is my fashion when I see a crab.

Petruchio
Why, here's no crab, and therefore look not sour.

Katherina
There is, there is.

Petruchio
Then show it me

Katharina   Had I a glass, I would.

Petruchio
What, you mean my face?

Katharina   Well aimed of such a young one.

Petruchio
Now, by Saint George, I am too young for you.

Katharina
Yet you are withered.

Petruchio   'Tis with cares.

Katharina   I care not.

Petruchio
Nay, hear you, Kate –
     She struggles
                      In sooth, you 'scape not so.

Katharina
I chafe you, if I tarry. Let me go.

Petruchio
No, not a whit. I find you passing gentle.
'Twas told me you were rough, and coy, and sullen,
And now I find report a very liar.
For thou are pleasant, gamesome, passing courteous,
But slow in speech, yet sweet as spring-time flowers.
Thou canst not frown, thou canst not look askance,
Nor bite the lip, as angry wenches will,
Nor hast thou pleasure to be cross in talk.
But thou with mildness entertain'st thy wooers,
With gentle conference, soft and affable.

     He lets her go
Why does the world report that Kate doth limp?
O slanderous world! Kate like the hazel-twig
Is straight and slender, and as brown in hue
As hazel-nuts and sweeter than the kernels.
O, let me see thee walk. Thou dost not halt.

Katharina
Go, fool, and whom thou keep'st command.

Petruchio
Did ever Dian so become a grove
As Kate this chamber with her princely gait?
O, be thou Dian, and let her be Kate,
And then let Kate be chaste and Dian sportful.

Katharina
Where did you study all this goodly speech?

Petruchio
It is extempore, from my mother-wit.

Katharina
A witty mother, witless else her son.

Act II, Scene i, lines 181–258

2 Fluency, quick-thinking	**2** Put the students into mixed pairs by initiating a kind of tag where you specify who will chase whom on a given signal. Call out names to pair people off and explain once they have been tagged they must start a quarrel with their partner, again using words from the previous line. After a few minutes, evaluate what differences there were between the two tasks, namely pace, volume, energy, facial expression, gesture.

Separating these two tasks allows students to appreciate the ingredients of this style. They are doing their own creating in parallel with the text.

3 Divide the group into two, the Petruchios and the Kates (Katharinas), each sitting in one half of the circle. Using the extract, begin reading one phrase from each respective character only up to the next punctuation mark. This is to be done in a quiet but firm voice.

Sharing of the reading in phrases allows everyone to succeed equally and prevents reading too much 'received' feeling or 'acting' into the text at this stage. The important thing is to listen and become aware of speech patterns. |
| 4 Projection, rhythm | **4** Students should then choose a line, phrase, or word, learn it and find a partner. (It doesn't matter whether the lines go together or not.) Ask them to keep repeating their lines while moving away from, and then closer to, each other. When they feel they have the most suitable pitch, projection and clarity, they should continue to speak, absorbing the musical patterns created.

Using much more space than students might have on the stage, and again working in a non-threatening manner, the scope of possible voice patterns becomes clearer. When they settle on the 'right' pitch and pace, the line will have taken on a rhythm of its own. |
| 5 Voice appropriate to situation
Communicating emotions effectively | **5** In mixed pairs, as far as possible, students using lines 195–202 play the extract by continuously moving, turning and attempting to tap each other on the back. Using the resources of the room, students can try to gain the upper hand by getting up on blocks, moving forward, moving faster, further. The aim is to keep the meaning in the words while trying to win the game. |

This extract is a battle of wits which later leads to Kate being held by Petruchio. The words are given appropriate actions; both are trying to score points. Language on the stage is given life and context.

6 Rehearsing text, movement, space, timing

6 Changing partners, divide the scene into tiny sections and allocate a section to each pair. In some cases this will be just a line each, in others much more. Ask the couples to rehearse their section to perfection.

You might have to narrow down the extract to, for example, the lines 215–26, 'Nay, come again . . .', depending on the size and skills of your group.

7 Concentration in performance

7 Run the scene in sequence using all your actors. The performance of the scene takes place with every pair standing ready to present their lines immediately the previous pair finishes. The students must collectively keep the pace of the argument by picking up their cues.

This is a technique for sharing and understanding the text without being intimidated by language or line learning. A high degree of concentration and sharp thinking by all members of the class allows them to be performers and audience simultaneously. Students gain great pleasure from experiencing the scene unfolding in this way.

8 Evaluate in terms of use of language, voice and movement and the implications for the relationship.

Here is an opportunity to focus on planned use of skills and why they were effective.

9 Evaluation of form

9 Ask each person to record in detail the actions, voice and space used during his/her specific extract.

Discovering the details required to present even one line of script is a useful training for students of all abilities in developing skills for evaluation.

10 Re-distribute the problem page letters to other students. For homework, ask them to write advice to this person. These letters will enrich the discussion during the forum.

The Sisters Quarrel

- Presentation skills
- Pair work arising from textual material geared at different levels

RESOURCES
Photocopiable Shakespearean text (Act II, i, 1–36)
Photocopiable cartoon story
Photocopiable modern translation of text

This is a multi-resourced lesson. It aims to equip the students for the forum in which a series of alternative meanings will be created in the text to examine gender roles.

1 Ask the students to improvise, in single sex pairs, a typical quarrel between sisters or brothers about boyfriends or girlfriends. They might tease or provoke each other. Spotlight the pairs after they have been improvising for a couple of minutes. Comment on use of physical intimidation.

This quick warm-up exercise introduces the students to the situation. A practical opening will relax them in preparation for the challenge of tackling the script. The physical skills will need to develop alongside the language skills. As far as possible, keep single sex siblings throughout the lesson. If an issue is not made of the fact that Bianca and Kate are female, the boys will apply their own experience of rivalry to the situation and think little of 'playing women'.

The Taming of the Shrew

Enter Katharina, and Bianca with her hands tied

Bianca
Good sister, wrong me not, nor wrong yourself,
To make a bondmaid and a slave of me.
That I disdain. But for these other gauds,
Unbind my hands, I'll pull them off myself,
Yea, all my raiment, to my petticoat,
Or what you will command me will I do,
So well I know my duty to my elders.

Katharina
Of all thy suitors here I charge thee tell
Whom thou lov'st best. See thou dissemble not.

Bianca
Believe me, sister, of all men alive
I never yet beheld that special face
Which I could fancy more than any other.

Katharina
Minion, thou liest. Is't not Hortensio?

Bianca
If you affect him, sister, here I swear
I'll plead for you myself but you shall have him.

Katharina
O then, belike, you fancy riches more.
You will have Gremio to keep you fair.

Bianca
Is it for him you do envy me so?
Nay then you jest, and now I well perceive
You have but jested with me all this while.
I prithee, sister Kate, untie my hands.

Katharina
Strikes her
If that be jest, then all the rest was so.
Enter Baptista

Baptista
Why, how now, dame, whence grows this insolence?
Bianca, stand aside. Poor girl, she weeps.
He unties her hands
Go ply thy needle, meddle not with her.
(*to Katharina*) For shame, thou hilding of a devilish spirit,
Why dost thou wrong her that did ne'er wrong thee?
When did she cross thee with a bitter word?

Katharina
Her silence flouts me, and I'll be revenged.
She flies after Bianca

Baptista

What, in my sight? Bianca, get thee in.   *Exit Bianca*

Katharina

What, will you not suffer me? Nay, now I see
She is your treasure, she must have a husband.
I must dance bare-foot on her wedding day,
And for your love to her lead apes in hell.
Talk not to me, I will go sit and weep,
Till I can find occasion of revenge.   *Exit Katharina*
Act II, Scene i, 1–36

THE SISTERS QUARREL
FROM 'THE TAMING OF THE SHREW'

KATHARINE AND BIANCA ARE SISTERS. THEIR FATHER HAS INSISTED THAT KATHARINE, THE OLDER SISTER, MARRIES BEFORE THE YOUNGER. KATHARINE HAS NO BOYFRIENDS, BUT THERE ARE PLENTY WHO FANCY BIANCA.

GOOD SISTER, WRONG ME NOT, NOR WRONG YOURSELF, TO MAKE A BONDMAID AND A SLAVE OF ME.

OF ALL THY SUITORS, HERE I CHARGE THEE, TELL WHOM THY LOVEST BEST. SEE THOU DISSEMBLE NOT.

BELIEVE ME, SISTER, OF ALL THE MEN ALIVE, I NEVER YET BEHELD THAT SPECIAL FACE WHICH I COULD FANCY MORE THAN ANY OTHER.

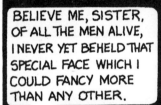

MINION, THOU LIEST. IS'T NOT HORTENSIO?

IF YOU AFFECT HIM, SISTER, HERE I SWEAR, I'LL PLEAD FOR YOU MYSELF, BUT YOU SHALL HAVE HIM.

O THEN, BELIKE YOU FANCY RICHES MORE. YOU WILL HAVE GREMIO TO KEEP YOU FAIR.

IS IT FOR HIM YOU DO ENVY ME SO? YOU HAVE BUT JESTED WITH ME. I PRITHEE, SISTER KATE, UNTIE MY HANDS.

The Sisters Quarrel

Bianca: (*with her arms tied behind her back*) Good sister, don't hurt me, you're hurting yourself by making me a slave and toy. I can't stand that. Just undo these ropes and I'll free myself of all other trappings. Yes, I'll strip right down to my underwear, or whatever you tell me to do. I know I must obey my elders.

Katharina: OK, of all the men who fancy you, tell me whom you love best. The truth!

Bianca: Honestly, sister, I haven't set eyes on Mr Right yet.

Katharina: Squirt, you're lying. You fancy Hortensio, don't you?

Bianca: Oh, if you fancy him, sister, I promise I'll ask him to marry you myself.

Katharina: I see . . . you're after the money then. Gremio's rich enough to keep you in designer clothes.

Bianca: Is that why you are jealous of me? For him! No. you must be joking. Yes, you've been teasing me all along. Please Sis, Kate, untie my hands.

Katharina: If this is a joke (*smacks her*) then I was joking!

Baptista: What the hell do you think you're doing? (*as he undoes Bianca's arms*) Don't mix with her, you are better off in your own room. As for you, you should be ashamed of yourself. Your sister has never done you any harm. Come on, tell me, when did she ever ever call you names?

Katharina: That's just it, she never says anything, she's so pathetic. I'm going to get my own back.

Baptista: Not when I'm here you won't! Bianca – go to your room.

Katharina: So you are going to stop me. I see. She is your favourite, your little pet, she will have a husband and I'll be left washing the glasses on her wedding night. And as far as your love for her is concerned, I hope you rot in hell. I'm going to go and cry until I get a chance for revenge.

2 Interpreting text

2 Distribute the textual resources to appropriate groups encouraging students to experiment with each role as they read through. Set up relevant tasks to help interpretation.
(a) Phrase – underline words which block understanding.
(b) Experiment with vocalising the lines while copying physical positions from the cartoon.
(c) Experiment with vocalising the lines and adding simple movements to illustrate the meaning.

The distribution is based on offering an achievable challenge to students of different abilities.
(a) To phrase, each speaker in turn reads aloud up to a punctuation mark; then another takes over. This helps to create sense. Students will have problems with some of the vocabulary and will need your assistance. However, they should be encouraged to make intelligent guesses around words to ease the flow of understanding.
(b) The cartoons/drawings are designed to provide a simple interpretation of the Shakespearean dialogue and encourage a practical process of understanding, still allowing students to work with the challenge of unfamiliar language.
(c) Without the burden of having to translate the complete language form, students can confidently begin to explore the interaction between the characters.

3 After allowing about ten minutes for group work, offer the opportunity to discuss the extracts, focusing on the content and possibilities for the form. Record the discussion on a poster or board.

This enables students to share the knowledge they have discovered from their specific resources with one another. The documentation will be useful in the main part of the lesson for reference.

4 Introduce the main task, which is to prepare a presentation of the extracts to take to the forum. Re-cap on the exercises previously experienced in 'The "Lovers" Meet' and 'A Husband Must Be Found' lessons and the need to apply personal experience to the text. Leave the students the rest of the lesson to work on this. The Baptistas can be most useful in the opening of the scene, by taking a directorial role. Move around the groups and focus in the following ways:
● suggesting suitable opportunities within students' own ideas for physical contact or eye contact;

- suggesting a re-read through of the lines in which the speakers begin over the last words of the previous speaker to create pace and tension;
- suggesting that students use a translation of the lines which cause problems to increase the appropriateness of tone
- concentrating on ways of making an impact with an entrance, and looking at how this re-directs attention and creates new tensions;
- exaggerating certain lines to effect differentiation in status.

In this way, your attention and expertise can be applied most effectively. Minimum 'interference' is best if students are working profitably. The aim of the whole lesson is for the groups to become experts on the extract for the forum. The length of the process is variable depending on student needs and time available.

Interpreting The Quarrel

- Active observation/responsive directing
- Forum

In this lesson, students bring their interpretations of the quarrel scene. The forum aims to deconstruct the story, searching for meanings through performance and discussion, and to discover why people behave as they do. Students will analyse this and advise one another on different courses of action. Change is based on the assumption that an actor can create the possibilities for a different form of action. People remain who they are, but their relationships and the power relations, in particular, can change. The degree of concentration, analysis and action involved make this a challenging lesson.

1 Allow each pair a few minutes at the start to refresh their work. Explain that everyone will be expected to chip in and that it is unlikely that the pieces will be played without interruption. During this time look out for work which will take close analysis, or which has a useful interpretation.

When students have spent a good deal of time preparing work it is important that their expectations are met. From the start, students should share in your thinking and understand the purpose of their work. During the last lesson they concentrated on form; movement and timing. What do these mean in action?

2 Call the students together and explain the nature and purpose of a forum:
- The actors and audience work together to analyse the drama.
- The audience gives advice based on personal knowledge, attitudes and experience.
- The actors use their skills to make the advice work as drama.

Agree some parameters for interventions in the work. In forum the audience have the right, normally reserved for the actors, to own and shape the scene.
Clear up the aims of the lesson so that students don't regard as a criticism any interventions that might take place.

3 Understanding dramatic communication

3 Begin by asking two or three groups to run the scene through without interruptions. Ask for comment after all three have been seen.
What was happening?
Why?

You are aiming to *generalise* about the quarrel. Seeing three versions of the same scene encourages this universality. We are not only looking at the specific problem for Shakespeare's characters, but at a more generalised and universal learning that can arise from it.

4 Using the drama form to communicate meaning. Acting. Directing

4 Using the issues that have arisen from the first discussion, ask another couple to play the scene. This time the audience can freeze the action any time there is a moment when a character does not need to respond in a negative way. The audience can call 'Freeze!' and then advise the character on a different tone, voice, gesture and so on. You will need to choose a confident group for this. During the course of the discussion, encourage reference to the other scenes studied and to the problem page letters.

The focus here is on how the theatre form can be used to bring about different meanings. The audience and actors are using their knowledge of the text to play with different interpretations. The atmosphere is collaborative, thoughtful and supportive. If the actors forget the lines, everyone else can help. If the actors need a break, another pair can take over. The quarrel is given the context of the play as a whole and the society it arose from, all viewed from a contemporary perspective.

5 Extrapolating from the drama to general attitudes

5 After up to 20 minutes' working time you will be considering the issues of:
— the 'need' to find a husband;
— unhelpful competition between sisters fostered by others;
— labelling of sisters as respectively shrewish and coy.
Give students a few moments to dwell on the implications of the situation. They know what the outcome of the play is. Need it have been so?
What do we want to change, the individual or the society?

After summing up the issues, allow some quiet time before the next phase of the lesson. The atmosphere in the forum is likely to have been lively and heated, and a chance to reflect is vital for everyone. Forums may not end in equilibrium.

6 Modifying actions within boundaries of the person

6 Divide the class into three groups, all the Biancas to work together, all the Baptistas and all the Katharinas. The sisters are to discuss the statement 'It would help me if you . . .' The Baptistas are to consider why their daughters are quarrelling and decide on five actions they could take to help the daughters get on better.

Continuing to stress the process of interaction encourages students to see they have the power to change things in their lives and the responsibility to interpret text from a value stance.

7 Direction

7 Select a student from each group to play the scene again. Call them away from the discussions and give them some tips on how they can improvise the scene for the class. Send the chosen Katharina to the Biancas for advice, the Bianca to the Katharinas and the Baptista to the Baptistas.

The personal perspective is maintained, giving the actors opportunity to respond to the same situation with the support of those advisers. The Baptista will need extra guidance; the timing of his entrance will be important and spontaneous. He might not need to enter until the quarrel is resolved.

8 Play the improvisation again. The audience must watch without interruption but with consideration of the question, 'Did our advice help?' Discuss the power of the theatre to change meaning and to change attitudes. The class are going to devise their own version of the remainder of the play, working with these characters and this situation. What are the issues they want to address?

The lesson is likely to have been quite challenging. We are encouraging a critical view of received meanings. Both the contemporary magazine style and the Shakespeare play are products of a particular culture. Both represent different forms of personal oppression. The *Shrew* uses humour to view bullying and psychological torture. We can see this arising from a particular historical perspective, yet having relevance for students' own lives. Taking a critical view of magazines designed for teenagers will enable students to appreciate the extent of the possibilities open to them personally and collectively. Central to this is the comprehension and application of the theatre form.

What Could Have Happened?

- Communicating analysis
- Making the play their own

RESOURCES
Sugar paper, felt tip pens
All documentation from previous
lessons

1 Awareness of value of the
drama experience in human and
theatrical terms

Having deconstructed the play and seen both where
meanings come from and how they are conveyed, students
are given the task of making the play their own with the
focus on the use of language. Their work will be recorded.

1 Discuss what the students have learned from working on
these materials. Where are they now? Question round the
circle, giving every student an opportunity to answer.
Accept all answers. From these replies, open the topic for
discussion.

It is important to discover what the students think they
have learned, both in terms of the drama and more general
human learning. This is a guide for your evaluation of the
content, though it is worth remembering that students may
well have learned things they are not aware of.

2 Explain that the students will have some time (this could
vary from one lesson to three or four weeks) to shape their
own piece of drama arising from the stimulus, which will be
recorded on paper as well as played. Each group will target
its work towards a specific audience. A lunch-time
performance? Parents? Assembly? Personal and Social
Education lessons? Make a video for each student? Suitable
tasks might be:
— a contemporary version of the second half of the play
   (with contemporary attitudes, not merely adding in
   airports and computers);
— the family relationships change;
— Katharina at 40;
— Petruchio's earlier years;
— resisting personal oppression.
   Other titles might well arise from your discussion. You
might give groups the same task, but for a different
audience.

The time-scale depends on the students' own interests
and skills. You do not need to re-stimulate their work at this

stage as the previous lessons have been rich in input. However, during discussions and their planning time, reminders of the issues and content at appropriate moments will help to keep students on the right track.

Your choice of task needs both to contain an element of where your students are at and to pose a challenge that will require students to engage in feeling and thinking as they shape their piece.

3 Agree the parameters of the task. What playing time are students to aim for? How long do they have to prepare? What is the purpose of this task? Do they have to work with Shakespeare's characters, or can they introduce new ones? The skill focus for the task will be use of language. Remind students of the language inputs they have encountered in this unit:
- Shakespearean language of different registers, e.g. formality of Baptista's public statements, lower register quarrel, crude remarks of Gremio.
- Magazine language, articles, cartoons.
- Language of drama; negotiation, discussion, critical evaluation.

Throughout this course you will have been changing styles and purposes of prepared work. Students are well able to respond to these changes and consequently develop a wider range of process and presentation skills.

4 The students begin to plan their work in groups of four to six. Listening in here will inform your teaching, enabling you to select from a range of inputs.

5 About five minutes before the end of the lesson, issue the poster paper to the groups and ask them to record what it is they intend their drama to say. These posters will become a working notebook over the preparation period.

- Supporting the development of prepared work
- Six ways of deepening work

During the developmental period the teacher has a range of tasks in addition to supporting the work and improving the skills.

1 Encouraging the use of the working noticeboard to ensure that the drama does not take on a life of its own, but continues to say what the students intend it to say (though this intention might well change).

173

2 Enriching the work with other resources: women's writing including plays by women can offer a modern perspective on the issue of sisterhood.

3 Using video to record and replay extracts from work in progress helps students to understand and develop their own work. This is particularly useful for those who believe they have completed all the thinking once they have constructed a plot. Videos are much more useful when they allow students to have a kind of dialogue with their own work. Merely recording their action for posterity is under-using a vital resource.

4 Using forum techniques between groups so that two groups can help to develop meanings in each other's work. This helps them become aware of and committed to a perspective.

5 Using hot-seating, distilling to the essence, teacher in role, with groups or whole class, to deepen work.

6 Instituting a session on enriching the use of language. Even within Shakespeare's play the characters adopt an appropriate register to their situation, e.g. Katharina when speaking to the guests or when quarrelling with her sister. Students can be reminded of this, the repartee, the paternalistic announcements, Gremio's crudity, Petruchio's satire. Encourage students to see language as a paintbox from which they can create their own pictures. An extra dimension is added to the art of language when voice is used creatively, e.g. whispering venomously during a quarrel rather than shouting all the time.

TECHNIQUES FOR RECORDING WORK

Use of language in this project has been rich and varied. This is an appropriate time to teach skills associated with recording drama.

The students can draw on the following resources:
- the working noticeboard;
- the video recording or tape recording of their work;
- the live playing and replaying of their scene;
- a series of photographs of their scene.

The task is undertaken as a group, encouraging attention to detail and being a two-way process where the drama enriches the writing and the writing clarifies the drama.

Unless students' drama has been well structured and meaningful, their writing will be superficial and too routine a task to be of any real value. The task is not 'bolted on', but of value to the drama itself and their understanding of drama.

Script

Writing from video, tape, or during live work by the group, the script writer uses different coloured pens for stage directions. As the recorders are getting down both what was said and how it was said, they become like neutral directors, encouraging actors to think exactly what they intend to communicate. The language itself can be reviewed during the enrichment lesson. Once students' work is recorded, they can evaluate whether that is the best way of saying what they want in terms of register, vocabulary and style.

Scenario

This records actions and events rather than words. Because it is language we are concerned with here, the group members should write the scenario together, then each character is given a photocopy to supplement by writing in, with coloured asterisks as a guide, the lines actually spoken at key moments in the story.

Comic strip

Use photographs of students' work (e.g. see page 176) with extracts from the script (pages 164–5) below each picture.

Subtext

A development of the idea above, where the picture shows what happens, the script shows what was said, and in the inset box a character reveals what they thought.

Video or sound recording

These are useful supports for students while they are constructing a piece of coursework. They can check exactly what happened in the drama and avoid merely describing what they see. Students tend to describe events as a way of preserving their work. If this is already done for them, using video, their description will automatically take on more evaluation.

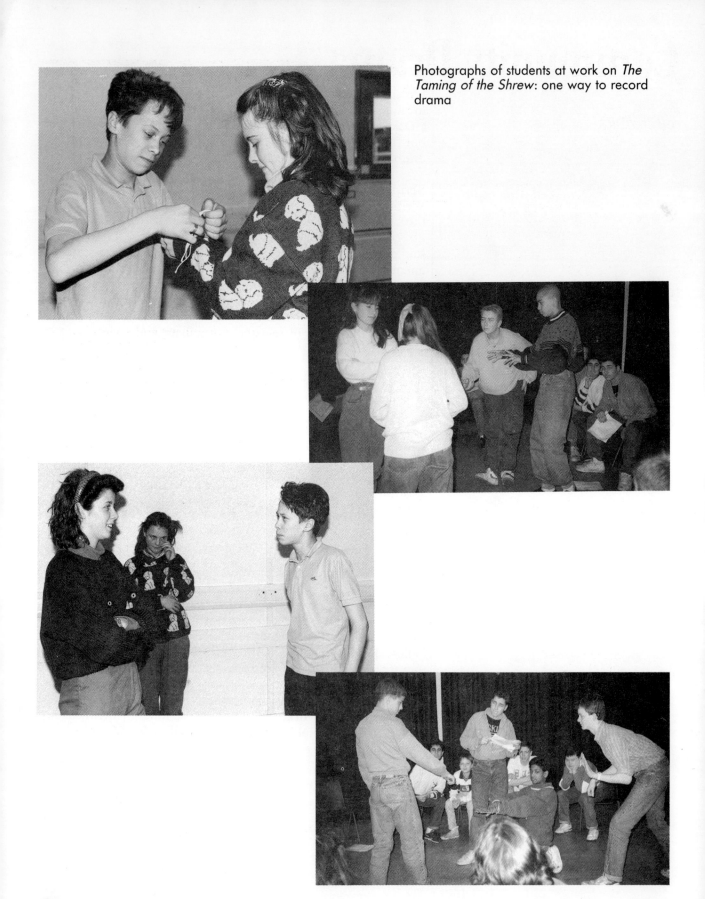

Photographs of students at work on *The Taming of the Shrew*: one way to record drama

Community Drama

NETWORK

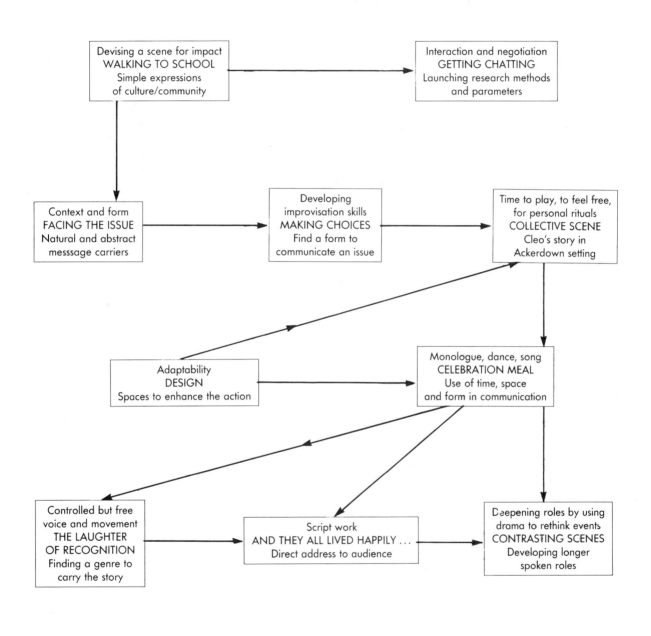

Devising a scene for impact
WALKING TO SCHOOL
Simple expressions
of culture/community

Interaction and negotiation
GETTING CHATTING
Launching research methods
and parameters

Context and form
FACING THE ISSUE
Natural and abstract
messsage carriers

Developing
improvisation skills
MAKING CHOICES
Find a form to
communicate an issue

Time to play, to feel free,
for personal rituals
COLLECTIVE SCENE
Cleo's story in
Ackerdown setting

Adaptability
DESIGN
Spaces to enhance the action

Monologue, dance, song
CELEBRATION MEAL
Use of time, space
and form in communication

Controlled but free
voice and movement
**THE LAUGHTER
OF RECOGNITION**
Finding a genre to
carry the story

Script work
AND THEY ALL LIVED HAPPILY ...
Direct address to audience

Deepening roles by using
drama to rethink events
CONTRASTING SCENES
Developing longer
spoken roles

A folio of responsibility
PRODUCTION TEAM
Making the work their own

Evaluating our work
SHAPING A PRESENTATION
Narrative or montage

WRITTEN TASKS

Prepare a Production Folio by the following stages:

Walking to School	Groups note learning from improvisation.
Getting Chatting	Research gathering, including transcription, diagrams of findings.
Facing the Issue	A collection of objects unfamiliar to the students because of their cultural origin.
Collective Scene	Jot down how a small improvisation was shaped and the sequence and rhythm of the composite scene.
Camel lesson	Development of form in stages.
Shaping a Presentation	Weather forecast, in role analysis, structured theatre review.
And They All Lived Happily . . .	Scripts photocopied.

Teachers might like to read:
John McGrath, *A Good Night Out* (Modern Plays series, Eyre Methuen, 1981)
Ann Jellicoe, *Community Plays* (Methuen, 1987)
Amrit Wilson, *Finding a Voice* (Virago, 1978)
Beverley Bryan and others, *The Heart of the Race* (Virago, 1985)

Teachers might like to view:
Motherland, Educational video available from Battersea CTV Centre (01 622 9966)
White Lies, Swingbridge Video, Suite 3, Norden House, 41 Stowell Street, Newcastle-upon-Tyne, NE1 4YB.
Black and White, a BBC Manchester *"Brass Tacks"* programme.

Community drama is a good motivator for students, as they see the link between school and life outside school in an immediate, creative and inspiring way. The students are already a part of that community, often more so than their teachers or theatre groups. Working creatively with people in the community is a growing trend in education and community theatre can be examined at GCSE.

Community drama is an opportunity to focus on the living culture and contribute to its shape. The value of doing your own research is enormous. As an idea grows from an overheard conversation or an impression of the atmosphere of the place into an integral part of a devised drama, creativity and excitement flourish. This chapter records resources and techniques used in creating/devising a community drama in a link project between an all-white rural school and an almost all-black inner city youth club. We used personal histories to create a non-documentary drama form. Some of the references arise from first-hand research. Others come from multi-cultural resources with a different research base, for example *The Writing on the Wall*. Through the life of a black girl it explores growing up as a process in which you deal with and find a pride in your origins and yourself. The work aims to give the students dignity in the same way as ethnic groups have begun to celebrate their culture rather than 'pretending' to be white or being made to feel invisible. As the drama grows, the black people are shown in positive and powerful roles, which is as important for white students as for the self-esteem of black students in your group.

Whether you decide to prepare your work with, for, by or about your target group it is important to find your own meanings from your research and improvisation. This involves finding what question the drama will raise rather than what problem it will solve.

Teachers are encouraged to use their professional judgement in the sensitive use of the resource material in 'Making Choices'. Your multi-cultural advisory teachers will have a wealth of resource material that can be substituted to meet students' needs. For 'Celebration Meal' teachers might like to read Seamus Heaney's poem 'Clearances' in *The Haw Lantern*.

Many of the lessons are shaped to allow you to devise a scene through drama and develop it through rehearsal techniques. You can adopt a variety of strategies to deal with these teaching points – for example, following the scene development in successive lessons, or using the rehearsal techniques to help maintain everyone's motivation once roles are cast. The shaping allows students to get results quickly and see further possibilities by application of form and development of roles. Each lesson has a design related input so that all students can share in this important concept.

OBJECTIVES
- Students will take responsibility for the development of a community drama.
- They will appreciate cultural diversity and the concept of community.

- They will use drama to entertain, with moral, social and aesthetic values implicit in content and form.
- In using their drama skills to present what the content offers, they will actively evaluate effective communication.

Walking to School

- Devising a scene for impact
- Simple expressions of culture/community

DESIGN
Promenade
Prepare before the lesson your chosen stimulus; your ideas on a target group.

1️⃣ Understanding of concepts

The objective is to create a working relationship and style that is both appropriate to community work and rewarding for the students, a kind of low-key enthusiasm. Students express themselves, generate ideas, and then use a 'form filter' to shape them just as they will do with the subject matter.

1 Explain to the group that we are going to make a play. That play is for a community and made by us. It will develop in small ways, but be something we want to share and that will help us and the community learn about one another while having fun.

What is a community? Discuss this with the group, drawing from their examples some of these categories:
— a group of similar people (their example, old folks' club);
— people from an area (their example, local estate);
— people with common interests (their example, swimming club);
— people dealing with an issue (their example, local action group).
Some you choose to belong to, others you are part of by circumstances.

Involving the students in tackling the concept of community from the start raises all the questions which they will face when working in the community, as well as allowing them a basis for the understanding of the concept. As the teacher, you can generalise from their particular statements as needed, giving their thoughts status in a shared consideration of the question.

2 To what communities do you belong? The answers will reflect a range of personal interests. How do you feel in those communities? Responses might include supported, warm, friendly, safe. Explain that we are going to look at the school as a community because we all belong there and doing some drama about school will help us to see how that community operates.

This improvision starts from where the students are at. In dealing with the familiar, the everyday, they have the opportunity to use form and concepts which will feature throughout this work, without concentrating on generating content.

3 Creating belief through life-rate drama
Evaluation

3 Using the whole room, students improvise the walk to school, recalling and replaying the experience. Play the scene, spotlighting moments which reveal something about the students themselves, their homes, how they feel about school. Evaluate these moments, 'What did that tell us about . . .?'

The open setting, at present unstructured, is useful in a final promenade use of space. Perhaps draw out comments on how the 'actors' and audience share the same space. The evaluation sets out to introduce another theme of this project, that of the need to develop more rounded characters than are possible in role-play.

4 Use of movement and language in form

4 Structure the work. First of all, focus on the opening of the door at home, as though that were the start of the play. Will students crash out? Will the door open slowly? Will we hear sounds from inside? Imagine students are going to perform in the school dining hall – what changes will they need to make? Create an impact by a punchy start. Ask groups to build the role-play into a prepared improvisation. You will get plenty of examples of use of form to build on. One class produced some funny moments when a small fourth year 'cycled' besides a very tall one. They almost danced on their bikes, showing their personalities and rhythms, and the final uphill ride to school was used to exaggerate their contrasting energies.

It helps the students if you work really hard to identify and appreciate any uses of form they are making. Their confidence will increase and they will take the skills further.

5 Evaluation of students' own work and that of others

5 After seeing the work, evaluate in terms of *content* (Would school pupils appreciate/recognise/enjoy the work?) and *form* (Would the work attract and hold attention in the dinner hall?). Begin to discuss the possible venues and community group for your chosen stimulus. Ask the students to note down, in groups, the knowledge gained from the walking to school scene that might be useful in their future work.

Students gain confidence from drawing out skills and techniques from a familiar area; this will enable them to approach their research in a more experienced manner.

Getting Chatting

- Interaction and negotiation
- Launching research methods and parameters

DESIGN
Expressions of community

RESOURCES
Notebooks, tape recorders, cameras

[1] Adopting and sustaining a role.
Evaluation

This lesson prepares the ground for effective and positive interaction with the community that will elicit useful source material and establish friendly relationships.

1 Students adopt a role in a queue. (The queue could be at a supermarket, chip shop, dinner queue, bus stop.) As teacher in role at the service point, you can control the movement of the queue. It is very slow. 'You don't know the people near you, except perhaps by sight. As the wait continues, you get chatting. After all, you are not in a hurry.' Allow this to run for a few moments, then evaluate. What were you able to learn about the other person? How did you feel as you began chatting? Record on a blackboard any tips that will be useful for approaching people in the community during research.

2 Divide the class into four equal groups, two groups to keep their roles, the other two to be themselves. Brief one of the groups in role to be preoccupied, shy, or busy, the other to be quite relaxed. Brief one of the student groups to interview someone, finding out as much as possible, the other to have a chat, remembering as much as possible. Pair the students half from each in role group working with half from each out of role group. You have all the combinations of researcher and respondent operating. Some combinations are likely to conclude their conversations sooner than others. Encourage the students to analyse why this is. From the evaluation of this task, draw up a list of criteria for good community research that the students will use. Reinforce the respect students have naturally for the communities to which they belong. Enlist the students' familiarity with the area as an advantage, encouraging them to initiate contacts and so on.

3 Explain that the play will be built on people's experiences, that they will have many different histories, and that we are going to use drama to explore how the past can help us change the future.

Draw up your list of people to talk to and places to go. You might include: The community artist
Youth Club leaders
Parents
Neighbours
Library
Community Centre
Local newspaper offices
Factories.
The next stage is to identify who would be good at what.

For further guidance on research see 'Soap' lessons, 'TV Researchers', 'Research Follow-up', 'Production Team Meetings'.

4 Explain that in devising their own play devices used in lessons like role–play, hot–seating, and freeze–frames can be used. Drama has to mean something, whether it is narrative or a series of scenes on a theme. When linking improvisations together, think about the audience.
What will they see?
What will they discover?
What will they think?
What will they feel?
What will they recognise?
Once the research is collected students will use drama to communicate their findings to an audience. This will mean experimenting and structuring to find meaning and form. In the sample material the link is between growing up and the multicultural society.

Facing the Issue

- Context and form
- Natural and abstract message carriers

RESOURCE
An object that reminds you of your roots

OBJECTIVE
- A consideration of cultural symbols as a key to personal histories and dramatic symbols to signify taking one's place in the world.

  Your multicultural advisory teachers can help resource and plan this work.

[1] Appreciating social structures in terms of personal values

1 'Our play is about growing up. Our audience are young mothers. Let's think about ourselves for a while. And let's start at the beginning. Where were you born?'

Collect responses on a blackboard. Note how not everyone is born in the local town. Go further – where were parents born, grandparents? Discuss the multiracial nature of Britain and how some people have to struggle against prejudice.

You will generally find students have origins outside your immediate locale. An awareness of the problems of racism and discrimination could be heightened by discussing how having black friends does not affect the employment statistics for black teenagers. This reinforces students' thinking about changes as gradual, not a characteristic of their times or of today's newspapers.

Alternatively, show the students an object that reminds you of your roots and talk through what the object means to you. Does it have symbolic value for the past? How does that affect the present?

The symbols and signs fundamental in drama and in affirming culture are considered. Are they a dangerous shorthand, or helpful holders of social meaning? In searching for meaning in these symbols, students are encouraged to bridge their understanding of the personal and the historical.

[2] Role-play in depth

2 Set up a role-play at a party, a meeting, a club – whatever social setting is appropriate for your theme. In this example, a group of parents wait outside the primary school gates to pick their children up. Identify three students to adopt the roles of newcomers. Introduce them to the improvisation one at a time. In the first instance, brief the group to pay no attention to the newcomer, as though she were invisible. The second receives a warm welcome, the third a mildly hostile response. Discuss how feelings were shown and how responses were communicated and record them for the portfolio.

Carrying the theme of the research material into an experience common for the target audience; in trying alternatives, students become aware of possible subtleties of response.

3 Movement and gesture with meaning

3 Develop the reactions and emotions into an abstract movement based drama that symbolises the response, e.g. turning your back, a group embrace.

The slight decontextualisation heightens the quality of feeling and the form of expression.

4 Individual semi-abstract expression of a poignant moment

4 Alone, ask each student to recollect a time when he/she was new to a situation, reminding him/herself of his/her feelings. Ask students to take up a position in that feeling, but using a role from the research, e.g. starting a new school. Freeze in a position that expresses these feelings without going over the top. Spotlight some students. 'How do you feel?'

Recontextualising the feeling gives students scope to express powerful feelings with simplicity and clarity.

5 Connecting ideas and action

5 In groups, develop a drama in which a young person begins a voyage of discovery. The work can include:
• cultural symbols which are positively valued;
• personal rituals which 'explain' what makes someone tick;
• a poignant moment of growing up.
You might need to introduce these criteria one at a time, depending on how your group grasped the concepts earlier on.

Consolidate the learning through drama in a way which carries universal meaning by focusing on the particular.

6 Evaluate (perhaps in writing): 'What questions does our drama ask?'

Making Choices

- Developing improvisation skills
- Find a form to communicate an issue

OBJECTIVE

- This lesson encourages students to appreciate how their drama must carry meaning. They develop a vocabulary of form to communicate this meaning.

RESOURCE
'The Writing on the Wall'

This is only a suggested resource. You may wish to identify alternative resources which are more suitable for their groups.

☐ Analysis
Not blocking in improvisation, using role to the full

1 'What questions does our drama ask?'
'Does your family help you take your place in the world, or hold you back?'
'Where do our values come from?'
'How much freedom do people have over things that happen to them?'

In pairs, begin a role-play. One is the parent, one the teenager. The parent describes an aspect of the teenager's behaviour as inappropriate. The teenager responds by accepting why the parent says this, but at the same time putting a personal view. Those in role as teenagers must ensure that no quarrel develops.

In learning the drama skill of going along with others in role, but working towards a positive solution, students are simultaneously developing their understanding of the theme: I am me and I respect you. This is helpful in addressing the relationship between people who came to Britain and their British-born offspring.

② Presenting a perspective
Shaping a drama to communicate meaning

2 Read or issue different extracts from Abiola Agana's story 'The Writing on the Wall' (see pages 188–9), so that groups within your class can reconstruct moments from Cleo's past. The action in the story is all female, unlike extracts often supplied to students. All your students could try out the roles, or you could ask the boys to play people who watch the action. Later we will introduce a white boy friend of Cleo's, Keith. If you use this story in place of research for a presentation, note that it refers to England.

Ask students to think through whether society gives equal status to groups from different origins. Ask groups to be aware of two levels, societal and personal, in preparing their improvisation. In shaping their work, they consider how the form adds to the meaning.

The Writing on the Wall

It was the first day back after the summer holidays, and Cleo Mothopeng had already begun to feel irritated surrounded by 500 girls the same colour as those who had killed her father.

Mrs Harding, the headmistress, dressed in her floral silk dress, stood at the far end of the assembly hall. She fiddled violently with her gold chain. It was obviously Azanian, thought Cleo, she could tell by the way it glistened like her father's forehead as he worked the mines, and like her mother's did when she had begged them not to kill him.

Cleo's train of thought was broken; the headmistress was reading Psalm 23. Cleo nudged Valerie when they heard the part about still waters, they both remembered last Wednesday when the pipe had burst in the toilets. The water was far from still. They laughed, shaking. Assembly ended and the pupils proceeded to leave the hall. Cleo got up. She prided herself on not having to use her hands. She used her legs; her lovely strong legs, the legs that had darted around policemen, over bushes, and run from intruders, 'those whites', as gran-gran used to say, 'would never quench dem thirst of Black man blood.' At fourteen Cleo was fit, she was approximately five foot six inches tall, whereas Valerie was only five foot and plump.

Cleo had joined St Clementine's school last term, and Valerie was the only one who seemed to notice. Valerie and Cleo often talked about their backgrounds. Cleo told her how in Azania there was never a day that someone in the family had not died, and how her father was killed for refusing to give their last four yams to a policeman. Valerie told Cleo how their family fled from Germany where they were constantly under threat.

Cleo often invited Valerie over to her mother's flat, where they would admire Cleo's mother Ntsikie's carvings and gold jewellery. She had made them, it was their livelihood. But Valerie did not care for the meals originated by the Cape Town people, nor the Kente cloth Cleo's uncle Kudame had bought from Ghana.

Ntsikie could see that Valerie was not the friend that Cleo thought she was. Ntsikie prayed that Cleo would not talk to the white girl, for it would only bring pain to Cleo. Ntsikie told Cleo this, but Cleo only thought that her mother was trying to destroy their friendship.

There had always been graffiti in the toilets, Cleo even wrote some herself. It was something to do during break. Valerie had never told her what 'WOGS' meant, but she seemed to find it funny, so Cleo too laughed absent-mindedly at the unknown.

That morning every one was whispering about a new group called the 'M.F.' or the 'N.F.' or something. Cleo couldn't quite catch it, but Valerie and a couple of white girls were all huddled together laughing and whispering. Cleo could faintly hear the words 'C-O-OON.'

Valerie did not talk to Cleo for the rest of the day, but when she did see Cleo, she said something like, 'You're right you know, she does look like an ape,' and then they would start to laugh. Cleo's eyes were stinging with tears, tears to flood her in self pity, because Valerie was not talking to her. But she would not, could not cry, for as her father had said, 'He who cries for the love of a white man is useless to the African struggle.' Valerie had been Cleo's only link to the other pupils in her class, and Valerie knew how reliant Cleo was on her.

Cleo looked at her smooth Black skin. She is beautiful; Josina Machel Cleopatra Neffertiti. She was them and they were her. Question upon question she asked herself. She had respected Valerie, why? She had wanted to be Valerie, why?

When Cleo got home, she told her mother everything. Ntsikie put down her half peeled potato, and grabbed her only child. She put Cleo's head on her chest, and wailed, 'Oh, oh Josina,' (that's Cleo's second name) 'From apartheid to apartheid!' Cleo also began to cry as she remembered her father and those who were put in tyres, and those who tried to take them out, who were branded traitors and filmed on television. Ntsikie told Cleo all the words that they have for Africans. Cleo felt ill when she thought of the amount of times she had been called 'Black Bastard' or heard another Black person called a 'Wog', and she had just smiled. Ntsikie had protected Cleo from this as a child, but in a country such as England, Cleo must become aware.

The next day, Cleo arrived at school early. She was fully aware of Valerie's hypocrisy although she still needed time to think. Cleo entered the toilets, her mind throbbing with strange thoughts, and there it was written on the wall:
'I LOVE P.W. BOTHA, KEEP BRITAIN WHITE'

'UMBONGO UMBONGO, RUBBERLIPS LIVE IN CONGO'

It was in red paint. Cleo stared. Valerie approached her. At first she was relieved to see her, but as Valerie grabbed her arm she felt the moist stickiness of paint. Cleo looked down at her arm, it was covered in red paint. Valerie smiled, 'What's up, Cleo?' Cleo made for the door; 'You and Botha have a lot in common.' Valerie continued, 'Was it something I said, Cleo? Talk to me.' Without looking back Cleo said with disgust, 'You don't need to say anything, because what you mean is written on the wall.'

by Abiola Agana (aged 13)

In choosing their way, your better students will identify subtleties of attitude and present them in a form able to carry meaning gently. Others will go for the committed absolute response and use a form that tends towards the abstract or stylised. You will need to discuss and identify how your target audience is going to be reached best, remembering that the aim is to ask questions, not to provide answers.

3 The students play the scene up to a moment of choice for someone in their scene. Give them a few minutes to decide where to stop, then share each group's work. Is choice a part of growing up?

Evaluate in terms of *form*:
- Direct address to audience?
- Time – how was this used?
- Space to convey meaning?
- Natural, or stylised, or somewhere in between?

and in terms of *content*:
- What was the drama saying?
- What was it asking?
- Who did we identify with?
- How did we feel?

4 Evaluation of meaning in action

4 Create new groups, consisting of representatives from the previous groups, to carry this evaluation further. Look at how the form and content carried the meaning together. Would the meaning change if space were used differently, for example? The groups create working notes and reconstruct moments in order to experiment with their view.

Everyone becomes involved in further thinking about the tools they have at their disposal for communication. This work is an excellent basis for theatre criticism and for deepening students' own work through awareness.

5 In groups, or as individuals, consider a piece of material from the research. Using the thinking just experienced, plan how the quality of feeling and the meaning behind the incident can be conveyed by content and form. Use the students' planning in a future lesson or rehearsal.

Collective Scene

Through every lesson you are teaching the development of drama skills, the exploration of the content and an awareness of the community's interests. This lesson helps all students to feel involved in a meaningful way in creating a scene. The focus is on Cleo and how the audience will begin to know and understand her.

Her individual work will be either created by the class in collaboration during the lesson, or by the student playing the part while the others are working on the given tasks. She needs to conjure up youth, individual strength, contentment, crossed with flashes of rebellion and spontaneity, all without words.

- Time to play, to feel free, to have personal rituals
- Cleo's story in Ackerdown setting

DESIGN
Large open space, rough, wild, with 'safe' enclosures

---

[1] Using movement and space to create reality and meaning

7 Using your discussions on growing up, remind the students of activities which characterised different stages in their lives. These become a series of extended tasks:

Sitting throwing stones	. . . . rhythm; direction.
Imaginative games	. . . . collective freedom, happiness, safety in groups.
Being 'cool'	. . . . establish your image – alone.
Admiring a friend's bike	. . . . apparent group solidarity, but influence of materialism and received culture evident.
Hurrying home from work	. . . . purposeful transition.
Young couple	. . . . counterpoint.

Ask students to recreate these, focusing on the age and outlook of the person, but working for the drama techniques indicated. Each of these suggested tasks reinforces the theme and helps to create the atmosphere of the Ackerdown, an open space, undeveloped. Every student has a role in creating this picture and the director will use her/his colouring box to highlight images.

The fact that everyone helps to present the scene is as much a part of the genre as it is of educational good practice. Students are part of the content, conjuring misty or clear images that arise from the themes. And part of the form is creating the wild free atmosphere, the setting for learning more about Cleo's destiny.

2 Communicating, in movement, action, and sounds, the atmosphere of the place

2 Experiment with each of the tasks, again rewarding students who do a particular one well. Encourage them to remember and develop their successes.

We all need reminding from time to time to say 'good work' to individuals. This series of tasks enables everyone to make a positive contribution to the scene, and to feel their particular contribution is significant.

3 Communicating through acting style

3 Once everyone has a task, ask students to polish their presentation on three levels:
(a) Playing the scene for audience attention.
(b) Playing the scene for atmosphere.
(c) Playing the scene to support (even if by contrast) Cleo's thoughts and action.
Tackle these in turn, so students have a repertoire of acting styles within their theme.

Evaluate in terms of differences between the three kinds of playing.

4 Ask the students to jot down now how ideas developed and how the acting styles differ.

Doing this in groups gives students the opportunity to go into the kind of detail required in written coursework with the experience fresh in mind and the support of their group. The note-making becomes a collective process.

5 Focus

5 Play the scenes again, giving different groups an opportunity to play their (a), (b) or (c) at different times. Introduce Cleo. At first, she is just another one of the children on the Ackerdown, but gradually we need to focus on her. Use yourself as a physical device for this, getting closer to her as the scene focuses in on her, rather as in film close-ups. On your way there, freeze and spotlight various pieces of action. After each one, ask the groups to say what they are adding to the scene, using their understanding of the content, the issue and the intention of this specific scene. What sounds can we hear? What parts of the space should you use?

6 Once you and the students feel you have got the scene right, play it through a couple of times. Everyone must record the sequence and rhythm of the scene for future reference.

Some students prefer to do this graphically. They could draw a plan of the set and mark their moves with asterisks which are explained in notes. Perhaps different lines for different paces, e.g. dotted lines for slow movements, lines with arrows for direct fast movement.

Rehearsal

The scene will need reinforcing over the next few days and Cleo's character and actions need devising. Looking at each of the components, Cleo could identify what she has in common with each other character, e.g. 'Like the children, I enjoy freedom. Like the lovers, I appreciate the space and the early evening light. . . .' Her personal history needs to be derived from the research material; this scene gives the audience an opportunity to observe her enjoying her own company and to reflect on thoughts about her already developing.

Some students can consider how to create intimate spaces while keeping the 'rough and wild' qualities; others can be polishing their individual piece. An input from the story-telling lesson in the *Theatre* chapter (pages 239–63), or from the role-play lesson in *Soap* (pages 30–53), will help to deepen roles. Self-help hot seating can be used by small groups of students.

Design

- Adaptability
- Spaces to enhance the action

See the approach used in the *Theatre-in-Education* project (pages 82–100) to prepare your resources. Creating a composite setting is possible in this piece. It really depends whether you will perform in a small space, with the audience closely directed to look at you, or an open space, where the acting will have to gain the audience's attention as in a carnival/promenade staging. The overriding rationale for all design work is that the ideas should develop with the devising process.

1 Identify the demands of each scene as devised on a design noticeboard. Below is an example.

Location	Concept – she feels it's great to be young	Design notes
Ackerdown	wild, rough, open, but with intimate spaces	levels, nooks and crannies
Cleo's home	comfortable but closed, feeling a bit hot to handle	lighting to close down
Precinct	organised, planned, structured, sterile; adult	smooth levels, etc.
Toilets	flowing people, girls only	invisible mirrors facing the audience

Your rough notes will enable you to see what spaces the actors designed for themselves when working. Some of them appear contradictory. Leave this question in the air for the moment. A student will be sure to pick it up in inspiration when you introduce the next problem. A useful individual/homework task would be to add a fourth column, 'acting style', which might include 'spotlighted' improvisations in the Ackerdown scene, sound collage in the precinct.

2 The audience: What is the venue?
               Where are we going to be as actors?
               Where will the audience sit?
               How many can we expect?
This is rather like planning a good party. You need people to feel the warmth of the other guests, to be aware of one another, to be able to respond with them, to feel they are part of an experience not to be missed. Your students will know their audience, even personally, and this could be turned to advantage, undermining the notion of encouraging

students to be 'professional' by keeping out of sight and so on. Anne Jellicoe gives help with dealing with a promenading audience.

In looking at the space, see its existing possibilities, exits, entrances, levels, rather than wishing it were a drama studio.

3 The acting style. What kind of sharing do you want to aim for? Will the audience participate? Observe? Pass judgement on the question? How will this affect acting style? Many community plays have something of a carnival atmosphere, harnessing cultural signals from the target group, celebrating this by entertainment, incorporating small scenes, promenade.

Everything the students have learned on their course about what exactly it is they are doing in drama could be consolidated through this point.

Try out scenes in spaces before final decisions are made. Encourage students to show in their portfolio how a piece of scenery, such as a bench, can become a sledge in the snow, a wall if turned on end and so on, with appropriate examples from the script to show how the scenery enhances the action.

Celebration Meal

- Monologue, dance, song
- Use of time, space and form in communication

RESOURCES
Several baskets or bowls, four or five large pieces of fabric

DESIGN
Linking the theme of received culture, home life, with target group, young mothers: a pram, a washing line, swing, a playpen, etc. In this example, a basket of colourful fruit and vegetables, with fabric for a tablecloth. Contrast with the wild, softer tones (browns, greys) of the Ackerdown. Tables and the shaping of an audience space

1 Demonstrating understanding of the research through drama skills

1 Students space out and adopt the roles of parents preparing vegetables for a meal; their baby is asleep nearby. Before beginning, talk through some of the ideas arising from the research to focus the students: the images children have of their parents, regularly performing such tasks, the great or small hopes parents have for their children. Working individually, the students bring the scene alive, talking aloud if they wish, just thinking about their child, if they prefer. Quietly identify and reward good work that you want to preserve for the final scene.

This lesson is going to create the content and structure of a scene. It can either be played to a target audience or improvised with them. The images are immediate and familiar to people of all cultures and, as the work grows from individual reflection to a celebration meal, the tempo builds. No sharing at this stage, the atmosphere created in the room is paramount.

2 Work in pairs, one retaining the role of the parent, the other a friend. The parent has seen the signs of change in the now 13-year-old and talks over hopes and fears with a friend. The parent has almost finished preparing the vegetables. Once again, reinforce good work by quiet reward.

The continuity of the vegetable preparation gives an idea of how time is used in drama. The child has grown 13 years in the time it takes to prepare a meal. The pair work generates drama from ideas. The research is given form in language, movement and space.

3 Expressive movement

3 Collect ideas from the students about the actions of the teenager. Enrich this with evidence from their research and

196

their own experience. Encourage an awareness of development of personal history. Working in pairs, prepare the scene 'Cleo/Keith grows up'. One student is the teenager and will perform the actions, the other is the narrator who will be largely still and address the audience. As the students are working, help them find an image in form that will reinforce their actions – for example, growing up is a journey, so Keith moves forward as the scene develops; it's also a struggle, so Cleo's movements will show her pushing aside toys, searching through a maths problem, and so on.

It is vital that the narrator/demonstrator technique is sufficiently deep so as not to look like a performing bear act – unless, of course, a child's growth felt like that! This scene again uses drama time and teaches a technique that will become part of the final scene.

4 Evaluation of concepts

4 Decisions will need to be made later as to whether you will have both a Keith and Cleo scene or just Cleo. A performance would be better if it focused on one, but, if you are sharing the work with the community in a more open or informal context, playing both could be useful. The decision then would be whether to play the scenes simultaneously, showing parallels and contrasts, or one after the other, which gives a sort of question-and-answer style. In the lesson everyone is contributing ideas towards the scene. Appoint a recorder to jot down effective work that the class, as a whole, wishes to preserve after seeing each pair. Include some discussion of the concepts, recording productive ideas:
'The street stands for acceptance from other kids. It's safe.'
'Society makes you grow up – it exposes you to worries.'
'Yes, and if you cope with the worries, you become grown up.'

In the evaluation you can really push your students' thinking. They often use simple language, and examples that can be generalised, to tackle more complex notions. For example, in one discussion, the idea was emerging that a middle-class upbringing convinces you you are right, and a working-class one convinces you you're wrong. Oversimplification, but an interesting notion.

5 Explain to the students that together you have been improvising the structure for a scene. In discussion, focus on how time can move at different rates in drama, how we can use various devices besides the naturalistic to tell the audience about Cleo's personal history. In this lesson, the devices that occur are the reflective monologue of the parent, the narrator/demonstrator, and later the possibility of song. 'We are going to weave all these ingredients into a scene. But first we must write the song.' Actually, this is a task for a small group of students, perhaps working with someone from the community, but the others can help get it started. In groups, ask the students to begin to compose a song for a celebration meal. You could divide the task up, or ask each group to be aware of the following criteria:

Content	— Images of the person, the food, the guests, the culture.
Style	— Upbeat, able to be sung by everyone, repetition so people can join in, music the community appreciates (soul music, rap?)
Instruments	— Voices? Music from the culture? Music from contemporary culture?
Atmosphere	— The song is part of the play. What do we want the audience to feel while hearing it?

You have taught the use of form by developing it parallel with content. The abstract has a link in the students' minds with the concrete. Try to set some students thinking about how the actors and audience might interact.

6 There is just one more teaching point before we are ready to run the scene. The celebration meal gives us an opportunity to illustrate the different effects of theatre space. A table for theatre in the round can have people sitting all around it, a table for arena staging needs an empty side. During the course of the scene, experiment with different layouts. A group of actors can play a small extract of a scene several times, with students moving from one side, to all around, to two sides and so on. Discuss how different feelings of identity are experienced depending where the audience is. All this is best done when the characters are seated. You can then add the dimension of a character moving away from the table as someone else speaks and see how this changes the audience perspective. Add to this the impact achieved by some actors leaning over the table, resting on the table, moving under it, standing on it, and the feel is changed again.

Once you have your music, the action can be planned as a kind of a dance where the stillness of the finished table arises from a buzz of movement that is the setting of the table.

7 In groups, use a piece of fabric and the baskets to 'set the table'. The scene begins as a parent finishes the vegetables, the other characters enter and transform the almost empty space into a celebration setting.

You now have all the ingredients for your celebration scene. Use rehearsal to decide the finer details – for example, are you having all the students on stage as parents at the beginning, or just one? Expect the students with individual pieces to prepare at home. They have the resources of everyone's ideas to draw on.

- Parent prepares vegetables: reflective monologue; child as youth.
- Table set for celebration: colour, movement, song; a rite of passage.
- Tension revealed: narrator/demonstrator; 'being you and being me'.

Could you have a meal with a community group as part of the play? Or a dance?

The Laughter of Recognition

- Controlled but free voice and movement
- Finding a genre to carry the story

The aim of this lesson is both to develop students' skills of presentation for a non-naturalistic theatre form and to look at the role of humour in conveying meaning and raising issues. The joke used as an introductory exercise was the start of a play, *The Conquest of the South Pole* by M. Karge, seen at the Traverse Theatre, Edinburgh Festival, in 1988. The play was about the effects of unemployment on individuals – the joke was their keynote greeting suggesting patterns of loyalty and logic. Any similarly non-sexist joke would do.

1 Begin with the joke – ask the class 'Why can't a camel ride a bike?'
Wait for a response. Repeat the question with louder voice, larger gestures, until you have a chorus in reply of, 'I don't know. Why can't a camel ride a bike?' Using much softer tones, say, 'Because . . . it's got no thumb to ring the bell!' Don't expect students to fall about the floor laughing. Play around with the form of telling the joke for a few more minutes; ask three students to say the first line, everyone to reply loudly 'because', and a small voice to deliver the punch line; ask four people to rush to the centre of the room, freeze, look around, then speak and so on.

The structured warm-up gets people moving, using their voices and experimenting with form.

2 Evaluation

2 Discuss the form and content of the joke. What meanings were created by the use of voice, movement and space? What clues were introduced about the people? The joke itself is harmless; discuss the nature of humour. It needs more meaning to be funny and yet we don't want racist or sexist jokes.

3 Use of chanting, repetition of rhythm, levels, action

3 Ask the students to work on the joke, using only those words, as though it were the start of a play. Brief them to concentrate on setting the tone for the play through pace and space, and to ensure that they know what group of people they are.

This starts from where any group is at, yet really pushes the use of form because students are given the content. The work will begin to take a genre.

200

4 Presentation
Evaluation of process and product

4 See every version. Evaluate in terms of form and skills. Ask the students to note down how their piece was developed and performed, by consulting with their group and taking account of their evaluation. This gives them a miniature model for writing a piece of coursework on performed work. The idea is developed through a series of stages – the process. The product is played and evaluated by the students themselves and their audience. Good coursework needs to reflect on both the process and the product.

5 Take the issue from your research material and begin to consider how humour, well presented, can raise the issues. Negotiate the criteria for students' next task, for example:
(a) People need to recognise something in laughter.
(b) The laughter should raise a question; that is, it should educate and entertain.
(c) The humour must support the material.
   For example: Using 'The Writing on the Wall', focus on Valerie. In discussing the possible reasons for her actions e.g. fear, ignorance, being bullied herself, the scene raises a general point – can being happy with yourself help you to be happy with other people as they are? Allow plenty of time for preparation, helping to shape students' work by questioning groups about the use of form, and taking on roles to help develop content.

Establishing the criteria for laughter in the drama is vital, not only in terms of the content of the scene from a drama perspective, but because of the moral implications involved in the issue. The gentle prod approach here does not make any racist in your class or prospective audience feel isolated as the butt of jokes, because this would reinforce some of the causes of that racism anyway. One put-down leads to another. A good example for the gentle, prodding style of theatre is the way the Hull Truck Company, whose work has a dynamic relationship with the local community, raises issues, presents characters to the recognisable community, and always has enough moral clout to attract a following amongst middle-class theatre-goers of the left.

6 Construct a scene with Cleo in a new relationship with other girls, one where her self-sufficiency has grown. Develop a matching scene with a group of boys. Both scenes draw out attitudes to mixed race relationships.

201

Some students will devise work with happy endings. By asking if life has such happy endings you can have a useful discussion of drama form. Perhaps, like Brecht, raise an issue, face it, but leave the audience to answer the questions for themselves.

7 Besides supporting the development of ideas in groups, it will be helpful to intervene with some general points. This can break problems some groups may have (e.g. discussing too much or being dominated by one person) and allow time for reflection on the criteria.

8 Whether or not you see all the work, ask the groups to record specific ideas, moments, lines that will fit into the play as a whole, and should therefore be involved in the one scene this lesson will provide. Point out that, while many scenes were good in themselves, this is a new stage: writing a scene that contains the best from all the rest. If you need to ensure more objectivity than your groups are capable of, ask one person from each group to leave the first group and join another. Their roles are to take notes and ask questions of their new groups, never simply refusing to note things down, but prompting the groups to justify their ideas in the context of the whole. These people could form a scripting group with the specific task of coming up with a scene based on the improvisations for the next production team meeting.

9 Whether you use a scripting group, plan the work with the class, or do the shaping yourself, don't miss out on the opportunity to increase awareness of how a story unfolds. This will teach students the basis of good improvisation and add a dimension to their evaluation. You might point out how characters are introduced, consolidated, developed; how counterpoint arises (the lovers talk apart whilst couples walk through the park); how the issue is raised openly in the middle of the play, making other experiences slot into place and preparing for development.

And They All Lived Happily...

- Script work
- Direct address to audience

RESOURCES
Levels created by boxes or a
trestle table made into ramp
Fabric hung vertically
Unfinished script

Research – either prepare a script, or use the lesson to devise one based on an appropriate scene.

|1| Being daring

1 Have some fun with the students saying 'I love you', but saying 's/he said' and the stage direction as they do so.
   E.g. '"I love you," she said, turning the pages of the newspaper.'
'As he offered her his last Rolo, he said, "I love you."'

Everyone is aware that we will work on a love scene; the Brechtian technique is introduced and the initial embarrassment which might have produced silly or flippant work later is given voice and worked out now.

|2| Giving life to a script

2 Evaluate in terms of belief – which ones were more believable? Issue the *Unfinished Script* (see page 205), saying to the class that the couple involved really care for each other. They have been friends and supporters for some time. They are attracted to each other but afraid. Read the script. Discuss the effect the distancing has on the meaning and on the audience reaction.

From the start, you are encouraging students to interpret text, in this case, by contrast with their own work.

|3| Communication through space

3 In twos (or threes, with one being a director), begin to play the scene. Focus on the use of space and levels and the use of movement by giving different pairs different challenges. The more experimental students can be left to their own devices; another couple can play the scene intimately, with eye contact; another, side by side facing the audience; another across a wide gulf; another with both facing in opposite directions.

This provides the dimension of directorial interpretation for the work and gives everyone a contribution to make, even if the lovers' roles are cast.

4 Alternatives: Both these tasks are required for the scene. Do one with the whole class while individuals work on the other.

(a) To keep everyone involved, ask each pair to work on until they have devised an ending in the same style. The criteria should meet the project's aims in terms of raising not resolving issues, showing someone growing up to take pride in him/herself, showing different cultures living in Britain.

(b) Discuss the notion of counterpoint. With close reference to the text, identify moments when, for example, the distant passing of an old couple holding hands would heighten the feelings of the audience about the main couple. Improvise possibilities and collect them in note form for scripting.

Rehearsals

The scene takes place in the Ackerdown at twilight. Experiment with the use of torches. The couple could use the torch, placed lens down, to simply 'leak' light, gradually lifting it to shine into the partner's face. Another approach which gives every student a task is to light the couple with torches shone by the group from various parts of the room. Fireworks, such as indoor sparklers, could be used as a special effect to heighten the distancing technique and draw attention to the 'happy end' as unrealistic phenomena. During this work you can discuss the role every actor plays when, in community theatre, he or she is seen by the audience when not acting. Such actors must become what Ann Jellicoe calls the 'ideal audience', responding to the scene in an appropriate manner. In the use of torches, students' timing and stillness add atmosphere to the scene.

Play with the pace – the space.

Unfinished script

The tablecloths that created colour and celebration in the previous scene are reversed by the actors in their linking entrance to create the effect of the snow-covered Ackerdown.

We hear their laughter before we see a group of children run into the space, playing with the snow. The last of their snowballs hits Kevin in the face. As the children disappear Kevin sits down in the snow. Glum.

Moments pass. The last drips of the melting snowball trickle down his face. Kevin looks at his new clothes, the very latest gear. He realises his bottom is getting wet, stands up quickly and adopts a new glum waiting pose.

Cleo enters at the other side of the space and pauses, looking at Kevin.

Cleo: Kev?

He doesn't answer. He is still waiting. Cleo throws a snowball into the space between them. Kevin and Cleo look at each other.

Kevin: Hello, black girl . . .

Cleo: Hello, white boy . . .

Kevin: Thought you weren't coming.

They go to sit down together in the snow but, quietly laughing, realise it's not a good idea.

Kevin: My mum had a benny on me for wearing this to school. I was doing the washing up n'all.

Cleo: Once isn't enough. It's not a miracle cure, you know.

[*From here to ★ is spoken to the audience.*]

Kevin: He looks at Cleo, her eyes grin back at him. He puts his hand in hers, inside the pocket of her coat. Like holding hands in the precinct, he thinks, but better.

Cleo: She holds his hand, and lifting her hand and his, looks at their black and white fingers criss-crossing. Like holding hands in the precinct, she thinks, only different.

Kevin: Kevin moves behind Cleo to whisper in her ear how beautiful she is. You're beautiful, you know, he said, feeling proud of her and quite warm.

Cleo: Cleo smiles and rests her head on his shoulder. What will her mother think if she marries a white boy, she wondered, feeling just a little colder.

Kevin: Kevin sighs. (*sighs*) Kevin knows his mum would like Cleo. His mother's a feminist and goes to lots of meetings.

Kevin: They almost kiss.

Cleo: They almost kiss.★

Cleo: (*moving towards a tree swing*) I've been learning things today.

Kevin: Cleo . . .

Cleo: (*swinging gently*) Yeah, but when you look at me you only see the girl from the youth club. When I look at me I see bits of me, bits of my mum, people who left, good times.

Kevin: And black skin (*Kevin has guessed what Cleo's thoughts are about*).

Cleo: And black skin. Mum hadn't said before. And I didn't either. We just got on. Then, yesterday, in the precinct we saw some graffiti, it was being cleaned off by the council, a Nazi cross. It got her talking about Uncle Edwin, he was in the RAF in the war. The family hero. They all wanted to come to Britain, a better life, help build Britain back up. Jobs in steel, coal, railways and buses, and not enough work in Jamaica. Cups of tea and hospitality, that's what she expected, not 'Sorry, it's not that I don't want to rent you a room, I support you, don't get me wrong . . .' Edwin was really upset when Trevor got arrested under the sus laws, suspicion, suspicion of being black. See, Kevin, it had to be written on the wall before you noticed it. I know Kevin, you're great, a good mate, good. But you can't solve racism by kindness and buying reggae records.

Kevin: . . .

Contrasting Scenes

- Deepening roles by using drama to rethink events
- Developing longer spoken roles

RESOURCE
Tape recorder to collect all feedback

Students used to the responsive style of improvisations need support to develop more extended pieces of speech. These tasks give the content and feelings to a more fully rounded portrayal of a role.

Throughout this task an alternative is suggested in brackets for the paired scene. This can be either worked on simultaneously, or perhaps more successfully at another session or rehearsal.

1 Adopting a role, creating belief

1 Individually, the students recall what it was like to be scared when walking home at night. How do they behave? What thoughts rush through their heads? Time plays tricks, rushing by, hearts beat faster. What is the atmosphere like? Perhaps it is misty. (Parallel scene: waiting for someone to come home, time moving slowly, worrying, the house is safe but prickles with anticipation.) Bring the scene to life.

This is a common human experience, though one that is heightened at times of strife, as in areas with racist problems, Northern Ireland and elsewhere. Students may involve an issue.

2 Finding meaning in action

2 Use the tape recorder to record the evaluation session on what people did, how they felt.

This will provide material for deepening role work later.

3 Application and appreciation of genre

3 Use your research to discover an action that someone was proud of, or deserved to be proud of. Discuss with the students the nature of pride. When is it good? When is it a negative emotion? Work in groups to recreate a scene – for example, washing racist graffiti off a wall observed by some of the perpetrators; an adventure in the street. (Parallel scene: a ritual in the home, washing your child's hair.) Heighten the quality of feeling in the scene by changing genre if necessary, even having something of the Western hero in tone (or the 'Last Mama on the Couch' melodrama, a scene from Wolfe's *The Colored Museum*). Consider unexpected genre, a domestic adventure showing nurturing and imagination. Stress the adventure/action base of the scene. Use video or tape recorder as you play the scenes.

In finding a form of entertainment familiar to the community, the students learn its limitations and possibilities, while enriching their understanding of how form affects meaning.

4 Role development

4 Return to the notion of pride and how it develops. Perhaps consider these continua:

    bitterness .... acceptance
    pride .... shame

Ask the students to devise a longish speech where the character thinks through negative feelings and, as the speech develops, comes to feel proud to be him or herself. The content of the speech can be gained from the recordings of the previous tasks. A way in could be to reconsider a number of experiences that have occurred to parents. How are they together? What patterns have grown over the years? Has parenthood changed priorities? Have opportunities that seem to be gone for ever been replaced by different experiences? Have parents come to accept what is good about the present, especially the hope for a future for the child? Questions will help students unable to shape experiences gained – for example, pride, or hide on the way home? How did I become me? (Answer in role.)

Once this extended speech is prepared, you can look for the right setting to bring it alive.

1 Supported role development

5 Alternatively, look at Cleo as a role model for someone younger. The characteristics admired in Cleo are also present in the younger girl. She begins to be proud of herself, enough to feel that her action or acceptance is appropriate. In each scene, look for the common human experiences, the place pride has in maintaining self-confidence to achieve independence. Use partners to help evaluate: What I thought I saw? How do we learn about you?

6 Find a situation into which the speech can slot. The ideal one is one where some of the same themes are underlying, but the superficial situation is simple, everyday, every person. This can be achieved by a good teacher in role work. For example:
(a) Set up a role-play where pride is at stake, people are being rewarded for achievement and so on, but one person feels like hiding – a mistake has been made.
(b) A person is going through his/her everyday rituals, things that signal how much we believe in ourselves. Something goes wrong. How do we react – when the drink is spilled, the toothpaste won't open . . .?

(c) Give a title, 'Home is the best place in the world'; 'The door step'.

(d) Give or devise a symbol – say, the swing, a symbol of freedom; the table, a symbol of family tradition.

Use research material and outline plot to make a device, but at this stage don't identify which characters need to be in the scene. This way new possibilities are thrown up and everyone is kept involved.

Rehearsal points
Concentrate on how change in focus from one of the parallel scenes to the other is achieved.

Experiment with the pace of the monologue.

Production Team

- A folio of responsibility
- Making the work their own

The production team meets the educational aim of giving students concrete work experience and responsibility for their own work. In the *Soap* chapter the roles were imaginary, in *Theatre in Education* they were content led. Here the students have full responsibility for the administration, too. Cross reference with the lessons in other chapters for how to run the sessions. The students gain individual responsibility and experience in collective decision-making. They may have to bargain, negotiate, or justify to one another the reasons for any actions. If you have a budget for this production, or can get a grant for the community work, hand over the financial decisions to the students, too. Arts administration is beginning to feature in examination syllabuses and represents an avenue of employment for students with drama qualifications. Local theatres and arts centres have their administration teams at work during school hours and are very helpful when you make contact. Your students are their future audience. The students will benefit from seeing how professionals do the job and their approach to the visit will be all the more meaningful, as each individual is likely to welcome advice and ask specific project-led questions.

The team sets its own goals, getting help from experts or volunteers as needed. They establish and maintain ownership of the material. They will have to consider the following topics:

- Research
- Community liaison
- Publicity
- Costing
- Venue
- An exhibition of work in progress
- Design – includes costume, stage props, etc.
- Scripting
- Technical – lighting, sound
- Transport
- Rehearsal time – plan
- Creating a positive image for themselves and the school
- Striking the set, returning borrowed things

The shaping of the material arising from research and these lessons is like making a collage.

- Evaluating our work
- Shaping a presentation
- Narrative or montage

RESOURCES
Postcards

7 Evaluation of form and content

The work in this unit has given you at least ten possible scenes, all of which the students have recorded in the production folio. In shaping a piece of drama for an audience, you will need to decide what the criteria are, what the form is, and what relationship with the audience you wish to set up. Ideas in these areas have been forming as the work has developed. It will help your students to evaluate their work and see the presentation as a whole if they join in the decision-making.

1 Using the portfolio as a source, write on a postcard the title of a good moment of drama, the form used to communicate it, and the message it carried. Students should work in small groups with up to a dozen postcards.

2 Lay the postcards over the floor. Consider the target audience and the time and venue you have for presentation. Use this discussion to consider the broad genre. If your piece takes place at a meal you share with the audience each 'table' can act between courses, for example.

3 What are we saying? How best can we say it? What will the audience be grabbed by most – a strong narrative line, or a series of sketches using dance, music, comedy and so on to create a sort of carnival atmosphere? Return to the postcards and juggle them to decide a sequence. At any point in this lesson, recreate a scene to help the decision-making process. Indeed, the outcome of your decisions might be that a message or context improvised in a naturalistic way needs reworking in a different genre.

This helps students understand just what drama is and see

rehearsals as a continuous creative process, rather than, 'remember your lines, speak loudly, stand in the right place'. Once again, they have been part of the critical decision-making process; all students see the production as a whole and not from the perspective of the scenes they are in.

4 For further advice concerning the last stages of rehearsal and performance see 'Jarrow March' phase 17 or read Ann Jellicoe's 'Community Theatre'.

Enrichment Tasks
To improve the quality of notes in the folio, three tasks, with a wider perspective than the particular lesson, can be targeted to meet individual needs.

1 The Weather Forecast
Students draw an annotated forecast map of each scene, indicating how hot it is, what the atmosphere is like – stormy, sunny, overcast and so on. This will help them plan for and evaluate dramatic action.

2 My Experiences in This Play
In role, tell the story from the character's point of view. Identify stages. What does the character feel at each point? How do I (the actor) get from one point to another? How do I share this with the audience?

3 Review a Play
If it is possible to see a play during work on this course, a task of analysis can be set to match the challenge your group are facing. The questions might consider how a message is interwoven; when do we first realise the issue, how were we engaged by it, etc.? Or the task might be to note how scene changes were carried out by the cast and how this related to the acting style. For example, Hull Truck's actors in 'Salt of the Earth' dance the furniture around very gracefully to period music, whereas the vibrant rock music of 'Conquest of the South Pole' has actors quickly and efficiently running scenery on and off. How was a particular character developed? How were the audience treated, addressed, involved?

Progress?

NETWORK

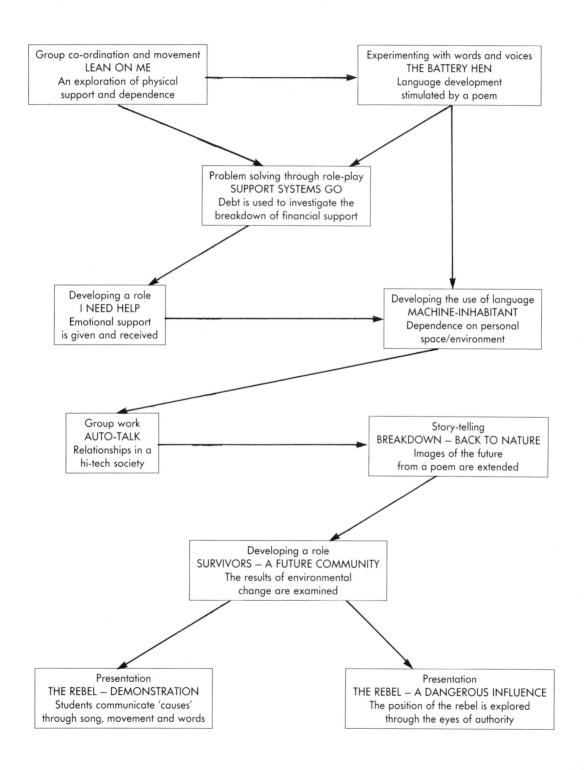

Group co-ordination and movement
LEAN ON ME
An exploration of physical
support and dependence

Experimenting with words and voices
THE BATTERY HEN
Language development
stimulated by a poem

Problem solving through role-play
SUPPORT SYSTEMS GO
Debt is used to investigate the
breakdown of financial support

Developing a role
I NEED HELP
Emotional support
is given and received

Developing the use of language
MACHINE-INHABITANT
Dependence on personal
space/environment

Group work
AUTO-TALK
Relationships in a
hi-tech society

Story-telling
BREAKDOWN – BACK TO NATURE
Images of the future
from a poem are extended

Developing a role
SURVIVORS – A FUTURE COMMUNITY
The results of environmental
change are examined

Presentation
THE REBEL – DEMONSTRATION
Students communicate 'causes'
through song, movement and words

Presentation
THE REBEL – A DANGEROUS INFLUENCE
The position of the rebel is explored
through the eyes of authority

The main objective of this project is language development. While it is important that students bring their own words and experiences to drama, we do not think these should be our only resources. In order to extend language skills, students must encounter new forms of expression and a wide range of vocabulary. In this project, experiments with story, dialogue, song and poem have been included, not as stimuli but as exciting dramatic events in themselves.

The theme of this project – a changing society – has been chosen to encourage discussion and debate. We want students to consider how hi-tech society is changing them, their language, relationships, and environment. Texts have been chosen not only for their language input, but because each challenges the reader to consider his/her perspective. In 'The Machine Stops' and 'The Horses' we look at a possible future and reconsider our own. In 'Song of the Battery Hen' we see what mechanisation has done to one creature and relate it to human experience. Along the way we touch on associated issues: money, authority, rebellion.

The overall aim must be that students will feel more confident about using new language, grappling with new ideas, using writing as a positive form of expression, experimenting with the creative use of words and voices.

Related reading:
Ray Bradbury, *Fahrenheit 451* (Panther, n.e. 1976)
Aldous Huxley, *Brave New World* (Study Texts series, Longman, 1983)
John Wyndham, *The Day of the Triffids* (Unicorn series, Hutchinson Education, 1975)
Doris Lessing, *Memoirs of a Survivor* (Octagon, 1974; Pan, n.e. 1976)

Lean on Me

- Group co-ordination and movement
- An exploration of physical support and dependence

1 Working as a group
Working with bodies in space

1 Students form pairs and experiment with support by leaning on one another's bodies, supporting one another's weight, and using balance.

In groups of four, eight, and then as a whole class, they form body shapes which depend on mutual support.

Students are introduced quickly and physically to the notion of 'support'. Physical awareness and a relaxed approach to working with others are important in this session. Set up a quiet atmosphere for this.

2 Co-ordinated movement and voice
Developing a physical vocabulary

2 Students go into small groups and form a machine containing:
(a) a wheel and piston;
(b) a production process.
Encourage clear actions. When the machine is in motion, students add sounds.

Spontaneous, concentrated activity is encouraged.

3 Use of movement, words and questions to focus understanding

3 As a whole class, a machine is formed which provides each person with a productive role. The qualities of the machine are discussed: size; components; function; sounds. On the completion of this task, the following questions are considered:
How does your movement change when you are working with one another?
What was the difference between working to support one another and working to produce something?
How does your movement change when you are machine-like?
When do people adopt these qualities?

Discussion and the use of language focuses the understanding of the task and its purpose. Questioning pinpoints important issues to be considered in the following activity.

|4| Recognition of concept
Exaggeration of concept in drama
form

4 Prepare a scene where people become automated.
Emphasise their machine-like qualities. (Some suggestions:
restaurant kitchen; office; checkouts in a store.) Encourage
awareness of what happens to people's voices, their eye
contact, perhaps introducing non-automated humans into
the scene. Look at how communication is affected.

The scene provides an opportunity to develop movement
skills within a dramatic context. A link is formed between
machines (physical environment) and human behaviour.

|5| Evaluation

5 The work can be shared effectively by spotlighting.

Spotlighting takes the emphasis away from performance
and leads to discussion of the ideas in the scene.

6 Draw up a list of opinions:
Technology gives us . . ./Technology takes from us . . .
Ask the question, 'Does it have to?'
Preserve this for the final lesson.

The Battery Hen —————————————

- Experimenting with words and
  voices
- Language development
  stimulated by a poem

RESOURCE
'Song of the Battery Hen' by
Edwin Brock

|1| Reading

1 Read 'Song of the Battery Hen' by Edwin Brock (see
page 216). Discuss first impressions.

Silent reading, followed by a fluent version aloud, offers
students opportunities to gather ideas and vocabulary.

2 Experimenting with voice: choral speaking, diction, expressing ideas and feelings Pinpointing themes in the poem	2 Work on the poem vocally. (a) One person reads, the others make sounds as the language suggests, e.g. on *rain drums on, fan blows*. (b) One person reads, others repeat important words, e.g. *concrete, dry, four walls*. (c) Read chorally in the roles of sales people. (d) Everyone makes a constant noise. Each person takes one or two lines, and fights to be heard. (e) Make a sound collage of the battery hen's home. Vocal experiments emphasise the richness and range of words and encourage the student to enjoy the dramatic use of sound. They also help the participant to understand the lonely position of the hen, and create an imaginative environment for the poem and the drama which follows. All this builds the students' own confidence in their voices and the possibilities of group/solo speech.
3 Extracting and using language appropriately Planning Rehearsing	3 Students form small groups and prepare *one* scene: — A scene in an estate agent's office, using the language of verse one to sell the hen's desirable home. — A scene in a geriatric ward, using the language of verse two to convey the isolation of old unwanted people. — A conversation between people looking back to their childhood with nostalgia, using the dream-like language of verse three. Each scene encourages a specific use of language – e.g. sales talk, insincerity, sarcasm – and requires the student to create a dramatic situation from the poem's themes.
4 Presentation Discussion	4 Ask the students to distil the essence, the feeling and intention of their work, allowing only two or three lines. Share the work, discussing the differences. Record the key lines for use in the final lesson of this project. An opportunity to analyse the contrasting use of language and relate this to the themes in the poem.
5 Focusing themes in writing	5 Writing task, 'Song of the High Rise Pensioner'. Using the poem as a basis, students change words to make it apply to a lonely old person living in a high rise flat. 'Old people' and 'looking back' have already been introduced in the scenes. Students now relate themes to a situation outside the poem and the drama, making a further connection between environment and human behaviour.

Song of the Battery Hen

We can't grumble about accommodation:
we have a new concrete floor that's
always dry, four walls that are
painted white, and a sheet-iron roof
the rain drums on. A fan blows warm air
beneath our feet to disperse the smell
of chicken-shit and, on dull days,
fluorescent lighting sees us.

You can tell me: if you come by
the North door, I am in the twelfth pen
on the left-hand side of the third row
from the floor; and in that pen
I am usually the middle one of three.
But, even without directions, you'd
discover me. I have the same orange-
red comb, yellow peak and auburn
feathers, but as the door opens and you
hear above the electric fan a kind of
one-word wail, I am the one
who sounds loudest in my head.

Listen. Outside this house there's an
orchard with small moss-green apple
trees; beyond that, two fields of
cabbages; then, on the far side of
the road, a broiler house. Listen:
one cockerel crows out of there, as
tall and proud as the first hour of sun.
Sometimes I stop calling with the others
to listen, and wonder if he hears me.

The next time you come here, look for me.
Notice the way I sound inside my head.
God made us all quite differently.
and blessed us with this expensive home.

Edwin Brock

Support Systems Go

- Problem solving through role-play
- Emotional support is given and received

RESOURCES
Bank and building society leaflets
Newspaper and magazine adverts
Video sequence of TV advertising
Scenarios

---

1 Listening
Expressing an idea or opinion

1 Teacher introduces the word 'security'. Students discuss support systems which make us feel secure.
What support networks do we have?
How do we use them?
What would we do if they collapsed?

The notion of emotional support is introduced through discussion and related to the students' own lives.

2 Sustaining a role
Adapting language and movement to a variety of situations

2 In pairs, students role-play a variety of situations:
(a) Someone is made redundant.
(b) A club is closed down. A retired person loses a hobby.
(c) Someone discovers that a member of the family is ill.
(d) A close friend lies to you.

Students go straight into role, without planning or discussing. The drama becomes a way of exploring the idea and the role, rather than a product to be examined later. In a fairly short time, each student experiences a range of roles and situations.

3 Identifying with role
Developing role imaginatively
Asking relevant questions to further the drama

3 Each person chooses ONE of the roles he/she played, and the role-play is shared through hot seating some members of the class.

Hot seating encourages the student to select an interesting role and develop it under questioning.

4 Collating ideas

4 The teacher introduces the idea of debt by a range of visual materials – for example, bank and building society leaflets encouraging credit facilities; newspaper and magazine adverts; a video sequence of TV advertising. How are we encouraged to spend more than we have? When does money fail to be a support?

A change in stimulus (verbal→visual) shifts the pace and direction of the lesson. A variety of visual materials will ensure the interest of most students. The questioning links the theme of the lesson to the new materials.

5 Story-making
Preparing an improvisation
Selecting appropriate forms for presentation

5 Three scenarios are presented as resource materials. A group is responsible for extending each scenario and presenting it to the class. This can take the form of:
(a) a scene with flashbacks;
(b) three improvised scenes;
(c) a series of enticing images or persuasive voices;
(d) a mixture of (b) and (c).
The group is asked to consider how the people involved lost their support networks.

The scenarios offer students basic information and the scope to select further roles and situations which sustain their interest and the drama. A suggested structure helps them to plan efficiently.

6 Presentation
Analysis

6 The presentations are shared and discussed. What could be done to help these people? How much are they victims of circumstances beyond their control? How did the different forms affect our sympathies?

7 Students are asked to write, in role, their feelings about their situation.

Scenarios for *Support Systems Go*

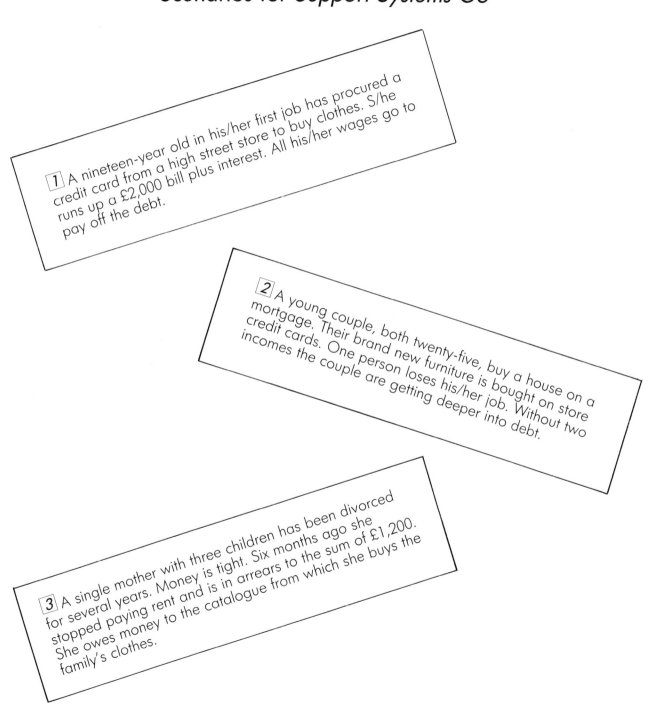

1. A nineteen-year old in his/her first job has procured a credit card from a high street store to buy clothes. S/he runs up a £2,000 bill plus interest. All his/her wages go to pay off the debt.

2. A young couple, both twenty-five, buy a house on a mortgage. Their brand new furniture is bought on store credit cards. One person loses his/her job. Without two incomes the couple are getting deeper into debt.

3. A single mother with three children has been divorced for several years. Money is tight. Six months ago she stopped paying rent and is in arrears to the sum of £1,200. She owes money to the catalogue from which she buys the family's clothes.

I Need Help

- Developing a role
- Emotional support is given and received

|1| Listening
Reading aloud
Evaluation

|2| Listening
Selection of role

|3| Decision-making
Use of space

|4| Developing a role imaginatively

1 In small groups, share the writing in role from the previous lessons. Students offer one another suggestions and questions.

Writing acts as a resource for the lesson. Sharing written work provides an opportunity for mutual encouragement/ sharing of ideas as well as a sense of responsibility for one another's work.

2 Teacher introduces the idea of a counselling service for people with financial problems. Some members of the class are to take on the role of counsellors, some are to sustain their roles from last lesson.

Students are offered the chance to re-shuffle roles and therefore sustain an interest in the drama. At this point the role of the counsellor is defined.

3 The space is organised by the students.
(a) A coffee area where counsellors and clients meet casually to chat.
(b) A meeting room where self-help and discussion groups are held.
(c) Two small offices where individual interviews can take place.

It is useful for students to see their playing space objectively and to be able to step outside it. The process of organising the space helps them to create their imaginative environment. The teacher can point out here the scope for a variety of relationships in the spaces.

4 Still moment/thinking aloud   Out of the playing space and before the drama begins, students are asked to think why they are coming to this place, and what has provoked them to do so. Some will have been many times before, for others it will be a new experience. As the teacher asks the following questions, *all* students respond simultaneously aloud and in role.

Tell me what's been happening to you?
Why have you decided to come here?
How do you feel about being here?

Both the setting of the space and the drama itself will be noisy. This is a useful focus for allowing the students to enter the drama confident of their role. It also defines a quiet 'thinking' area outside the playing space.

5 Working as a group
Sustaining a role
Developing dramatic situations

5 The drama begins   It is 6.30 p.m. The counsellors arrive for the evening session. Some are experienced, some are new. They talk to one another. Gradually clients arrive. Some know one another and meet here regularly. Some are lonely, isolated, maybe unfriendly.

Students play out their roles within the situation. The teacher can use both spotlighting and thinking aloud to focus the work at various points.

The teacher may find it useful to have a signal for spotlighting or thinking aloud. The students' quality of work will be heightened by moments of stillness and reflection.

6 When the teacher feels enough useful work has been achieved, the students are asked to leave the playing area, and spend a few moments thinking quietly. They can then dismantle the playing spaces before discussion.

The quiet, followed by the physical activity, helps the students to come out of role before discussion. This is particularly helpful if some have been very intensely involved in the drama.

7 Discussion:
Counsellors: How did you respond to the people and problems which faced you?
How did you attempt to offer support?
Clients: How much were you able to trust the counsellor?
All: If you were in this drama again, would you choose a different role? Why?
Can you think of circumstances in which you might seek help from an organisation?

Machine Inhabitant

- Developing the use of language
- Dependence on personal space/environment

RESOURCES

'The Machine Stops' by E.M. Forster (extracts 1 and 2)
Tape recorder
Blank cassette

---

[1] Accepting and developing a dramatic situation
Appropriate communication
Working as a group
Building an imaginative environment
Identifying with a dramatic situation

[1] Students work in role as either mother or an adult son or daughter. Separate the mothers from their offspring as far as possible. Use a tape recorder to act as an answerphone. First the mothers' group leaves a message for the others: 'Haven't seen you for a while' and so on. Record this. Take the tape to the other side of the room. Record a message from offspring to mother. Repeat this process working for a sense of expectation and use the slowness of reply to focus on how communication that is not interactive affects people's feelings. While the mothers are preparing and recording their final message, brief the others to try to persuade mother to leave her condemned house for her own safety. Record this message. Ask the mothers to establish a place where they feel at home. They are safe and comfortable. Play the message.

[2] Using and extending the language of the text
Using and extending the imaginative ideas in the text
Listening
Identifying with and adopting a role
Working successfully with different members of the group

[2] Read extracts 1 and 2 from 'The Machine Stops' (see pages 223–6).
The class is divided in two; half take the role of Vashti, half that of Kuno.
Students work in pairs.
Vashti and Kuno describe their rooms to each other.
Students change partners.
Vashti describes her own appearance, Kuno his.
Students change partners.
Vashti tells Kuno what she thinks of his life and opinions. Kuno replies.

THE MACHINE STOPS

Extract 1

Imagine, if you can, a small room, hexagonal in shape like the cell of a bee. It is lighted neither by window nor by lamp, yet it is filled with a soft radiance. There are no apertures for ventilation, yet the air is fresh. There are no musical instruments, and yet, at the moment that my meditation opens, this room is throbbing with melodious sounds. An arm-chair is in the centre, by its side a reading-desk – that is all the furniture. And in the arm-chair there sits a swaddled lump of flesh – a woman, about five feet high, with a face as white as a fungus. It is to her that the little room belongs.

An electric bell rang.

The woman touched a switch and the music was silent.

'I suppose I must see who it is,' she thought, and set her chair in motion. The chair, like the music, was worked by machinery, and it rolled her to the other side of the room, where the bell still rang importunately.

'Who is it?' she called. Her voice was irritable, for she had been interrupted often since the music began. She knew several thousand people; in certain directions human intercourse had advanced enormously.

But when she listened into the receiver, her white face wrinkled into smiles, and she said:

'Very well. Let us talk, I will isolate myself. I do not expect anything important will happen for the next five minutes – for I can give you fully five minutes, Kuno. Then I must deliver my lecture on "Music during the Australian Period".'

She touched the isolation knob, so that no-one else could speak to her. Then she touched the lighting apparatus, and the little room was plunged into darkness.

'Be quick!' she called, her irritation returning. 'Be quick, Kuno; here I am in the dark wasting my time.'

But it was fully fifteen seconds before the round plate that she held in her hands began to glow. A faint blue light shot across it, darkening to purple, and presently she could see the image of her son, who lived on the other side of the earth, and he could see her.

'Kuno, how slow you are.'

He smiled gravely.

'I really believe you enjoy dawdling.'

'I have called you before, mother, but you were always busy or isolated. I have something particular to say.'

'What is it, dearest boy? Be quick. Why could you not send it by pneumatic post?'

'Because I prefer saying such a thing. I want –'

'Well?'

'I want you to come and see me.'

Vashti watched his face in the blue plate.

'But I can see you!' she exclaimed. 'What more do you want?'

'I want to see you not through the Machine,' said Kuno. 'I want to speak to you not through the wearisome Machine.'

'Oh, hush!' said his mother, vaguely shocked. 'You mustn't say anything against the Machine.'

'Why not?'

'One mustn't.'

'You talk as if a god had made the Machine,' cried the other. 'I believe that you pray to it when you are unhappy. Men made it, do not forget that. Great men, but men. The Machine is much, but it is not everything. I see something like you in this plate, but I do not see you. I hear something like you through this telephone, but I do not hear you. That is why I want you to come. Come and stop with me. Pay me a visit, so that we can meet face to face, and talk about the hopes that are in my mind.'

She replied that she could scarcely spare the time for a visit.

'The air-ship barely takes two days to fly between me and you.'

'I dislike air-ships.'

'Why?'

'I dislike seeing the horrible brown earth, and the sea, and the stars when it is dark. I get no ideas in an air-ship.'

'I do not get them anywhere else.'

'What kind of ideas can the air give you?'

He paused for an instant.

'Do you not know four big stars that form an oblong, and three stars close together in the middle of the oblong, and hanging from these stars, three other stars?'

'No, I do not. I dislike the stars. But did they give you an idea? How interesting; tell me.'

'I had an idea that they were like a man.'

'I do not understand.'

'The four big stars are the man's shoulders and his knees. The three stars in the middle are like the belts that men wore once, and the three stars hanging are like a sword.'

'A sword?'

'Men carried swords about with them, to kill animals and other men.'

'It does not strike me as a very good idea, but it is certainly original. When did it come to you first?'

'In the air-ship –' He broke off, and she fancied that he looked sad. She could not be sure, for the Machine did not transmit *nuances* of expression. It only gave a general idea of people – an idea that was good enough for all practical purposes, Vashti thought. The imponderable bloom, declared by a discredited philosophy to be the actual essence of intercourse, was rightly ignored by the Machine, just as the imponderable bloom of the grape was ignored by the manufacturers of artificial fruit. Something 'good enough' had long since been accepted by our race.

'The truth is,' he continued, 'that I want to see these stars again. They are curious stars. I want to see them not from the air-ship, but from the surface of the earth, as our ancestors did, thousands of years ago. I want to visit the surface of the earth.'

She was shocked again.

'Mother, you must come, if only to explain to me what is the harm of visiting the surface of the earth.'

'No harm,' she replied, controlling herself. 'But no advantage. The surface of the earth is only dust and mud, no life remains on it, and you would need a respirator, or the cold of the outer air would kill you. One dies immediately in the outer air.'

'I know; of course I shall take all precautions.'

'And besides –'

'Well?'

She considered, and chose her words with care. Her son had a queer temper, and she wished to dissuade him from the expedition.

'It is contrary to the spirit of the age,' she asserted.

'Do you mean by that, contrary to the Machine?'

'In a sense, but –'

His image in the blue plate faded.

'Kuno!'

He had isolated himself.

For a moment Vashti felt lonely.

Then she generated the light, and the sight of her room, flooded with radiance and studded with electric buttons, revived her. There were buttons and switches everywhere – buttons to call for food, for music, for clothing. There was the hot-bath button, by pressure of which a basin of (imitation) marble rose out of the floor, filled to the brim with a warm deodorized liquid. There was the cold-bath button. There was the button that produced literature. And there were of course the buttons by which she communicated with her friends. The room, though it contained nothing, was in touch with all that she cared for in the world.

Extract 2

By a vestibule, by a lift, by a tubular railway, by a platform, by a sliding door – by reversing all the steps of her departure did Vashti arrive at her son's room, which exactly resembled her own. She might well declare that the visit was superfluous. The buttons, the knobs, the reading-desk with the Book, the temperature, the atmosphere, the illumination – all were exactly the same. And if Kuno himself, flesh of her flesh, stood close beside her at last, what profit was there in that? She was too well-bred to shake him by the hand.

Averting her eyes, she spoke as follows:

'Here I am. I have had the most terrible journey and greatly retarded the development of my soul. It is not worth it, Kuno, it is not worth it. My time is too precious. The sunlight almost touched me, and I have met with the rudest people. I can only stop a few minutes. Say what you want to say, and then I must return.'

'I have been threatened with Homelessness,' said Kuno.

She looked at him now.

'I have been threatened with Homelessness, and I could not tell you such a thing through the Machine.'

Homelessness means death. The victim is exposed to the air, which kills him.

'I have been outside since I spoke to you last. The tremendous thing has happened, and they have discovered me.'

'But why shouldn't you go outside?' she exclaimed. 'It is perfectly legal, perfectly mechanical, to visit the surface of the earth. I have lately been to a lecture on the sea; there is no objection to that; one simply summons a respirator and gets an Egression-permit. It is not the kind of thing that spiritually-minded people do, and I begged you not to do it, but there is no legal objection to it.'

'I did not get an Egression-permit.'

'Then how did you get out?'

'I found out a way of my own.'

The phrase conveyed no meaning to her, and he had to repeat it.

'A way of your own?' she whispered. 'But that would be wrong.'

'Why?'

The question shocked her beyond measure.

'You are beginning to worship the Machine,' he said coldly. 'You think it irreligious of me to have found out a way of my own. It was just what the Committee thought, when they threatened me with Homelessness.'

At this she grew angry. 'I worship nothing!' she cried. 'I am most advanced. I don't think you irreligious, for there is no such thing as religion left. All the fear and the superstition that existed once have been destroyed by the Machine. I only meant that to find out a way of your own was – Besides, there is no new way out.'

'So it is always supposed.'

'Except through the vomitories, for which one must have an Egression-permit, it is impossible to get out. The Book says so.'

'Well, the Book's wrong, for I have been out on my feet.'

For Kuno was possessed of a certain physical strength.

By these days it was a demerit to be muscular. Each infant was examined at birth, and all who promised undue strength were destroyed. Humanitarians may protest, but it would have been no true kindness to let an athlete live; he would never have been happy in that state of life to which the Machine had called him; he would have yearned for trees to climb, rivers to bathe in, meadows and hills against which he might measure his body. Man must be adapted to his surroundings, must he not? In the dawn of the world our weakly must be exposed on Mount Taygetus, in its twilight our strong will suffer euthanasia, that the Machine may progress, that the Machine may progress, that the Machine may progress eternally.

from *The Machine Stops* by E. M. Forster

The text acts as stimulus. Students use its language and ideas as a basis for their own imaginative work. This frees them from any need to 'stick to the story', and makes the following drama their own. Listening to a number of partners helps them to receive a wide range of ideas and language in a relatively short time.

Description rather than conversation acts as a discipline and links with the writing process which follows.

3 Selection of appropriate language
Writing skills

3 Students find a part of the room to work in alone, a space they feel comfortable in, that they can call their own. The students complete notes for a piece of creative writing: a description of Vashti's or Kuno's room.

The teacher introduces the experience of de-personalised communication in 'The Machine Stops'. A dependence on an environment is demonstrated.

4 Discussion
Evaluation
Writing

4 Whilst the students are working quietly draw their attention to their use of space. What would your reaction be if someone took away this space?
What are the risks in leaving them?
When would you take those risks?
Evaluation. Completion of written task from (3) for next lesson.

Auto-Talk

- Group work
- Relationships in a hi-tech society

RESOURCES
'The Machine Stops' by E.M. Forster (extracts 1 and 2)
Tape recorder
Blank cassette
Blocks (optional)

1 Working as a group
Co-ordinated movement and voice
Adapting to a variety of activities

1 Read extracts 1 and 2 from 'The Machine Stops'. The class is divided into groups. Using only bodies, blocks and chairs, one group sets up Vashti's room and the other Kuno's. In each group students are numbered 1, 2, 3, 4 ..., each number having a specific role, e.g. 1 is Vashti, 2 a receiver, 3 a screen. The room with its automatic apparatus begins to function. The teacher may suggest a number of events which could take place:
(a) the human being takes a bath;
(b) the human being is fed;
(c) the human being talks to a friend;
(d) the human being prepares to go to sleep.
 After some time, at a signal from the teacher the students rotate, taking on a different function in the machine.

 Students extend skills explored earlier in the scheme. They experience an automated environment as a human being and a machine component. The human being's dependence is reinforced.

2 Sustaining a role
Using appropriate language

2 Using the structure set up in (2) in the previous lesson, Vashti and Kuno now talk to each other about Kuno's disobedience:
(a) seated in their rooms;
(b) face to face.
 As before, each student takes the role of Vashti or Kuno at some time during the encounter. The conversation is taped.

227

The problems with communication become clear. Supported and separated by machines, human beings find it difficult to have a relationship. You may bring to the students' attention the lack of contacts, such as eye contact and touch.

3 Listening
Discussion
Evaluation

3 Students listen to the tape and discuss questions:
How has this society distorted the mother/son relationship?
Are these people secure or are they prisoners?
Are we like them in any way?

Students have an opportunity to assess their individual and group contribution. The effects of automation on people's bodies, voices, relationships and use of language are discussed.

4 Summarising
Role identification

4 Students complete a statement about Kuno's disobedience and/or a short script based on this encounter.

The tape and following discussion act as a stimulus and language resource for writing.

5 Use of form

5 Play the scenes again using the statement to form a Brechtian introduction or a climax to the scene.

The choice of forms may apply to different coursework requirements. The writing crystallises ideas discussed.

Breakdown – Back to Nature

- Story-telling
- Images of the future from a poem are extended

RESOURCE
'The Horses' by Edwin Muir

THE HORSES

Barely a twelvemonth after
The seven days' war that put the world to sleep,
Late in the evening the strange horses came.
By then we had made our covenant with silence,
But in the first few days it was so still
We listened to our breathing and were afraid.
On the second day
The radios failed; we turned the knobs; no answer.
On the third day a warship passed us, heading north,
Dead bodies piled on the deck. On the sixth day   10
A plane plunged over us into the sea. Thereafter
Nothing. The radios dumb;
And still they stand in corners of our kitchens,
And stand, perhaps, turned on, in a million rooms
All over the world. But now if they should speak,
If on a sudden they should speak again,
If on the stroke of noon a voice should speak,
We would not listen, we would not let it bring
That old bad world that swallowed its children quick
At one great gulp. We would not have it again.   20
Sometimes we think of the nations lying asleep,
Curled blindly in impenetrable sorrow,
And then the thought confounds us with its
    strangeness.

The tractors lie about our fields; at evening
They look like dank sea-monsters crouched and
    waiting.
We leave them where they are and let them <u>rust</u>:
They'll <u>moulder</u> away and be like other loam.
We make our oxen drag our <u>rusty ploughs</u>,
Long laid aside. We have gone back
Far past our fathers' land.
                         And then, that evening   30
Late in the summer the strange horses came.
We heard a distant tapping on the road,
A <u>deepening drumming</u>; it stopped, went on again,
And at the corner changed to hollow thunder.
We saw the heads
Like a <u>wild wave</u> charging and were afraid.
We had sold our horses in our fathers' time
To buy new tractors. Now they were strange to us
As fabulous steeds set on an ancient shield
Or <u>illustrations in a book of knights</u>.   40
We did not dare go near them. Yet they waited,

229

Stubborn and shy, as if they had been sent
By an old command to find our whereabouts
And that long-lost archaic companionship.
In the first moment we had never a thought
That they were creatures to be owned and used.
Among them were some half-a-dozen colts
Dropped in some wilderness of the broken world,
Yet new as if they had come from their own Eden.
Since then they have pulled our ploughs and borne
  our loads,
But that free servitude still can pierce our hearts.
Our life is changed; their coming our beginning.

                                        Edwin Muir

| 1 Listening | 1 Before reading the poem aloud the teacher asks the students to imagine that they are the last survivors on earth. |

1 Listening Reading Adapting to a variety of vocal registers	1 Before reading the poem aloud the teacher asks the students to imagine that they are the last survivors on earth. 'You are speaking out of a silent world. You are telling your story – there are no cars, planes, televisions, only the sounds of humans, animals and the elements.' Students read the poem aloud, several times, taking lines or sections: (a) as if the poem is a fireside story; (b) as if it is a mystery, chilling, but exciting; (c) as if the reader is beginning to hope, after experiencing despair. The teacher provides an imaginative context and a fluent version of the poem. Students experiment with story-telling, using words and voices to create atmosphere.
2 Using and extending the language of the text Working in a group Choosing appropriate roles/ experiences	2 The class is divided into groups. Each group is responsible for preparing a description as eyewitnesses of some of the events in the poem. Group 1 will describe the day the radios failed. Group 2 will describe the sight of the warship. Group 3 will describe the last plane falling into the sea. The groups should consider some questions: Where were you living? Did you know one another? Was the experience the same for all of you? What had you been doing just before? How have you changed since that day? The events described in the poem are transferred by students into people's experiences. A simple description becomes the stimulus for a role and a history.
3 Identifying with the role and situation Problem solving Decision-making Spatial awareness	3 The class now sets up a camp/living place for the survivors. Students consider the space available, the living arrangements and the relationship with the land. The layout could be drawn on/discussed over a large sheet of paper. The camp is set up to provide a context for the material prepared in (2). Having considered their role's past, they now consider present experiences and conditions. Discussion around a diagram helps the students to visualise their ideas and examine potential problems.
4 Accepting and developing a role Using material prepared in (2)	4 The teacher now enters the camp in role as a stranger looking for shelter. Survivors have to decide whether to share their resources and to trust the outsider. They tell the stranger their experiences and ask for his/hers.

The context is now set for the sharing of material from (2); you are acting as the stimulus, providing an opportunity for the description to be recounted in role and in context.

5 Discussion
Evaluation

5 All come out of role and discuss some questions:
How would a group like this regard their camp?
Is the stranger welcome, or a threat, or an item of curiosity?
What would be the criteria for trusting the stranger?

Students identify with people whose environment has radically changed. Relationships with the environment are discussed – a sense of home, security, the threat of the outsider.

Survivors – A Future Community

- Developing a role
- The results of environmental change are examined

RESOURCES
'The Horses' by Edwin Muir
An object unfamiliar to students because of its age, culture, or context
An everyday object for *each* student, e.g. bottle, kitchen utensil, a book

1 Reading
Listening

1 Recap on the previous lesson. The poem is read again, and roles as survivors discussed.

The roles and experiences become immediate through discussion and the reading of the poem.

2 Discussion
Analysis

2 Teacher brings in an object which unfamiliar to the class because of its age, cultural origin, or context. Students try to

232

identify it and its purpose. Once this is established, students are asked how they viewed the object, how they handled it, what they felt about it.

Students adopt the position of the survivors. They discuss their attitudes and feelings towards 'strangeness'. The work is introducing the idea of objects as symbols.

3 Adopting an objective view

3 Each student finds a space and is given an everyday object (a bottle, a kitchen utensil, a book . . .). Students are asked to handle the object as if it is completely strange. Perhaps they are looking at this twentieth-century object through the eyes of someone from the past, or the future.
What can you tell from the shape, from colours, from the place you discovered it?

The identification with the survivors is extended. Students adopt an objective viewpoint. They make the everyday item strange to them, and therefore perceive it differently.

4 Analysis
Relating the poem to the experiences of (2) and (3)

4 Read the poem again and discuss:
Why did the horses seem strange to the survivors?
What were they used for?
What difference did they make?

Students relate their own experiences to the survivors.

5 Adopting and sustaining a role
Identifying problems
Spatial awareness

5 The students set the camp and assume their roles as survivors. The teacher introduces the role-play by saying: 'You are holding a meeting to discuss your use of the land. You are people who lived in an automated society. Now, there are no machines left in good condition, no fuel to make them operate. How are you going to eat, build, make what you need?'

Ideas are collated: automation, dependence on the environment. In role, the students discuss the problems of an automated society plunged into a world devoid of machinery.

6 Preparing an improvisation
Problem-solving

6 In groups of four or five, prepare an improvisation about the change in the survivors' lives after the coming of the horses.
The improvisations are presented to the class. Back-tracking (see *Teaching Devices*, page 3) could be a useful way of evaluating the drama.

Students explore the results of environmental change. You may suggest that they consider changes in relationships; use of living space; posture; leisure time.

7 Relaxation and writing   The students relax in a space while the teacher says:
'While you are relaxing, imagine the landscape we have been working in. Think of what this room has represented – colours, contours of hills and land, buildings, sky, wildlife, trees and plants, redundant machines. Think of words and phrases which describe this place. You have ten lines in which to describe it. When you are ready, write those ten lines.'

Relaxation helps the students to concentrate. The change in environment is expressed in written form.

The Rebel – Demonstration

- Presentation
- Students communicate 'causes' through song, movement and words

---

RESOURCES
Cassettes or records of protest songs
Tape recorder or record player
Newspaper headlines
Photographs
Percussion instruments
Large sheets of paper
Marker pens or paint

---

1 Listening
Discussion
Analysis

1 Students listen to some protest songs. They discuss language, rhythm, the power of singing in unison.

Students are introduced to a form of expressing rebellion. They are asked to consider the choice of words and their effect. The strength of the group rebellion is made clear. Choosing simple songs will encourage students' confidence in writing their own.

2 Spatial awareness
Forming ideas into physical shapes or movement

2 Teacher hands round some newspaper headlines or photographs which illustrate rebellion. Using phrases such as, 'I won't', 'Who do you think you are?' and 'We're together on this', students construct a series of freeze frames.

Thinking aloud, or asking the students to 'unfreeze' and improvise spontaneously, could usefully extend this section.

Students consider how rebellion looks. Visuals are used to stimulate ideas in terms of movement and shapes.

3 Selecting/collating ideas
Visualising ideas
Co-ordinating rhythm and language

3 Students form groups and decide on a reason to rebel. Encourage them to use resources gathered in earlier lessons, 'Lean on Me' (pages 213–14) and 'The Battery Hen' (page 216), as well as concepts developed elsewhere in this project. Using percussion instruments, students construct a protest song about their cause. They write, or paint a banner.

By setting these tasks, you provide the groups with material for their presentation, and help them to link language, rhythm and visual material in the context of the drama. You have the opportunity to assess their appreciation of the concepts taught.

4 Rehearsal
Selecting movement, visuals, rhythm appropriately

4 In the same groups, students devise a presentation entitled 'Demonstration'. They use their song, banner, and freeze-frame, extending it as they wish.

5 Presentation
Analysis

5 The presentations are shared with the class and discussed.

This is an opportunity to express rebellion and to evaluate the success of the presentations in communicating it.

The Rebel – A Dangerous Influence

- Presentation
- The position of the rebel is explored through the eyes of authority

RESOURCE
'The Accusation of Kuno'

[1] Adopting a role

1 Recap on the last lesson. The teacher introduces another kind of rebel – the person who doesn't seem to care, or who laughs at authority.

In pairs, the students work on short scenes:
(a) teacher with disruptive child;
(b) employer with a difficult employee.

The notion of rebellion is considered in a different context, but related to previous work. Students investigate simple situations with which they are familiar.

[2] Discussion
Analysis

2 Use the forum technique to share and evaluate the above. Discuss: Could the child or employee be considered dangerous? Why? Who uses these methods of rebellion? Why?

Students are put in the position of authority. They begin to see the rebel from a new perspective.

[3] Analysis and extension of written material

3 The class divides into groups. Each group is given a copy of the document 'The Accusation of Kuno'. Students work out how the accused has rebelled and what the rules of the society are. They write down the rules.

The document is a language stimulus and helps students to form rules and use language appropriately in the following role-play.

[4] Adopting and sustaining a role
Discourse and debate
Working as a group

4 Students adopt rules as the governing body of this society. In the same groups, they hold a meeting to discuss their intended action against Kuno.

236

The Accusation of Kuno

The prisoner is accused of failing to apply for an Egression Permit.

The prisoner is accused of taking action which is not initiated and ratified by the Machine.

The prisoner is accused of exercising the body, and therefore not wholly relying on the Machine.

The prisoner is accused of leaving the Machine and going to the Outer Air without permission.

The prisoner is accused of saying that the Machine will stop.

The prisoner is threatened with Homelessness.

Students are now in role as rulers in contrast to their roles as rebels in the previous lesson. They begin to recognise their power over others.

|5| Structuring material
Preparing an improvisation

5 The groups are asked to prepare a scene entitled 'Owning today for tomorrow'. During the scene Kuno is interrogated; he describes:
(a) his decision to rebel;
(b) the action he took;
(c) being caught.
These descriptions can be acted out as flashbacks.

Through preparing this presentation, the position of the rebel is again explored but from the perspective of authority and punishment. Shaping is guided to heighten students' awareness of the impact of form.

|6| Presentation
Evaluation
Analysis

6 The scenes are presented and discussed.
Why is Kuno considered dangerous?
Why did you as rulers take the action you did?
What should society do with its rebels?
Do causes need heroic acts?

Theatre: A Collective Form of Story-telling

NETWORK

PHASE I

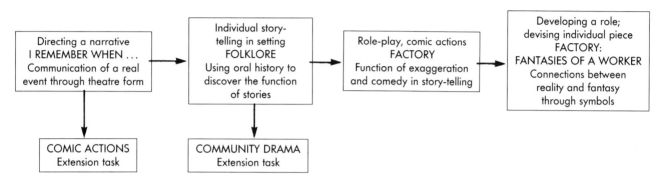

Directing a narrative I REMEMBER WHEN ... Communication of a real event through theatre form	Individual story-telling in setting FOLKLORE Using oral history to discover the function of stories	Role-play, comic actions FACTORY Function of exaggeration and comedy in story-telling	Developing a role; devising individual piece FACTORY: FANTASIES OF A WORKER Connections between reality and fantasy through symbols

COMIC ACTIONS
Extension task

COMMUNITY DRAMA
Extension task

PHASE II

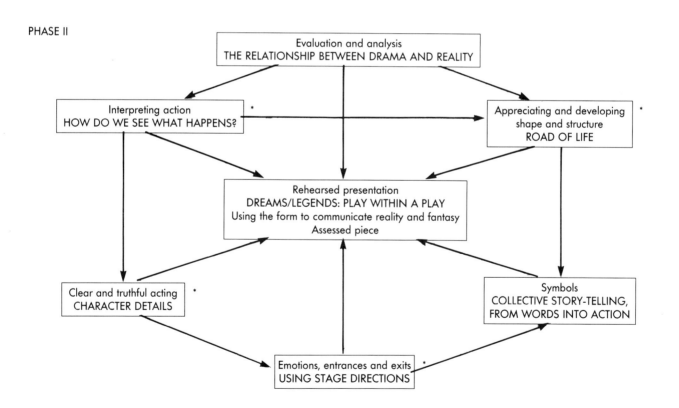

Evaluation and analysis
THE RELATIONSHIP BETWEEN DRAMA AND REALITY

Interpreting action
HOW DO WE SEE WHAT HAPPENS? *

Appreciating and developing shape and structure
ROAD OF LIFE *

Rehearsed presentation
DREAMS/LEGENDS: PLAY WITHIN A PLAY
Using the form to communicate reality and fantasy
Assessed piece

Clear and truthful acting
CHARACTER DETAILS *

Symbols
COLLECTIVE STORY-TELLING,
FROM WORDS INTO ACTION

Emotions, entrances and exits *
USING STAGE DIRECTIONS

*These lessons can be adapted to help with analysis and appreciation of theatre seen. More ideas are given in the secton *Documenting Drama* (pages 101–116).

A Collective Form of Story-Telling ——————————

RESOURCES
Winnie Mandela's autobiography, *Part of my Soul* (Penguin, 1985)
Recordings of local people talking to an 'oral newspaper'
ID card (page 246) and sound effects of factory (optional)
Extract from Nell Dunn, *Poor Cow* (page 249)
A3 paper
Extract from the *Mahabharata* (pages 254–5)
Extract from Anton Chekhov, *The Cherry Orchard* (page 257)
short extract of character actions*
A text extract about one page long with a key entrance*
Edward Bond, 'A Story', from *The Woman* (page 261)
scenario from a scene in the text*

* alternatives for set text work

SUMMARY OF WRITTEN TASKS
Students may keep working notes for every lesson but specific tasks are set in these lessons:

'Factory Fantasies'	– notes on belief
'Road of Life'	– annotated drawing
Dreams	– opening moments, situation, message
Character details	– rehearse decisions
Emotions	– stage directions
Symbols	– working notes

This project is a stepping-stone between role-play and theatre. The stepping-stone is the concept of narrative; in role-play, events and attitudes unfold at life-rate, in theatre, form can be used to interpret reality and explore meanings in events and actions.

Phase I (pages 241–250) is an introduction to the concept of story-telling in the theatre. In Phase II (from page 250) you can use the content supplied or find comparable examples from any text the students are working on. The assessed task can be introduced after Phase I or after Phase II.

AIMS
By collective story-telling to:
- understand the nature of belief and willing suspension of disbelief and its relationship with form;
- use form to understand, explore and interpret reality;
- gain tools for the use and appreciation of form.

- Directing a narrative
- I Remember When . . .
- Communication of a real event through theatre form

Phase I

Students recollect, then recreate an experience communicating their knowledge and experience to the audience.

1 Concentration

1 Students recollect a childhood memory, perhaps feeling embarrassed by something they did in primary school. Once they have chosen one, they think through the event in detail, as though they were telling the story. They might mutter the occasional word and show on their faces how they feel about the event.

By keeping the stories private, students can relax. The premium on the quick thinker is removed, allowing all students freedom to enjoy the experience.

2 Summarising

2 Everyone turns to the person beside him or her and says in one line only what his/her memory was. Go around the group with each person saying, again in one line, what the partner's story was – for example, 'When Rani was seven, she got her tongue stuck in the fridge.'

This generates interest in everyone's story and gives value to everyone's experience.

3 Co-operative group work
Resource gathering

3 Group the students in clusters of four and give them a few minutes to find out about one another's stories. Listen in to the groups, giving status to all experiences.

4 Converting a dramatic episode into dramatic action
Rehearsal techniques
Recreating truth

4 Ask the clusters to select a story with no more than three characters in it. The 'owner' of the story is the director and must ensure the event is recreated as accurately as possible. The director can have a role as narrator but must not play him or herself. The story is to be told, not relived.

The criteria for selecting a story is a dramatic one, not one the most dominant pupil suggests. The experiments with the use of narrator will demand both accurate portrayal and the use of form to encourage reflection and comment on an event.

5 Play the scenes.
Is drama like real life?
Using a narrator: What techniques were used?
How did this affect our belief?

241

Watching work should always be focused. These questions form the basis of understanding the theatre form.

6 For next time, students should find a story that is not their own, one told to them as children, family folklore, an interview with an older member of their community about childhood.

COMIC ACTION
Extension Task
To encourage students to be more physical in their expression and introduce comic skills, take another memory and retell the story in groups with this alternative approach.

1 Adapting movement for meaning and clarity
Experimenting with bodies in space
Pacing action and words

1 Select a memory that has plenty of details, but where only one or two people are involved. Enact the story in groups with every object being acted as well as the people. The students become the fridge, the taps, the sunshine and so on. Rehearsal time will need to include how an actor changes from one object to another and a consideration of the important moments shown in the pictures. The narrator is more detached from the action. As you circulate, encourage large and clear actions and enjoy students' efforts.

Comic techniques are taught with the emphasis on the content not the joke – this usually produces more effective humour. The fun of the physicality, given pace by the narrator, frees those students who tend to be cerebral.

2 Evaluate in terms of the relationship between comedy and the truth. How did the narrator feel when the story was being exaggerated? Can comedy affect the feelings? Is comedy true?

Folklore

- Individual story-telling in setting
- The function of story in oral history

RESOURCE
Working notebook

<u>1</u> Appreciating function of story

<u>2</u> Communication through words

<u>3</u> Devising a setting and style for narration

Folklore is not only a means of recording events; the retelling of a story has meanings for present relationships. The task is to find the life and meaning in a story and communicate it, using narrative and setting.

1 Introduce the importance of story-telling, from the bedtime stories told to children, the story-tellers in market places in Morocco, to the religious stories of the *Mahabharata* or the Bible. Reinforce the value stories have for adults and children. A good example of a negative function of story common to all students is the stories they heard about secondary school just before they were about to begin.

To appreciate deeper meanings, students need to see that stories fulfil a purpose and entertain – just what they will attempt in their own drama.

2 In pairs, the students simply tell their story to one another. Discuss what makes a good story, well told,
- shaping;
- descriptions to create belief/atmosphere;
- eye contact;
- introducing new ideas;
- simplicity, clarity.

Reinforce good practice and highlight specific techniques.

Getting the story told before working on techniques of communication is safe and reassuring. Positive clues are given before individuals are exposed to more listeners.

3 The partners give each other advice from the list of tips discussed. As individuals, ask the students to consider where they would like to tell their story – standing under a tree, sitting on the floor and so on. Allow time for individual work, supported by working notebooks.

Working alone is difficult. The partners should be used as advisers, but responsibility for decisions remains with the individual.

4 Communicating through space, symbols and words

4 Intervene with a discussion on symbols. Encourage partners to point out symbols in each other's stories. A symbol is only useful if it helps the story along, rather than distracting from the meaning. After further individual preparation, cluster the students in fours or fives so that they can hear one another's stories. The listeners jot down key words that made each story work for them.

The concept of symbols needs to be taught in context. Where they arise naturally, the students will have confidence in their understanding and use of symbols. Telling stories in clusters allows everyone enough time to share the work. The report-back task ensures everyone appreciates the skills used.

5 Discuss the techniques employed and their relationship with other drama work. Look at space and setting – what atmosphere was created?

COMMUNITY DRAMA
Extension task
These two sessions could make an effective launch into the *Community Drama* project (pages 177–210). Many recordings and transcripts have been made with a local flavour and are available through libraries. Students could launch their own oral history research by interviewing people in their communities. Once the stories have been gathered, they can be processed for drama work with, by, for, or about the target community.

A story arising from experience in another culture can provide a vibrant resource for comparison and contrast. Such simple tales, honestly told, as in Winnie Mandela's autobiography *Part of my Soul* (Penguin, 1985), have much to teach our own society. These stories can be dramatised using the technique from the sessions on 'symbols' or 'interpreting action'. An audience might be a school assembly, or a community group, for example.

Factory

- Role-play, comic actions
- Class role-play

RESOURCES
Rostra, chairs, etc.
Sound effects recording of factory
ID card for Health and Safety Inspector
Clipboard

The play within a play technique allows concentration on an event so that its meaning can be considered through comic action.

[1] Negotiation
Adopting a role
Communicating through movement

1 Using all the resources available in the room, the students set up the space as a sewing factory. After agreeing all the necessary stages in the production line, students adopt a role and begin working on a routine job. A recording can be used to create the loud noise of a factory and encourage actions rather than words as the communication style.

This is a physical and impersonal start for a session which will concentrate on physical communication.

[2] Sustaining belief in role and situation
Communicating through movement

2 Allow this exercise to run until the students' belief in the work makes the drama begin to take on its own life. Using the ID card, approach a worker saying you have come to make a routine inspection for health and safety in the factory. Begin your inspection, noting down such things as jewellery, suitable footwear, machine guards, staff facilities. At the same time, observe how your tour is being received, if people are working as normal, or if word of your visit is travelling ahead of you.

Adopting a role as an outside establishment figure allows you to intervene with authority and escape to allow the students to take their own decisions.

[3] Evaluation of role-play skills: sustaining a role, building on ideas of others

3 Stop the drama and evaluate students' responses:
Why did you adopt that role?
How believable were the actions?
How did the workers feel about the inspection?
How did others who hadn't seen your ID know who you were?

Focus attention onto the meaning of an incident that will become the raw material.

HEALTH AND SAFETY EXECUTIVE
IDENTIFICATION CARD

Chris Evans is an officer of the above executive and, as such, has the right to visit all manufacturing premises to ensure that the health and safety of the staff employed therein are protected.

4 Large gestures, coded language, belief

4 Discuss how people might communicate in a factory. Remind students about the noise and the demands of the machine; payment by piece work. Encourage the idea of an exclusive language which helps workers cope with visits from management or outside agencies. This should be largely non-verbal owing to the noise. Replay your visit with the focus on workers' actions on seeing you, while maintaining belief in your authority.

5 Using story-telling techniques and comic actions
Shaping material collectively

5 Regroup the students in the canteen where they will tell one another what happened when the health and safety officer visited their part of the factory. Allow them time to prepare this 'story', stressing comic actions, mimicking the officer and their own responses, exaggerating to the point of actually acting out the inanimate objects in the scenes as well as the people.

A change of groups refreshes the work and gives purpose to the initial retelling of story. Prepared work deepens consideration of the event.

6 Concentration and focus

6 Run the scenes in the canteen using the spotlight technique. First let the scenes begin simultaneously – people getting their snacks and so on – and then spotlight snippets of action, taking a sample from everyone's work while keeping the belief in the role-play. The coffee break can end with a hooter tape recorded to signal a return to work.

7 Discuss the nature of comedy. How does it help us to learn? Does drama have to be real to tell the truth? How does comedy increase the truths we know? Students will have their own experiences to draw upon in responding to establishment figures in school. You might like to point out the tradition of Grammelot, a 'language' used by thirteenth century players to discuss ideas censored by the Church and State. Here, words were replaced by sounds, but the tone of voice, actions and expression made the meaning clear. Dario Fo's work is full of examples of comedy to enlighten the relationship between those with power and those apparently without.

Evaluation continually feeds students' developing understanding of the relationship between form and reality.

Fantasies of a Worker

- Developing a role, devising an individual piece
- Connections between reality and fantasy through symbols

RESOURCE
Extract from 'Poor Cow' by Nell Dunn

Students have narrated, re-enacted and exaggerated stories. Language is used in this session to draw the social connection between reality and fantasies and the symbols apparent in both.

1 Assuming a role
Rhythmic movement

1 Re-establish the factory. Before the role-play begins, discuss how students cope with boredom, or with having to be somewhere they don't like. (One day there'll be a school where students don't automatically give lessons as an example for this.) Begin the role-play. Conversation is to be kept to the minimum. The place is noisy and everyone wants to earn as much as they can for Christmas, or the holidays.

Action and repetition are stressed to allow the mind to drift.

2 Picking up clues about dreams and the form of presenting them

2 Spotlight some students to discover what they were thinking of whilst working. Don't comment, merely listen and sample, so that all contributions are accepted for the drama, and no additional 'challenge the teacher' games sneak in. Let the role-play run again to reinstate belief before stopping the drama while you read the extract.

You'll need to make your own decisions about the reading of the language depending on the climate of your school. The extract expresses simple dreams in vernacular language and hints at the meanings of these fantasies.

3 Discuss the form and content. How would this piece be played by one of the workers in the factory play? What do people dream of? Where do these fantasies come from? What do they do for the people who own them?

Students will be familiar with fantasies in our culture, often concerned with the easy money or romance themes. Other examples can be found in techniques for selling newspapers, Edward Bond's play *Derek*, *After the*

POOR COW

I've always been a daydreamer, me, Joy – Joysy as my Auntie calls me. Daydreamed about – oh, loads of things – just to have something, to be something. I don't want to be down and out all the time I want – I don't know what I do fucking want but I dream about driving a car, that I'm in this big car driving around. When you've got a car you kind of feel something. It's a marvellous thing. I feel independent, let's put it that way. I feel like, well, it's mine. And I feel like pulling up at a bus stop and saying 'Do you want a lift?' Potty really, but I do. Oh and I day-dream about the sort of house I'd like to live in. I know what sort of house I'd like. A house in the country. One of these old-fashioned houses. You know these old cottages, you remember the ever-so-old cottages, with little tiny windows, and I'll tell you what, they've got a long pathway and you know the trellis what goes over like that, that's the sort of house that I want. Ever so plain, I don't want nothing fancy, but just nice, like a proper little home. I'd have fitted wardrobes and I'd have all pale colours, I'd have blue and pink 'cause I like them. And I'd have a white dressing table, very very long, fit it in the windows. And I'd have just an ordinary bed and a white painted headboard. Oh yeah. Flash curtains I'd have. Coloured curtains I suppose, no, plain curtains. Oh, and a fitted carpet. Must be a pale colour, pale blue or something like that. Nice white bed-spread. Look lovely. What would I do all day? Well first thing I'd get up in a morning to get little Johnny to school, then I'd do all my work and what would I do then? Let me think. Do me work and my washing and bleeding ironing. Then make meself up, and go out in me car. Shopping, go round my mates, then I'd come back and cook the dinner. I just like to feel that if I wanted something I could go out and buy it. Terrible when you ain't got fuck all, you ain't got nothing.

From *Poor Cow* by Nell Dunn (Virago)

Assassinations (Methuen Theatrescript, London 1983) in which a latter-day Jack and the Beanstalk gets a million pounds by outwitting a computer, and, on the Cinderella theme, the films *Letter to Brezhnev* and the dream-come-true ending of *An Officer and a Gentleman*.

[4] Use of form to indicate change from 'reality' to fantasy
Using form to illuminate the truth of the content in terms of people and issues
Group work

[4] Remind the students about the story-telling techniques they have used so far – narrators, comic actions, re-enactment, direct address to an audience. With the skill focus on the use of form, the students prepare an improvisation located in the factory, using their present roles. Someone's dreams become known through drama without destroying belief in the play (that is, the factory) itself. The play within the play should both be fun and deal with the problems the people are faced with. It allows for a liberating change in style and possibilities of using inanimate objects as part of the fantasy setting. Students don't have access to the techniques of the soft focus and theme music of films and must use drama skills to cue in and out of the fantasy.

[5] Play the scenes with students noting techniques used and how belief was created and sustained. Look for analogous situations, symbols. Use all the notes taken in this project to start Phase II.

The Relationship between Drama and Reality —

- Evaluation and analysis

RESOURCE
Students' notes

Phase II

In the last four lessons students have learned about the nature of story-telling, how the stories arise from a real event or a fantasy, and the function they perform for the teller and the audience. Stories tell us about the world we live in, whether as a fairy-story to encourage girls to be afraid of 'wolves', or as a piece of theatre where interpretation can mean that a play written in another time can have meaning and resonance for our own time. The next section looks at elements of how a playwright tells a story; it can be taken in any order and adapted to illuminate any text. First of all, though, it is important to discuss with the students belief and story-telling in the theatre. Don't reserve this for academic students; you will be encouraged by how sharp and immediate the responses of all students are to this discussion.

Discuss how we tell a story through drama, encouraging students to give examples from their own work and their notes. Keep the process open; after all, it is something that changes with society. Some questions worth addressing might include:

- What makes an audience interested?
- How do we encourage an audience willingly to suspend disbelief?
- How do we communicate with clarity and honesty.
- What is the relationship between entertainment and issue?
- Whom do the audience care for or identify with?
- How close should the audience come to the situation?
- What happens?
- What is the effect of the narrator, of comedy, of setting?

There is always more to be learned, for student and teacher, from this discussion, and students enjoy being rewarded for thinking through something which began when they first realised Santa Claus did not exist.

From here, select the tasks and sequence that best suit your students' needs. They may fit into the context of a set text studied, or enrich or inform the development of the devised work.

How Do We See What Happens?

• Interpreting action

Symbols of human relationship are more open to question when looked at through unfamiliar or distanced eyes. This lesson aims to help students see the art of devising or interpreting drama.

Theatre samples   Brecht affects our seeing by informing us what is to about to happen. The Greek tradition had momentous events occurring off stage and in our contemporary theatre Edward Bond says:
'The play comes to a halt if we play each scene with the emotional urgency we would use to tell someone their house was on fire. Very few blows should be struck in the play because when they are struck they should be a knockout. So most of the blows occur before the scenes. The scene itself is the reeling effect of the blow. This is very simple. It is what happens in human affairs. Most of our lives are spent reacting to events.' Edward Bond, *The Woman* (Modern

Plays series, Methuen, 1979)

Students will be familiar with thrillers; sometimes we know who the murderer is before the victim, sometimes not until the detective solves the mystery.

1 Interpreting dramatic action
Identifying clues

1 While the class is settling down with notebook and pens, privately brief two or three students to perform the following series of actions:
Sit on a chair. After a few moments turn and look over your left shoulder, then your right. Stand. Turn to the left, then to the right. Wave. Step a few paces down left, turn and run out of the door.

Ask one of the performers to play the scene. Without comment or discussion, ask the spectators to write down what they think is happening.

2 Before seeing the scene played again, tell the audience, but not the performer (you want the simple actions with no elaborate or superficial actions), that this person has done something wrong. Again, ask the spectators to record what they believe was happening.

3 Now tell the audience what is happening, but again not the performer. A person is sitting in the garden when he or she hears a wasp, turns, gets up, tries to get away from it, and ends up indoors for safety. During this version, the audience might well laugh, to the bemusement of the actor. Discuss how knowing what happens is affected by context and information.

4 Using the theatre form
Experimental group work

4 Encourage the students to experiment in groups, reworking either an improvisation from their existing repertoire, or an extract from a text they are working on. The focus is on changing the experience for the audience by timing the giving of information.

5 Evaluate in terms of story-telling in the theatre. Where do we begin? How much do we tell? What do we want people to think and feel while watching our work? Can we dwell on the implications of an action? Can we explore moments in detail?

6 Take a simple action like showing your identity card at a turnstile. What can we tell about the person? What can we tell about society?

Road of Life

• Shaping a drama/appreciating shape

RESOURCES
Cartridge paper, pens
Mahabharata extract

|1| Recording of value for drama

1 Ask the students to draw a 'Road of Life' on the paper. On this they note memorable events for themselves, a role they are playing or a character in a play they are working on or have seen (see the chapter *Documenting Drama*, pages 101–116). The events recorded will be not only births, deaths and weddings, but personal signposts with personal significance.

|2| Spotting the potential in material
Early shaping

2 To tell the story of that life, students will need to take some decisions. Where to start? What clues to give about the past? How to suggest what the future might be. In groups, the students discuss their ideas for starting a drama arising from this road. You might like to read them the opening two and a half pages of the *Mahabharata* where Vyasa faces the problem of how to begin a play. The play is an example of simple, honest and direct communication. The first scene is even called 'The Beginnings'.

3 Try out one or two of the opening moments, constantly encouraging only the barest minimum of action. Discuss how one thing might lead to another, opening possibilities for development of content and form.

THE BEGINNINGS

A boy of about twelve enters. He goes toward a little pool. Then a man appears. He is thin, wearing a muddy loincloth, his feet bare and dirty. He sits thoughtfully on the ground and, noticing the boy, he signals him to come closer. The boy approaches, slightly fearful. The man asks him:

Vyasa: Do you know how to write?

Boy: No, why? *The man is silent for a moment before saying:*

Vyasa: I've composed a great poem. I've composed it all, but nothing is written. I need someone to write down what I know.

Boy: What's your name?

Vyasa: Vyasa.

Boy: What's your poem about?

Vyasa: It's about you.

Boy: Me?

Vyasa: Yes, it's the story of your race, how your ancestors were born, how they grew up, how a vast war arose. It's the poetical history of mankind. If you listen carefully, at the end you'll be someone else. For it's as pure as glass, yet nothing is omitted. It washes away faults, it sharpens the brain and it gives long life. *Suddenly the boy points, indicating a strange form approaching in the distance.*

Boy: Who's that? *It is someone with an elephant's head and a man's body, who comes strutting toward them. He has writing materials in his hand. Vyasa greets him warmly.*

Vyasa: Ganesha! Welcome.

Boy: You're Ganesha?

Ganesha: Rumour has it that you're looking for a scribe for the Poetical History of Mankind. I'm at your service.

Boy: You're really Ganesha?

Ganesha: In person.

Boy: Why do you have an elephant's head?

Ganesha: Don't you know?

Boy: No.

Ganesha: If I've got to tell my story too, we'll never finish.

Boy: Please.

Ganesha: Right. I am the son of Parvati, the wife of Shiva.

Boy: The wife of the great god, Shiva?

Ganesha: Himself. But Shiva's not my father. My mother did it alone.

Boy: How did she manage?

Ganesha: It's not easy. To cut a long story short, when I arrived in this world, I was already a fine, sturdy boy, just about your age. One day, my mother told me to guard the door of the house. She wanted to take a bath. 'Let no-one in,' she said. An instant later, Shiva was standing in front of me, wanting to come into the house, his house. I blocked the way. Shiva did not know me – I'd only just been born – so he said 'Out of my way! It's an order. This is my home.' I answered, 'My mother told me to let no-one in so I'm letting no-one in.' Shiva was furious. He called up his most ferocious cohorts. He commanded them to flush me out, but I sent them flying. My force was superhuman. I blazed, I glittered, I exploded – horde after horde of demons withdrew in shame, for I was defending my mother. Shiva had only one way left: cunning. He slipped behind me and suddenly he chopped off my head. My mother's anger had no limits. She threatened to destroy all the powers of heaven and smash the sky into tiny splinters. Shiva, to calm her down, ordered a head to be put on me as quickly as possible, the head of the first creature to come by. It was an elephant. So there we are. I'm Ganesha, the bringer of peace. *He positions himself with great care and says to Vyasa*: I'm ready. You can begin. But I warn you: my hand can't stop once I start to write. You must dictate without a single pause.

Vyasa: And you, before putting anything down, you must understand the sense of what I say.

Ganesha: Count on me. *A silence falls and lasts a few moments.* We're expecting someone?

Vyasa: No.

Ganesha: So . . . ?

Vyasa: There's something secret about a beginning. I don't know how to start.

Ganesha: May I offer a suggestion?:

Vyasa: You're most welcome to.

Ganesha: As you claim to be the author of the poem, how about beginning with yourself?

From the *Mahabharata*

Character Details

• Clear and truthful acting

RESOURCE
Photocopied extract from *The Cherry Orchard* by Anton Chekhov

Students sometimes colour their acting with an intensity of extraneous gestures in an attempt to show it is not themselves but someone else who is speaking. They may have learned from role-play that honesty and simplicity is the best. Alternatively, they may have been aware that, in role-play, it is often difficult to distinguish whether it is they or their roles who are speaking, as the drama demands a responsive pace. Some students, when faced with a challenging script, may feel that they need to limp, twitch, or stutter to convince the audience that they are acting. We see characters that approach the farcical details of Dario Fo's maniac in *Accidental Death of an Anarchist*, (Modern Plays series, Methuen, n.e. 1987), whose false eye, leg, arm, are the subjects of a theatrical joke. Awareness of form will help students to pitch their work appropriately, as well as to understand the rehearsal process where experiment both throws up and disposes of any false or superfluous gestures. This task enables students to find and value sincerity. They become aware of how a playwright indicates, through use of pause, stage directions and language, what we need to know and feel about the character.

[1] Research through self-observation

1 Students have each been given a large sum of money. They carry it safely with them. When they arrive somewhere, they forget for a moment exactly which pocket they put it in. Play the scene. Discuss those awful moments when you think you have lost your money. What do you do? How do you feel?

[2] Interpretation
Teamwork

2 Issue the extract to pairs, each of them to support the other's acting. The extract can be learned effortlessly by working on it, so no need to mention learning it. Give them the following additional information: Pischik has been asking for a loan to pay off his debts since the start of the play, despite the fact that others are selling off their homes to make ends meet. He tries to impress and become involved, but is too self-aware to be popular.

The task allows students to decide how much to stylise a portrayal of character. It is useful to remind them of the work on this in sessions on the factory (pages 245–7) to enable them to relate appropriateness to context.

THE CHERRY ORCHARD

Pischik Do you know Nietzsche says – the philosopher, you know, great man, very famous, first-class intellect – he says . . . somewhere . . . one has the right to forge banknotes?

Trofimov You've read Nietzsche then?

Pischik No, not exactly. Dashenka told me . . . about it. But at the moment I'm in such a mess I might be forced to follow his advice, I can tell you. I've got to find three hundred and ten roubles for the day after tomorrow, and so far I've managed a mere hundred and thirty . . . (*Pats his pocket, to indicate them; feels nothing.*)

Oh my God, I've lost it, it's not there, I've lost the money. (*Hands feverish around other pockets.*)

Sweet Jesus, where's the money . . . (*Shout of relief, as he locates it.*)

Aaah! It's here! Inside the lining! Look at me, I'm sweating. Oh.

From *The Cherry Orchard* by Anton Chekhov
(ed. Trevor Griffiths)

3 As they are working, encourage interpretation that arises from the printed extract, as well as experimentation. Perhaps suggest two extremes of experiment: one to play the scene completely over the top, and the other to give an absolutely minimalist portrayal. After this, if students re-read the text they will be able to decide on an appropriate pitch and quality of feeling.

4 Play the scenes. Ask each couple to explain decisions made while rehearsing and the reasons for these. Record these in note form in working notebooks. A discussion of plays seen in performance could be compared with students' own work, as part of a developing understanding of the search for meaning through form.

Using Stage Directions

- Emotions, exits and entrances

RESOURCES
If you are working on a set text, choose an extract of about half a page, with a key entrance, to work on. Group the students, including one recorder who writes down what actually happens at the point of entry. Use the first part of the lesson to read and discuss the text instead of the improvisation suggested, and join at (2) below.
Pens and notebooks

1 Adopting a role
Building an environment for role-play
Responding to clues

1 Divide the class into groups of four or five, one person in each group to retain his/her role from the factory, one person to become the playwright/recorder, the remainder to adopt roles as people whom the worker would meet with socially. The friends and family students are briefed to set

up a space with an entrance and begin a life-rate drama of the early evening. Meanwhile, brief the recorders in their task. They must write down what is said and done by everyone in their group immediately before and after the entrance of the factory worker. Allow them a few moments to share ideas with one another for this, and to get set up in a comfortable position. Now brief the workers privately in role as shop steward. The factory has lost an important contract because workers did not keep to safety regulations. This means that, one month before the holiday time, 40% of the workers will be laid off. There will be a meeting tomorrow to decide how to respond. The workers have to time their entrance and decide what to say when they rejoin their groups. Let the scene run.

2 Stop the work. Actors only discuss what clues they received from the person entering about what has happened. The recorder can be asked for specific information. Leave this unresolved so students continue the thought process when they play the scene again. The recorder notes what happens in the second run through.

Keeping the recorder apart draws the contrast between subjective and objective experiences as a learning process for interpretation.

3 Detailed evaluation of students' own work

3 Stop the work. As the recorders, read to the group precisely what happened. As groups, then as a class, discuss how the atmosphere is changed by the entrances and the clues to the reasons for the change.

4 Appreciating the link between text and action

4 In groups, get together to write a refined script, with stage directions, around the moment of entry. If working on a text, compare the recording of events with the playwright's description.

5 Play the scene again. Either share the work, or report to the class what was learned by this. Written evaluation notes could be compared with those taken on *The Cherry Orchard* extract.

From Words into Action

● Symbols

RESOURCES
'A Story' by Edward Bond
Notebooks and pens

The story selected as stimulus has the two key ingredients that this lesson seeks to teach: the use of symbols and the mixture of legend and analogy that the students are using in their prepared work. The location of the story gives scope for the design of sound and space and movement work and, being set in a workplace, builds on the role-play. The story carries the message of seeking knowledge in order to improve the quality of life.

[1] Picking up clues

1 Having decided how long you plan to spend on this piece, tell the class that you will tell them a story and that as a group, with you available to help and advise, they must dramatise the story in the time available. You will read the story twice; they must be silent and jot down any ideas they have for story-telling style, sound, action, space and so on.

[2] Searching for meaning through form

2 This is where you begin to walk the tightrope in the way that drama teachers do so well. Let students take the decisions about how to organise their work and structure the story, with you being there to question, assist and guide, but definitely not to lead from the front. Have the courage of stillness at moments of apparent chaos, but intervene with supportive questions, or reminders of the time limit, at other moments.

Pressured time avoids self-indulgent actions and (because this is not a film set) limited resources encourage the use of the actors' art.

3 The possibilities are many. These questions might help students to keep the clarity, directness and interest implicit in story-telling.

Questions
concerning setting:
How do we know it is a mine?
How do we create a shaft?
How do we show the contrast with the surface?

concerning action:
How can we tell that the miners could imagine the palace?
When do we focus on the young miner and when on the charge hand?
What about the transition?
How do we show the passing of time?

A STORY

In the mine there was a rumour that the mine owner had built himself a white palace next to the sun. This caused great confusion to the miners. They could imagine what a palace looked like. It would be like the holes they cut in the rock. But the holes would be bigger and even longer. (It was said that a man might stand upright in some of them.) But what was sun? And what was white? The miners had never seen white. Nor had their families who lived at the bottom of the shaft below the mine owner who lived near the top.

And one day a young miner decided to go to see the palace and come back to the miners and tell them what sort of thing white was. After his shift he started to climb up the shaft. It was a hard climb. Whenever he tired he slept in a crack in the side of the shaft. Sometimes there was a low roaring below him as a cage loaded with ore came up. At such times he hid in the side. At other times he heard a gentle sighing above him as an empty cage came down. Then he had to move very quickly to reach a hole. His shoulders and elbows were scraped raw by descending cages because he couldn't move quickly enough.

No one searched for him. In the weeks before he left he had hollowed out the roof of his tunnel. On the last day he had knocked it down. The charge hands had assumed he was buried under the fall of rock. One of them had marked the fallen rock with a piece of iron. The piece of iron meant that other miners should not be sent into this tunnel. Charge hands were punished (deprivation of food or, in the case of joking with miners, demotion to the job of miner) if they lost miners through unnatural causes. Natural death in the mine was through routine work. Accidents were not only against nature but even against regulations.

After a few days of climbing, the miner realised he could drop onto one of the roaring cages going up and in this way be carried to the top. He thought about it for a time. Four cages passed him before he risked jumping on to the next.

At the top he found the mine owner. The mine owner was paying his six-monthly visit to the mine. The mine owner threw a rock at the miner. He knew what a miner looked like because his father had insisted he learn the job from the bottom and so he had once been shown a drawing of a miner.

For some reason the miner knew he must be the mine owner. He said, 'I have come to see your palace. And please sir, what is white?'

The mine owner smiled. Here was a good fellow, he thought, and he remembered how his father had told him to think favourably of miners. 'Well . . .' he said, looking at the sooty miner. 'White? . . .' he mused for a moment and then smiled and pointed to his head. 'My face,' he said, 'is white.'

With a whoop of joy the miner reached out, cut it off and dropped it down the shaft to the miners.

It would be better for them if those who know what white is also knew what black is.

From *The Woman* by Edward Bond

concerning sound:
Cages roar when loaded, sigh when empty.
Sounds of work.
Sounds for atmosphere, building tension.
Sounds reflecting concepts or key words: this helps the students to picture the story free of self-awareness.

concerning meaning:
What does the mine symbolise?
What does the palace symbolise?
Why does Bond use black and white?
What do feelings reveal?

concerning form (subsumed, of course, in all other questions):
How are we going to tell this story together?
Where shall we begin?
Do we need a narrator?
Who speaks?
Who will listen?

4 Play the scene for its intrinsic value for the participants; they become the audience for their work. Evaluate working methods, decision-making processes, effective use of form, symbols and symbolic action.

Dreams/Legends: Play Within a Play —————

- Rehearsed presentation
- Using the form to communicate reality and fantasy

RESOURCES
Blackboard
Students' working notebooks

This task can begin any time after the 'Factory: Fantasies of a Worker' lesson (pages 248–50), using the second phase of lessons to enrich working content. Alternatively, introduce it at the end of the module as a major assessment piece, allowing students to work autonomously while the teacher assesses the focus skills.

Your preamble may sound something like this:

Your preamble may sound something like this:

1 'We've been looking at story-telling in theatre. We talked about belief: in what we do, in the scene portrayed, how theatre allows us a better look at real life. We talked about how theatre should entertain and have meaning, how we can enjoy understanding more. Let's agree a list of objectives for our work. What shall we use from what we have learned?'

Record the students' ideas on a board. Our own list included these skills from previous sessions:

use of narrator	knowing what is going to
simple setting	happen
entrances and exits	using pauses
comic actions	where to start
acting the 'right' size	what does it mean?
real life?	symbols
working together	sound effects

Encouraging students to define assessment criteria is a feedback to you of their learning and an important motivator for their work.

2 Set the task of preparing a rehearsed presentation that is quite short so the skills get detailed attention. The piece should include analogy, fantasy, or parable. This is using the theatre form within a piece of theatre, a play within a play. Examples abound, from Shakespeare to Brecht. Encourage the students to see the possibilities offered by these connections in terms of acting style and of understanding reality. It might help to remind them of parables, or legends, or Joy's fantasy (page 249). The important point is that the new dimension of the analogous has a dynamic relationship with real life and reveals meanings by allowing reflection and comment on the 'reality'.

3 The students will either work on this presentation with you, assessing the process and the product, or will use it as the content for the enrichment activities in Phase II.

On-going documentation tasks:
Record as a group the opening moments of your scene.
What is the situation you are working on?
What are you saying?

These should be note-form tasks which can be used in essay writing later.

A PROJECT PLANNER

The lesson is the link between the students and the syllabus. The planning undertaken by the teacher translates aims into action relevant to the students. This example shows one method of planning that can give ownership of the content to the students, while the teacher has the responsibility of developing skills and attitudes and providing experiences which will meet the syllabus aims. It was designed to accommodate selected aims from the Norfolk TVEI proposed GCSE (mode 2) in the Arts.

Select your objectives

2.2 To develop the capacity for creative thought and action; the ability to innovate, initiate and make effective personal responses.

2.3 To develop the education of imagination, feeling and sensibility, and to establish an appropriate relationship between emotional and intuitive responses and those derived from intellectual and analytical processes.

2.4 To develop an ability to assess social, cultural, . . . and aesthetic values through the practice and appreciation of drama and theatre arts.

2.5 To develop an understanding of cultural change and diversity.

3.2 To develop a critical self- and cultural consciousness, through the exercise of and engagement with the dramatic aesthetic.

3.4 To use the arts to challenge and revalue cultural assumptions, notably those concerning race, gender, class and attitudes towards disability.

A flow chart, devised after discussion with the students, is made, skills identified and a network finally drawn up.

Identify skills your students need

The students need to work on:
clarity, expression, meaningful but not contrived gestures; their use of space in role-play and the need to translate that for an audience (it is likely that some of them need encouragement to see more possibilities in a space); how they can make analysis a more independent process than when teacher-led; script work, making language and content thoroughly accessible; consolidation of language work begun in the *Progress?* chapter.

A sample of a teacher's working notes and a sample network follow.

Easy Money £££

freedom = racing through the supermarket
having won one minute's free choice

pools: wishing for luck to solve problems,
euphoria

escapism: appeals to
students

The Big
Match

Fate → Brecht → drama to question + empower

↓

'SPEND! SPEND! SPEND!'

problems — poverty = no choice, legislation || feel. respond. act.

Adverts — create appeal, create products, create information

ADVERTOCRACY

culture package

THEME PARKS

all you need to know
about... Eurotunnel, Sellafield...

nostalgia (buy a souvenir of the past)
what history is about

push back   drama cf. entertainment
the boundaries
of responsive role play (eg. a group of students approaches
a person in role with their own perspective on that history).
Ownership of history; talking about ourselves / others / events
rich experiences   identity

Big build-up to year 2000 — tension, excitement, atmosphere
of change, new possibilities

People on the periphery v. Designer Lifestyle

Old photos — access to meaning — not always immediate

responses — to individualism — to oppression — me
the real me
live for today?

Truth?
reorganising events / pictures
values — £1 when I was young / now.

Values

Objective: To use presentations of history as a means of investigating and experiencing the moral and aesthetic values in the entertainment industry and in drama as entertainment-with-purpose.

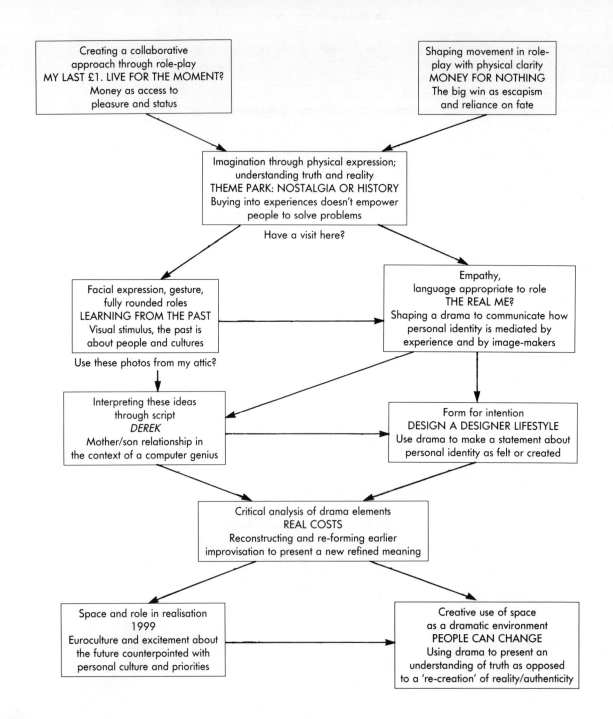

Creating a collaborative approach through role-play
MY LAST £1. LIVE FOR THE MOMENT?
Money as access to pleasure and status

Shaping movement in role-play with physical clarity
MONEY FOR NOTHING
The big win as escapism and reliance on fate

Imagination through physical expression; understanding truth and reality
THEME PARK: NOSTALGIA OR HISTORY
Buying into experiences doesn't empower people to solve problems

Have a visit here?

Facial expression, gesture, fully rounded roles
LEARNING FROM THE PAST
Visual stimulus, the past is about people and cultures

Empathy, language appropriate to role
THE REAL ME?
Shaping a drama to communicate how personal identity is mediated by experience and by image-makers

Use these photos from my attic?

Interpreting these ideas through script
DEREK
Mother/son relationship in the context of a computer genius

Form for intention
DESIGN A DESIGNER LIFESTYLE
Use drama to make a statement about personal identity as felt or created

Critical analysis of drama elements
REAL COSTS
Reconstructing and re-forming earlier improvisation to present a new refined meaning

Space and role in realisation
1999
Euroculture and excitement about the future counterpointed with personal culture and priorities

Creative use of space as a dramatic environment
PEOPLE CAN CHANGE
Using drama to present an understanding of truth as opposed to a 're-creation' of reality/authenticity

Acknowledgements

The publishers would like to thank the following for permission to reproduce copyright material: Grafton Books and BBC TV for extract from *Boys from the Black Stuff* by Alan Bleasdale (pages 46–9), *The Guardian* for articles (pages 72 and 89), *New Statesman* for article (pages 74–5), Margaret Ramsay for extract from *Our Day Out* by Willy Russell (pages 94–5), Bede Gallery for 'The Jarrow Marchers' and Jarrow petition (pages 128–9), Afro-Caribbean Education Resource Centre for 'The Writing on the Wall' by Abiola Agana (pages 188–9), Secker & Warburg for 'The Song of the Battery Hen' by Edwin Brock (page 216), Faber for 'The Horses' by Edwin Muir (pages 229–30), Virago for 'Poor Cow' by Nell Dunn (page 249), Methuen for extracts from *The Mahabharata* trans. Jean-Claude Carriere and Peter Brook (pages 254–5), *The Cherry Orchard* ed. Trevor Griffiths (page 257), *The Woman* by Edward Bond (page 261), Norfolk TVEI Unit, for extracts from their proposed GCSE mode 2 for the Arts (page 264) – contact David Shepherd for details.

Photographs courtesy of Oxfam (page 29), Shelter (page 60), AA Picture Library (page 85), Bede Gallery (pages 122, 127 and 135).

The authors would like to thank all those who helped them, especially Joan Bird. Thanks also to the following: Steve Birch, LEAG, GCSE Training Video for the original idea behind 'Expedition', WJEC for 'role-making and role-taking' in 'Making It Home', A. Boal (see his *Theatre of the Oppressed*) for device used in the 'Sisters Quarrel' section of 'The Taming of the Shrew', M. Karge for the joke from *The Conquest of the South Pole* used in 'Community Drama', Dario Fo (see his *Riverside*) for ideas used in 'Theatre: A Collective Form of Storytelling', Peter Chippindale and Chris Harrie in *New Statesman and Society* for the term 'advertocracy' used in 'A Project Planner'.